The Politics of Inclusion

The Politics of Inclusion

THOMAS H. KEAN
Governor of New Jersey

THE FREE PRESS
A Division of Macmillan, Inc.
NEW YORK

Collier Macmillan Publishers
LONDON

The Free Press
A Division of Macmillan, Inc.
866 Third Avenue, New York, N.Y. 10022

Collier Macmillan Canada, Inc.

Printed in the United States of America

printing number
1   2   3   4   5   6   7   8   9   10

Library of Congress Cataloging-in-Publication Data
Kean, Tom.
   The politics of inclusion.

Includes index.
   1. Kean, Tom—Political and social views. 2. New
Jersey—Politics and government—1951–
3. Republican Party (U.S.: 1854–   ) 4. United
States—Politics and government—1981–   I. Title.
F140.22.K43A3   1988   974.9′043′0924   88–3556
ISBN 0-02-918341-3

The Politics of Inclusion

THOMAS H. KEAN
Governor of New Jersey

THE FREE PRESS
A Division of Macmillan, Inc.
NEW YORK

Collier Macmillan Publishers
LONDON

The Free Press
A Division of Macmillan, Inc.
866 Third Avenue, New York, N.Y. 10022

Collier Macmillan Canada, Inc.

Printed in the United States of America

printing number
1   2   3   4   5   6   7   8   9   10

Library of Congress Cataloging-in-Publication Data
Kean, Tom.
    The politics of inclusion.

Includes index.
    1. Kean, Tom—Political and social views.   2. New
Jersey—Politics and government—1951–
3. Republican Party (U.S.: 1854–   )   4. United
States—Politics and government—1981–   I. Title.
F140.22.K43A3   1988   974.9'043'0924   88–3556
ISBN 0–02–918341–3

To the People of New Jersey

Contents

Preface

I love to talk with people. I get great and intense pleasure from pulling up a chair with an old friend or a new acquaintance and listening to them talk about what matters in their life, and in turn sharing what matters in mine. Real conversation is not always easy when you are governor of a big state like New Jersey. The demands of the job often make it impossible to sit down, relax, talk, and listen.

That's why I decided to write this book. I want it to be a conversation with the kind of people I meet every day: people who are interested in politics, the state of New Jersey, and other people.

The book is divided roughly into two parts. In the first, I talk about my development as a politician and the transformation that has occurred in New Jersey in the 1980s. In the second, I write about public issues that have preoccupied my working life for quite some time. Throughout, I'll introduce you to the people and events that have shaped my life, share with you my thoughts on problems I feel we must recognize and tackle, and explain to you the philosophy I've developed after twenty years in public life.

I want to thank a number of people who helped me. My editor, Grant Ujifusa, patiently awaited the manuscript and always understood the pressures on a governor's schedule. I envy Grant's facility with the English language, and I appreciate his ability to turn my sometimes diffuse thoughts into what I hope is now clear, straightforward prose.

I also want to thank Mike Meagher, Dr. Zachary Narrett, and Peter Begans for their editorial comments and Janice Abbott and Louise Loriquet, who worked overtime to help prepare the manuscript. Janice and Louise have a unique ability to decipher my handwriting.

Above all, I want to thank Steve Provost, who worked nights, weekends, and vacations to help me with this project. To him I owe a special debt of gratitude.

1
The Road Taken

WHEN I was a child, one of the most important realities in my life was a train. Every Sunday in the fall, beginning in the third grade, my mother would put me on the DeCamp bus in Livingston, New Jersey, for the forty-minute ride to Newark's Pennsylvania station, where I would board the 4:00 P.M. train to Washington, D.C. In my pocket was a ticket for a parlor car seat and two dollars. Upon arriving in Washington, I would be met by the boarder in our house at the time, with whom I would live during the course of the school week. On Friday, the trip was reversed and I would catch the 4:30 Congressional back to Newark.

I was an eight-year-old commuter, living apart from my parents, five days a week, because my father was a member of Congress. Like many congressional families, we had two homes, one in Washington and one in Livingston. In those days, Congress stayed in session from January to July or August. For the balance of the year, my father felt he had to be in Livingston among his constituents.

My parents obviously didn't want me going to two schools in one year. So I went to elementary school in Washington and spent the fall commuting back and forth from Livingston. At Christmas, the entire family would join me to live in our Washington home. Then, when school let out in June, my family, me included, would move back to Livingston and my father became the commuter, until Congress adjourned a few months later. Both of us took the train because the country was at war, gasoline was rationed, and automobile travel was virtually forbidden.

I grew to love the commute. I was usually the youngest passenger on board and almost always the youngest traveling alone. So the Pullman porters and the conductors befriended me, and I looked forward to seeing them every week. I also figured out a way to pocket a little spending money. My mother said I was to spend my two dollars in the dining car. But if I bought my sandwich from the vendor working the aisles, the price was thirty or forty cents. The rest was mine for the week.

My father was elected to the U. S. House of Representatives in 1938 when I was two years old. He served for twenty years, concentrated on tax matters, and eventually earned the nickname Mr. Social Security. His father and uncle had both served in the U. S. Senate, politics being very much in the Kean family tradition. Yet anybody who knew me as a child would never have predicted that I would become a politician. I was shy, often lonely, and generally unsure of my place in the world. Living in two places didn't make things easier, because it meant I could make few friends my own age.

At school in Washington, I was unsuccessful at almost everything I tried. And I stuttered badly. Only people who have had the problem know the terror of being called on in class and not being able to get a word out of your mouth. As stutterers know, you usually don't have trouble when you sing or have mental time to pick the word you want to use. But the problem becomes severe when you are asked by someone else to say a specific word. As a second- or third-grader, I remember when the teacher would ask each child to call out their name. I would break out in a cold sweat as my turn approached. Then came that terrible moment when as the class watched and listened, I struggled to get out the word "Kean."

Eventually I got over my stuttering, but I always remained the fifth of six children. I watched as my older brothers and sisters were given piano, golf, and tennis lessons. Yet I don't remember my younger sister Katharine or me ever having a lesson in anything. When I was older, I remember asking my mother why. She said, "When the first four children said they didn't want to go to piano lessons, your father and I forced them to go because we thought it was good for them. By the time you came along, we were a little older and a little more tired. When you said you didn't want to take piano lessons, we said fine."

With few friends, and with my older brothers and sisters preoccupied with their own lives, I was left on my own. I grew to love animals, and probably read every book on dogs in print. I liked books of all sorts and enjoyed taking solitary walks in Rock Creek Park in Northwest Washington or in the Livingston woods.

At twelve, I was sent away to school in Massachusetts. While there and in college, I followed my father's career with some pride. But I had no desire to work in his campaigns or to get involved in his Washington work. When my father hosted political meetings in our home, I would go upstairs or leave the house. In fact, I followed politics much as I followed baseball. Both games were interesting, but I never expected to actively participate in either. A political career was the last thing I wanted for myself. After I graduated from Princeton and finished my military service, I decided it would be either teaching or business.

And yet ten years after I left Princeton, I was elected to the New Jersey state assembly. A number of things had happened to convince me that politics could be fun, rewarding, and important, including my father's campaign for the U. S. Senate, John F. Kennedy's presidency and assassination, and Bill Scranton's long-shot bid for the presidency in 1964.

In the fall of 1957 I found myself stationed at Fort Dix. On leave after basic training, I told my father that I was thinking about interviewing for a job with a large company in the Midwest. He suggested that I first get some experience in a Wall Street firm. Then he told me that the rumors were true. He planned to leave his seat in the House and run for the Senate.

My father had never asked me to help in any of his campaigns. But his announcement coincided with my release from active duty, and as a young man I had no pressing commitments of any kind. So with little enthusiasm, I found myself in my father's Newark campaign headquarters, working side by side with the very people, professional politicians, I thought would never become part of my life.

My responsibilities were mundane. I stuffed envelopes, answered the telephone, and ran errands. As time passed, I actually began to enjoy the work. A political campaign is a group of people, many of whom barely know each other, thrown together for six months, twenty hours a day, working toward one all-consuming goal. A genuine sense of community and camaraderie develops and then in one evening, it's either all over or you earn the right to go on. Few things in adult life are so intense and clear-cut. For me, the only comparable experience is getting a play ready for Broadway.

As time went on, I began to develop an interest in campaign strategy and the nuts and bolts of our operation. The candidate's son was never knowingly excluded from important meetings, because no one ever thought that I was going to run to our opponent with anything important.

Then too, I found that people interested in the campaign were eager to speak to a member of the family. So if they couldn't talk to the campaign manager, they would ask for me, not knowing that my big job was to get to the mailbox on time.

As an undergraduate at Princeton, I read Socrates and Cicero, Hobbes and Rousseau, and studied the Lincoln-Douglas debates. Politics, I was taught, was an arena where lofty ideals espoused by earnest and brilliant men clashed. In my father's campaign, I learned something else, perhaps more important, which was, as Tip O'Neill put it, that "All politics is local." I learned that most people get into politics not out of principle, but because it in some way affects things that make a difference in their daily lives: a better school, a new town hall, another policeman on the corner, or the hope of a government job.

All this is doubly true for New Jersey. Living in the shadow of New York and Philadelphia, New Jersey voters had always had a hard time developing any sense of statewide identity. But our twenty-one counties were small enough so that people could get to know their elected officials. County leaders, in turn, dispensed jobs and other forms of patronage to loyalists. Accordingly, nominations for statewide offices like governor or senator usually went to politicians in both parties who could put together the strongest coalition of county political leaders.

In short, New Jersey politics was very personal. In some towns or counties, political loyalties sprang from feuds whose original participants were long since dead. To win statewide, you had to know who was on whose side in each county, who disliked the chairman, who in the local community wanted a new road in town, and so on.

My father had always tried to stay above politics as practiced in New Jersey. He liked government itself, public service in the true sense, and much preferred spending time debating tax law in Congress to the chicken-dinner circuit of shaking hands, making friends, and engaging in small talk. He believed people knew his record and respected his hard work. So he was surprised to discover that he was an underdog in the Republican primary, even though he had more government experience than his opponents. He found himself running against Bern Shanley, President Eisenhower's former appointments secretary, a man well liked by political people throughout the state, and Robert Morris, a young conservative who thought the Republican party under Eisenhower had drifted to the left. With only two or three exceptions, all the county chairmen preferred Shanley.

One job at campaign headquarters was to try and crack some of the county organizations. The campaign chief, a former newspaperman named Joe Sullivan, had the radical idea that we could win without the support of the county leaders by taking my father's record directly to the people. At the same time, we worked to win the support of the disaffected organization people in every county. Oddly enough, I was to pursue the same strategy in another Republican primary twenty-three years later.

Someone would call from Hudson County and say that if I would only call the Republican chairman of Bayonne, we might get his support because the Hudson County Republican chairman would not give the Bayonne politician's brother a job. Picking off disaffected Republicans became an art form. I was naive, of course, and once put down the telephone and ran to Joe Sullivan to tell him that an old woman in Ocean County had just told me she could deliver five-thousand votes if my father would attend a certain meeting. Joe quietly said to me that the same lady had been saying the same sort of thing for thirty years, and I had just spent an hour on the phone with a kook.

One day my father got a last-minute chance to appear on television, and had to cancel a scheduled speech to a meeting of the Fanwood Republican Club, which asked for a member of the family to stand in. My brothers were not available and, though scared, I agreed to appear. The last time I had spoken in public was in a high school debate. Anyway, I remember stuttering a bit as I spent ten minutes telling the group why I thought my father was the best candidate. The response surprised me. People came up later and said how impressed they were that the candidate had such an articulate and thoughtful son. The mayor even called headquarters to say how well I'd done, which for me, someone who was never much in the limelight in high school or college, was wonderful. Up to that evening, no one had ever complimented me on a public performance. I suspect it was then that the political bug bit for the first time. I got my first indirect taste of what it was like to be a candidate for public office, enjoyed it, and learned I wasn't half bad at holding forth.

Joe Sullivan asked me to speak for my father regularly after that. My mother remembers sitting in campaign headquarters while speaking assignments were discussed. I was asked which group I thought I appealed to most. I looked at my mother and admitted, not without embarrassment, that I thought for some reason I did best among older ladies.

My father, in an upset, won his primary that year but lost in the general election to a Democratic congressman named Harrison Williams. The year was bad for Republicans all over the country. Sherman Adams, President Eisenhower's chief of staff, was trying to explain where his expensive vicuna coat had come from. Sputnik had just been launched and Americans were worried that we were losing a technological race with the Russians. Nevertheless, I think my father would have won the election if he had spent as much money as his opponent. But he hated to raise money and was absolutely no good at it. Although he had a fair amount of money himself, he refused to spend any of it on his own campaigns. He thought that that somehow insulted democracy. So he was badly outspent, especially during the final weeks.

I remember my father sitting on election night with his friend Clifford Case, who had been elected two years earlier by the closest margin in New Jersey senatorial history. The night of the election, several newspapers had announced that Case had lost. He didn't prove them wrong until early morning. When the first returns came in on our election, my father studied them and shook his head sadly. Senator Case turned to him and said, "Those don't mean anything. At this point two years ago I thought I had lost." My father replied, "The difference is, this year I know I have lost."

I was disappointed, even bitter. I took the loss personally, and felt that there had to be something wrong with the democratic process if going through it meant that someone with my father's ability ended up losing. I remember promising myself that somehow I was going to get even with Harrison Williams. Over the years, of course, that desire left me. I got to know Pete Williams, who became a good friend of my father. One of the things you discover in politics is that when you get to know people, any animosity bred of partisan politicking soon disappears.

The experience in my father's campaign did away with the antipathy I had always felt toward politics and politicians. No longer the spectator, I continued as a participant. Even though I accepted a job on Wall Street, I continued to stay involved in New Jersey politics during the evenings. I maintained a close friendship with Herb Roemmele, who had been youth director in my father's campaign. Herb was chairman of my county's Young Republican organization, and I became chairman of the Livingston chapter. In those days, the Young Republican organizations were a powerful force at the local and state levels. We had well over a thousand members in our Essex County organization alone. I still didn't think I would ever run for office on my own, but I did notice myself starting to enjoy my Republican nights more than my Wall Street days.

After about a year on Wall Street, I got a call just before Thanksgiving. The head of the History Department at St. Mark's, the high school I had attended in New England, had suffered a heart attack. They needed a teacher right away. The pay was about $3,500 a year with room and board. Would I come?

Here was a chance, I thought. I had always wanted to teach, and now I could do so at a school I knew. Shaking a little, I went with the news to the head of our Wall Street firm. His response: "I've lost good young people to Merrill Lynch and even to Kidder Peabody, but this is the first time I've lost somebody to a goddamn school."

So I became a teacher, and experienced a time that proved to be among the most productive and rewarding in my life. I loved the work and made lifelong friendships among both faculty and students. In the classroom I learned how to present complicated ideas in ways that people could understand. I found that students learned more if you laced the lessons liberally with humor and anecdotes. The fact is, if you can hold the attention of twenty teenagers at nine in the morning day after day, you're prepared for any audience. Once again, politics became a spectator sport—with one exception. Like many of my generation I was taken with the young senator from Massachusetts. So in 1960, I became school chairman of the Kennedy for President club. It was to be my only deviation from the Republican party.

I stayed at St. Mark's for three years, taking advantage of my summers to travel; once to Greece with a group of history and language teachers, once to Japan, and once around the world on my own, visiting Burma, Cambodia, Thailand, India, and Iran. Although I never worked harder or was happier, by 1962 I was worried. I was single, planning to devote my life to teaching, and yet I had no professional credentials. In one of the hardest decisions I have ever made, I decided to leave St. Mark's for graduate school. I chose Columbia University, which boasted such luminaries as Richard Hofstadter, William Leuchtenburg, Richard Morris, Garrett Mattingly, Jacques Barzun, and Richard Neustadt. Once again I found myself a student, this time living in New York City.

Columbia in those days could be a very cold place. I remember being in awe of Professor Hofstadter; to me he was the epitome of the accomplished scholar. One day at the beginning of class, Hofstadter leaned heavily against the lectern. "Ladies and gentlemen," he began, "you'll have to excuse me but I'm not feeling very well. I'll see you all next class." All gathered up notebooks and started to leave. I turned around and saw the professor stumble. I went back and asked him if there was anything I could do. By this time, he and I were the only ones left in the room. "Thank you so much," he said. "I think I'm having a heart attack." He refused to go to the hospital, so I got him to my car and took him to his home nearby. Fortunately, it turned out to be only a case of severe indigestion. But what if it had been a real heart attack? Some of the people in the class must have known him well. Yet not one stayed to find out if he was all right. The university seemed such an impersonal place that I was not surprised when riots erupted at Columbia some years later. Of course the impersonal atmosphere did have one advantage. I buried myself in my work and did reasonably well academically for the first time.

My political activity was limited to late-night discussions on various topics of the day. It was, of course, rare to find a Republican at Columbia. My lonely defenses of conservative principles really recemented my allegiance to the Republican party. Democrats at Columbia, I found, were basically elitist. They seemed to feel that what the poor needed was a group of wise men, I should say wise Democrats, who would dole out sustenance from some altar of government. They were forever talking about what government should do for people, not how government could help people do things for themselves. They seldom talked about creating opportunity. I argued that government's role was to create conditions for an individual to succeed, not attempt to guarantee success for everyone.

One day while working on a paper in a midtown library, I heard a commotion downstairs. Things grew so noisy that I went down to see what was happening. "The president's been shot," I was told. I walked back across Central Park to my small apartment near 72nd Street and Broadway. Cab drivers leaned out their windows to shout the latest news to passersby. That day there were no strangers in New York City. Only after I got home and switched on Walter Cronkite was the terrible news fully confirmed. John F. Kennedy was dead. For me, as for so many others, Kennedy was more than a man. He was a symbol of our hopes and dreams, transcending partisan politics and political ideology. For the next two days I never left my apartment. I watched television and did a lot of thinking. I didn't realize it at the time, but I suspect it was during those two days that I definitely lost whatever misgivings I still had about public service, and decided that if I ever got a chance, I would one day run for public office.

I earned my master's degree and completed the courses for my teaching certification from New York State. Working year round, I did most of the course work for my doctorate. Ahead lay my orals and dissertation. But I knew I was getting stale. Needing a break, I decided to take a term off before completing my Ph.D. It was early 1964. Barry Goldwater and Nelson Rockefeller were the main contenders for the GOP presidential nomination, along with some dark horses, one of whom was Governor Bill Scranton of Pennsylvania.

At that point, I remembered the advice of a teacher of mine at Princeton, who told me that the best experience of his life was the time he spent working on Averell Harriman's quixotic bid for the presidency in 1952. The professor said he was given a lot more authority and gained much more experience working on an underdog campaign than would have been the case for a front-runner. I decided to spend a few months working for the Scranton campaign.

The year was a contentious one for the Republican party. I admired Goldwater, but like many Republicans, I felt that he could not win a November election. Rockefeller was a fascinating, vibrant man, but to me he was too willing to spend the public's money. I admired the way Governor Scranton had used state government to promote economic growth in Pennsylvania. He was also a superb manager and I thought he would use his skill to great effect in the White House.

I was told to get in touch with a fellow named Warren Sinsheimer, a young, ambitious New York attorney. When we met he reminded me that the Wendell Willkie for president boom had started as a press conference in a New York lawyer's office. With Willkie in mind, Warren held a press conference in New York one day in 1964 to announce the formation of an organization to support a leader he admired greatly, Bill Scranton. The press was not told that the organization's only member was Warren Sinsheimer. The historical parallels end there, because Warren in no way ignited an explosion of national support for Scranton. In fact, when I met Warren he was still the entire organization.

I asked how I could help. He told me to open a campaign headquarters in New Jersey, which I did, but it was discouraging. I would sit at the headquarters day after day making phone calls to people who didn't care who Bill Scranton was or what he was doing. I was just about to give up when the phone rang. It was Warren, asking if I could afford airplane fare to San Francisco. I said yes. He said, "Good, you've just become the national youth coordinator for the Bill Scranton for president campaign."

Suddenly I found myself smack in the middle of national Republican politics. Nelson Rockefeller was getting divorced and had lost the California primary. He dropped out of the race and left behind a huge campaign apparatus, for which he had already paid the bill. He turned the entire operation over to Scranton. I became the liaison to the Spencer Roberts Organization, the forerunner of modern political consulting firms. The Spencer Roberts people, veterans of many a political war, set about to teach me a few things.

Because Governor Scranton had little support from the Republican leadership, our job was to convince the media that the grass roots were with him—which wasn't easy in San Francisco in 1964, when the name Bill Scranton was just slightly better known than my own. Nevertheless, we became masters at organizing crowds. For one thing, we arranged to have the public-address system at the airport announce repeatedly that all television cameras and media personnel were to proceed to Gate 6 to cover the arrival of Governor Scranton. A few cameras went to Gate 6, of course, but so did everyone at the San Francisco airport with time on their hands. After the governor stepped off the plane into a throng of people, the media dutifully reported Scranton's surprisingly large airport crowd on the evening news.

Later in the week the campaign staff announced a reception for the governor at his hotel. Spencer Roberts sent out small engraved invitations to every Republican in the city inviting them to a personal get-together with the governor. The result was a mob scene, as thousands of people showed up for what each thought was a small, intimate reception with Scranton. The hotel owners eventually had to call the police. The press meanwhile noted that they hadn't yet seen anyone try to mob Goldwater's hotel.

Organized labor had been among Barry Goldwater's bitterest foes. So the Goldwater people made a point of using nonunion labor to put the convention together. To print the tickets for the various sessions, they picked a small nonunion shop. They didn't know its owner had been the first San Franciscan to support Bill Scranton publicly, and had thus become one of my earliest contacts when I came to town. You can imagine what then happened. The Goldwater forces tried to restrict entry to the convention floor for all but a few Scranton supporters, to minimize dissent in front of the cameras. Thanks to my friend the printer, I suddenly had as many tickets as we needed. I then recruited demonstrators from the ranks of the Young Republicans at Stanford and Berkeley. The furious convention organizers knew there were illegal Scranton people on the floor, but not how they had gotten there. Once a frustrated sergeant at arms noticed that I seemed to be at the center of the Scranton support, tore up my ticket, and literally carried me off the floor. I pulled another ticket out of my pocket and used another entrance.

Governor Scranton was soundly defeated, and a lot of the young people on our campaign left San Francisco discouraged. I was not. I had seen the kind of influence one person could have on the electoral process. I had met and worked with people who made a difference. I felt again the irresistible tug of politics.

Looking back now, I realize that convention was the first solid indicator of some of the changes that were going to move and shake our country during the next twenty years. The Northeast would no longer be able to dictate things, economically or politically, to the rest of the country. People tend to remember most vividly the 1968 Democratic convention in Chicago, but the San Francisco Republican convention of 1964 was in many ways more of an indicator of the country's direction. I sensed as much when I stood on the convention floor and heard Nelson Rockefeller booed. There was the sometimes intolerant enthusiasm of delegates from states like Texas and California, who felt they were finally in control. Never again, they asserted, would the South and the West allow the Northeast to dominate a Republican convention.

☆

That summer I decided not to return to graduate school right away. Instead, I went home to live in Livingston and took a job with an investment real estate firm in Elizabeth. But I really wasn't interested in real estate; I was interested in local politics. I asked the Republican state chairman, Webster Todd, how I could help. He suggested that I work with my local county chairman. So I spent the next eighteen months learning the real estate business and working in the evenings for the county organization. I ran and was elected to the Republican county committee in Livingston.

But not all my evenings were devoted to politics. It was after I returned to Livingston that I met my future wife, Debby. Debby grew up in

Wilmington, Delaware, but when we first met she was working in New York as a salesclerk at Tiffany's. I soon unaccountably found myself burdened with all sorts of reasons to go into the Fifth Avenue store as well as to spend evenings or weekends in the city.

Nineteen sixty-seven became the most important year of my life. Debby and I were engaged late in 1966, and planned a June wedding. The winter was full of good times as our families and friends met at various gatherings. When I asked Debby to marry me I told her I was not planning a nine-to-five life. She said that was okay, but had no idea of what she was getting into. An only child, she was marrying into an immediate family that already contained some twenty-eight people. A very private person, she was all too soon to become a center of public attention. I know the adjustment has been difficult, but her love and support have always been there. I cannot imagine my life without her.

Debby and I got married and spent a wonderful three-week honeymoon in Ireland. Meanwhile, politics in New Jersey was coming to a boil. The Essex organization faced a serious challenge. The antiorganization forces had found an angel. The ambitious president of a large drug manufacturer was willing to finance a serious primary challenge to the Republican organization ticket. The organization was forced to look for people who could attract primary voters, and the Kean name was highly regarded in the district. Republican leaders knew I was playing an active role in politics. Shortly after my return from Ireland, I was asked to run for the state assembly.

The decision was relatively easy to make. My early aversion to politics was gone. Being asked to run was exciting, I suppose in the recesses of my mind I envisioned a young John Kennedy, enthralling voters with impassioned speeches. Besides, I knew that the assembly job was only part-time and that I could continue my real estate business and perhaps eventually return to teaching. Let me say that I think there is nothing sadder than a young person who gets involved in politics, in either an elected or appointed position, without an established career to fall back on. Five years later they or their candidate may lose, and they are out on the street. In my case, I figured if I won I would stay in the state assembly for a few terms and then go back to the private sector.

In New Jersey there are two assemblymen for each district. As my running mate, the Republicans chose a young graduate of Yale and Yale Law School who was already making a mark in New Jersey business circles. Phil Kaltenbacher and I became close friends. We ran as a team.

When most Americans think of politicians, they think of a U. S. senator or a governor who works under the media's spotlight. Most people know little of the politicians who represent them in their state legislature or in their county or town government. But local officials are truly the backbone of our democracy. As de Tocqueville noted 150 years ago, local and state politics glue a huge democracy together, giving all a stake in our nation's future.

But my father thought I was foolish to run for the assembly. He didn't think too much of state government except as a stepping-stone to national office—which wasn't surprising. His time of service in the Congress had been one of rapid growth for the national government, while state government had often been either corrupt or meaningless. In the 1960s, the New Jersey legislature met once a week for about half the year and members got $10,000 a year in salary and expenses.

The campaign strategy was rather simple. Phil and I would get home from work and spend a good part of the evening walking around neighborhoods, banging on doors, and getting to know people. We had a couple of flyers printed up advertising our qualifications. We would also try to get invited to meetings of local community groups where we would have a chance to talk for five minutes to an audience of fifteen or twenty people. The opposition ticket did things differently. They had a ton of money to spend on the campaign and hired a lot of people, including a young New York advertising consultant named William Safire.

The district we wanted to represent consisted primarily of comfortable middle-class suburbs like Livingston. But our largest town by far was the blue-collar town of Irvington, next to the city of Newark. Phil and I made it a special priority to win votes in Irvington, which we simply worked to death. We attended meetings of the Italian-American organizations, the Irish, the Jewish, and the Ukrainian. We stopped by most weekends at the Polish-American hall, and spent Sunday afternoons at the senior-citizen projects. The highlight for me was being chosen by the local monsignor to draw the winning numbers for the raffle at St. Leo's, the largest parish in the district. About five hundred people attended the drawing that night. I picked the number of someone who not only wasn't present, but didn't even live in the district. That was followed by groans. I was sure we were going to lose the election.

Anyway, that's the way assembly campaigns are waged. There are no television debates or commercials—at least there weren't then—but you really get to know people in your constituency, what they do for a living, how old their kids are, what their hopes and dreams are. I remember in particular both young and old people living in poverty, but too proud to ask for welfare. I began to genuinely appreciate problems people struggled with, and the ways in which government might make a difference.

You cannot be shy in a campaign. To be effective, you have to have the confidence to knock on doors of hundreds of houses and spend sometimes an hour or two in the living rooms of strangers, listening to whatever they have to say. Of course, not everyone was happy to see a politician. Once state senate candidate Alex Matturri and I stopped to shake hands in front of a shopping center. Its owner, a gruff and loud man, came out and said he didn't "want any damn politicians around here." It was the end of a long day and Alex had endured one too many hassles. He turned to the owner and said, "Look, we are going to get elected. Then we are going to the state capital and become very important people. When that happens, the first thing we will do is build a superhighway right through your place." The owner was so taken aback he agreed to let us stay. Matturri later became a judge.

The big moment of our campaign was the League of Women Voters debate, for which we studied and practiced for three weeks. We arrived and found that thirty-five people had shown up. Fifteen of them were our supporters, fifteen supported our opponents, and the other five showed up on their own initiative. A reporter from the local weekly newspaper was also there. That was enough to make our evening. This kind of campaign goes on year after year in every town in America. I have great respect for anyone who runs for a school board or a town council or a state legislature. Candidates don't do it for glory and money, but because they know active involvement makes democracy work and getting involved is rewarding and fun.

Our organization ticket lost the primary, but Phil and I won. We also won the general election. I had never before set foot in Trenton, the state capital, and arrived for my orientation session not really sure of myself. Still it had been a big year statewide for the Republicans. We had captured almost two-thirds of the assembly and control of the state senate.

☆

Bismarck once said that there are two things that no one should watch being made: sausage and the law. The German chancellor might have spent time in New Jersey. The lower body of the state legislature in New Jersey is the people's house—democratic government at its coarsest and most unrestrained, unruly, unkempt, and raucous. It is sometimes chaotic but never boring. In those days the New Jersey assembly was called, with some affection, the Zoo. Serving were legislators as diverse as the state itself: German farmers from southern New Jersey elbowing Italian machinists from Hudson County, corporate executives cheek by jowl with day laborers. To all, discipline and order were alien notions. We would go for weeks without doing anything and then pass one hundred bills in one marathon twenty-four-hour session. Not much of our legislation was read, let alone understood.

During my first term in the assembly, the speaker of the house was a fellow from Atlantic County named Al Smith, someone who cried publicly when we failed to pass one of his bills. Another speaker was Bill Dickey, who was fond of dressing in all-white linen suits which made him look like the Good Humor man, and who fined people who were late. One of the most important debates of my entire assembly career was on whether to adopt a state income tax. The debate was contentious, tempers were short, and we argued back and forth for almost twenty hours. Finally, an assemblyman rose in the back of the room. The room fell silent. "Why do you rise?" the speaker intoned. "I rise to aerate my shorts," came the reply.

When I first arrived in Trenton most of the politicking and decision making was still done in the back rooms, in party caucuses. Committee meetings were just for show. Moreover, the legislators had no professional staff to help them understand issues; lobbyists took their cases directly to the floor, making no attempt to disguise what they were doing. I remember a fellow legislator who boasted that he never paid for his own meal during an entire legislative session. There was always a lobbyist available to pay, he said. Then there was Al Merck, an assemblyman from Morris County, who at the invitation of the League of Women Voters stopped in one day to have a sandwich and coffee at their local offices. After a discussion of some of the League's good-government positions, Merck pulled out $1.75 and handed it to a startled League president, saying, "Nobody pays for my vote."

I was a bit of an odd duck in the assembly. I had gone to an Ivy League school, while most of the legislators had learned their various lessons on the streets of the big cities. I wore old tweed jackets, while the cloth of choice was polyester. I tried to be cerebral in a place that was known to value aggressive persuasion over reasoned argument. When a session was over, Phil and I usually stopped for dinner on the way home rather than join our colleagues' spirited get-togethers that lasted well into the night.

As a young assemblyman, I figured the best thing I could do was to keep my ears open and my mouth shut. And I began to develop respect for my colleagues and for the legislative process. Regardless of their background or education, legislators wanted to be treated with dignity. Although we went about our work in different ways, most of us were in government for the same reason: to try to leave a better state for our children. Because I believed in that goal, I always tried to understand the various points of view held by my colleagues.

After one legislative session, I remember having dinner with two legislators, one black and one Italian, from Newark. Earlier that afternoon I had seen both of them cast a vote that I considered simply wrong. Both had gone along with a lobbyist who had little regard for the public interest. I started to kid them a bit. Both suddenly became angry. The black tore into me first. "What happens if you lose the next election?" he asked me. "You may be a bit unhappy, but you go back to your real estate firm. You may make even more money. Your life doesn't change. For me it's different. I've got no college education. My assembly salary is important. I've started a small public relations firm. Local businessmen hire me to speak for them to the black community. They hire me because I'm an elected official. I make around twenty thousand a year. Combine that with my assembly salary and it gives me a total of thirty thousand. If I lose this legislative seat, I lose my public relations firm. I'm back to nothing. I'm broke."

The Italian assemblyman interrupted the black, saying, "He's absolutely right. I'm a schoolteacher. My salary was eleven thousand. Since I was elected to the assembly I've been hired for an administrative job by the board. It pays me another sixteen thousand. With my assembly salary of ten thousand, my wife and I are living on fifteen thousand more than we have ever earned in our lives. We've got a new home with a mortgage. Our kids have a chance at college. If I lost my seat, I'd lose that administrative job as well. We'd lose our home. You just don't understand," he said. "This is the best job we've ever had or probably will ever have. I'll do anything to keep it. You're different and have no right to question our motives."

So I listened and I learned. The lessons were different from the lessons taught in the classrooms at Princeton or Columbia, and also unlike the talk of government service I had heard from my father. And as I listened I reached out. I genuinely liked my colleagues despite any and all differences in background. To my surprise and satisfaction, I found I could often bring people together on contentious issues.

I started to devote a lot of attention to issues that were neglected at the time. My priorities were education, environmental protection, urban aid, and clean government. I was a conservative, especially on fiscal matters, but I have always strongly felt that a real conservative must care deeply about children, clean air and water, and preservation of open land for future generations.

I had some early successes. I remember having a sandwich with the president of our local community college. He was distressed that good minority students were unable to attend college because they were too poor. He said that not only would these young men and women never reach their individual potential, but the community would be denied their leadership. Later, I sat down with the chancellor of higher education and we came up with something called the Education Opportunity Fund.

The fund was divided into two parts. The first set up a program to provide basic skills training to poor students who had done well enough to gain entrance to college, but who couldn't handle the course load because they had not really learned how to read and write in high school. The second part set aside some money that would be used to provide grants to low-income students. I felt that no one in New Jersey should be denied a college education because they couldn't afford it. The fund was a radical idea in those days, and difficult to sell to suburban voters. Yet it went to the heart of what I believe government should be about. We had to create opportunity for those who had been historically denied. In any case, the Education Opportunity Fund has been a success: more than 200,000 New Jersey students have been helped. It was my proudest accomplishment.

I was brought up a conservationist. My father knew the name of virtually every bird and tree. My brother Hamilton has been a lawyer for the Natural Resource Defense Council, one of the country's most respected conservation organizations. And I have always been a nature lover. Since I was a child I've always experienced contentment whenever I walk in quiet woods. In the late 1960s, I felt strongly that we needed prompt and strong government action to protect our air, water, and open space. This was back before Earth Day, and my strong conservation stands amused and surprised some of my fellow legislators. Responding to the first bill I sponsored to protect the environment from too much development, the Democratic leader rose on the floor of the assembly to remark, "Now I've seen everything. Essex County has sent a bird-watcher to the state legislature."

My earliest efforts were to preserve open space. The state's largest utility had a plan to develop one of the few natural glacial ponds in the state, a place called Sunfish Pond. It made no sense to me that out of all the places to build a power plant they had picked this beautiful, fragile pond in the middle of a state park. The fight to save Sunfish Pond was led by an ordinary yet extraordinary man named Casey Kays, whose dedication to the preservation of natural beauty combines religious fervor and poetry.

In early 1967 we convened a meeting of conservationists to put together an agenda. We had a writer, two or three college professors, the head of the Audubon Society, Casey and me. We began by going around the room and asking everybody to say why they thought conservation was important. What people said reflected a particular expertise; they spoke about the environment in a scientific or philosophical framework. Casey Kays spoke last. "I don't really know what I'm doing here," he said. "I'm not in the same class as the rest of you people. I work in a factory eight hours a day. I make about fourteen thousand dollars a year. My family and I live in a small house. We have no backyard. I've always considered our state parks my backyard. Whenever anybody tries to take away this land, they're taking away the backyard that my children and I enjoy. Those who want to preserve the land will always have my support." Since that day I have often remembered Casey's simple and eloquent case for conservation. Our world is becoming more and more crowded, many of our children will have no "backyard," and that's a reason why preserving and acquiring open space is so impor-tant.

My crusade to save Sunfish Pond caused me more than a little grief. Because the Kean family had been in the utility business for a number of years, the utilities thought they had a friend in the legislature when I was elected. So I received a couple of angry phone calls, as did members of my family in the business. "What does your brother think he's doing?" was the question. It was even suggested that a certain utility might no longer contribute to the Republican party in my home county

if I didn't drop the issue. All this I ignored. After a couple of years of public wrangling and after I had gotten a bill through the assembly four different times, the utility agreed to give Sunfish Pond back to the state. Eventually, it was designated a national landmark.

Sometimes a good piece of legislation has a strange history. For years a few people said that having a state Department of Conservation and Economic Development was schizophrenic and that it should be split in two. I felt that environmental protection should have a separate voice, but there was little support in the late 1960s for my point of view. In 1969 the candidates for governor were Congressman Bill Cahill and former Governor Robert Meyner, and neither of them seemed to care about the issue.

Some conservation leaders asked me how to get the candidates to say something about the environment. I said that other organized groups sent candidates questionnaires asking them for clear answers to certain questions. So we drafted a series of questions for the candidates. The first was, "Would you support the creation of a separate Department of Environmental Protection?" The questionnaire went off to the candidates in late June. We heard nothing for three months. Then in early October I received a phone call from a person who said that he was candidate Cahill's research director. "I've got a questionnaire here," he said, "and none of us seems to know how to handle it. You're a conservationist. Would you draft the answers?" I said yes, and ended up not only writing the questions but supplying the answers.

After Cahill was elected, I became his assembly majority leader. Early on I told him I was going to introduce a bill for a new department and I needed his support. He seemed surprised when I reminded him of his campaign pledge for such a bill, but I produced a copy of the questionnaire as proof. Weeks later I introduced the bill with the full support of the governor. I still have the pen that Governor Cahill used to sign the bill into law. Ever since, my attitude toward the Department of Environmental Protection has been a little paternal.

☆

When I arrived in the assembly in 1967, a large contingent of freshman Republicans arrived with me. I became personally close to several of them, in particular an able young assemblyman from neighboring Bergen County named Dick DeKorte, who had graduated from the University of Chicago Law School in two years. He was, in my judgment, a devoted public servant. I remember once he pushed for a change in the state's divorce laws, which were antiquated and forced people into painful, costly, and unnecessary court battles. An older legislator told him to forget the issue. "There are no votes in divorce law," he said. Dick looked at him for a while and replied simply, "People are getting hurt and I've got a responsibility to do something about it." Later he helped to create the Meadowlands Sports Complex. Dick died of cancer several years later. Had he not, I suspect that someday he would have served as governor.

Dick and I and the other freshmen discovered that we all shared an aversion to the custom of closed caucuses. We didn't like the seniority system either, because it produced too many leaders who were stuffy, unimaginative, and too closely tied to the county bosses. We organized an insurrection of sorts, with the idea of opening up the leadership slots. Shortly thereafter I was surprised to read an article in the *Newark News* suggesting that I was one of the candidates for legislative leadership. I really hadn't thought about running until I read the newspaper. Within weeks, a number of legislators approached me and asked me to declare and the more I thought about the idea, the more I liked it. My friends seemed to like the idea too, and after only two years in the assembly I found myself elevated to the position of assistant majority leader. The following year I became majority leader. The next session I would use that post as a springboard to become speaker of the New Jersey Assembly.

The speaker of the assembly, like the speaker of the House in Washington, is the most powerful member of the legislature. He or she sets the rules, hands out committee assignments, and determines what legislation will be considered on the floor. Traditionally, the speaker was picked by the majority party.

Nineteen seventy-one was different. There was no majority party. On election day the voters had chosen forty Democrats, thirty-nine Republicans, and one independent. A stalemate ensued. As time went on, it began to look as if the assembly would never be organized and the voters would have to endure two years of rancor. This was particularly bad news for the Republican administration of Governor William Cahill, who was entering the final two years of his term with an ambitious legislative agenda.

The Democratic party was preoccupied by tension within its own ranks, violently split into two factions: the Democrats from the industrial cities of Hudson County and the rest of the party. For one hundred years Hudson County has produced a pantheon of classic political bosses, led by the legendary Frank Hague. The latest was John V. Kenny. The Hudson Democrats had some allies, but for the most part the other Democrats resented them for what they saw as too much power in party caucuses. The bottom line was that Hudson County controlled most of the legislative patronage. By 1971 the feud was out in the open, the two sides refusing to talk to each other. So, despite our one-seat deficit, the Republican party was in a strong position.

The previous session, the Democratic floor leader had been Hudson County's David Friedland, one of the most controversial and enigmatic characters in New Jersey political history. Friedland was bright, flamboyant, magnetic, and extremely agile in debate. He wrote poetry in his spare time and was the flashiest dresser in Trenton, always surrounded by beautiful women. He was smart, too. He successfully argued the one man–one vote decision before the New Jersey Supreme Court.

Friedland had a great sense of humor. Once he introduced a bill to turn the Statue of Liberty around so, as he put it, "her rear end would face New York instead of my hometown, Jersey City." Another time he gave a passionate twenty-minute speech on the assembly floor in support of a particular bill. As he was concluding, one of his Hudson County colleagues tapped him on the shoulder and whispered that John V. Kenny was upset: the Hudson delegation was supposed to oppose the legislation. Friedland never missed a beat. He simply turned to the speaker's chair and said, "Those are the arguments for the bill. However, there are even better arguments against it." He went on for another twenty minutes in opposition.

For every trait that people admired in Friedland, there was another one they deplored. He could be mercurial, unprincipled, egomaniacal, and, it was rumored, he was not above using his public office for considerable private gain. Just how much of a rogue Friedland could be was proved in 1980, when he and his father were convicted of accepting $365,000 in kickbacks in return for arranging a $4 million loan from a teamsters' pension fund. David Friedland cut a deal with the FBI to reduce his seven-year prison sentence by gathering information on corruption rings in Hudson County. Friedland allegedly gathered evidence that Wally Lindsley, the mayor of Weehawken, had received kickbacks for helping secure development rights for a chicken-processing plant along the Hudson waterfront. Lindsley had been quoted in public as calling Friedland "my dearest friend."

As if that weren't enough, even as Friedland was gathering evidence for the FBI, he allegedly began to extort another $3 million from the same pension fund he had bilked seven years before. Even here the story doesn't end. In September 1985, just weeks before he was to appear before a federal judge who was to determine whether he had to serve his full seven years, and with a new indictment staring him in the face, Friedland, a skilled scuba diver, flipped over the side of a boat off the Bahamas and disappeared. "Friedland Drowns" read the headlines. Those who knew him wondered. Sure enough, a few months later he called a newspaper to say he was alive and well and somewhere in Europe.

None of this mattered back in 1971. What did matter was that David Friedland and his followers were not about to make peace with the rest of the Democrats. Meanwhile, of course, members of the Cahill administration realized that a rudderless legislature was not good for them or the state. Surprisingly for a Republican administration, they enjoyed cordial relations with the Hudson Democrats; in fact, the entire Democratic leadership in Hudson County had supported Cahill in the last election. Working behind the scenes, a number of people tried to work out a compromise.

Most of the Democrats wouldn't talk to us, but the Hudson Democrats and their allies agreed to supply enough votes to make me speaker in exchange for their normal number of committee chairmanships and a proportionate amount of patronage. Dick DeKorte and I saw this as the only way to break up the logjam. So did the Cahill administration. That January, I became speaker of a bitterly divided legislature.

The newspapers vilified us. One of them ran a cartoon of a burning cigar labeled El Stinko, with a cloud of smoke called Kean-Friedland Assembly Deal. The *Bergen Record* headlined its editorial "The Sellout." Other editorial writers all over the state told their readers that Tom Kean, the ultimate nice guy and good-government type, had signed a Faustian pact with the prince of darkness, David Friedland.

The truth was that Friedland and his forces got exactly what they deserved, proportional representation in the committees and in patronage jobs. There were no "deals" to give Friedland veto power over legislation, no agreements to give Friedland extra power. But the truth was lost in the uproar. In retrospect, the funny thing is that, six months after I was pilloried in the press, no one mentioned a word about the alleged dirty deal. The assembly was not only running smoothly but productively, as I did my best to be fair to both parties. My efforts were appreciated, especially on the Democratic side of the aisle. Once the dust was settled, the committee assignments made, and the jobs handed out, the press realized that Hudson County had gotten nothing to which it was not entitled.

I learned a couple of lessons from the brouhaha. One is that in politics the facts will finally win out. I kept telling reporters what was happening and eventually they saw I was telling the truth. Six months later I found reporters treating me favorably. Why? I suspect because many of them regretted what they had written earlier. The fact is the vast majority of reporters want to be fair. But they expect honesty in return. The hardest thing for a politician to learn is when to say, "I can't tell you that," or, "I don't know the answer." Too often, politicians choose instead to bend the truth or to tell only part of the story and that, of course, gets you in trouble.

I learned something else in 1971. I learned a lot about managing and motivating people. I knew I was sitting on a powder keg. The press was hungry and ready for blood. The traditional Democrats were absolutely livid. No one knew what the Hudson Democrats were going to do, and some of the Republicans were excessively partisan. The only way to operate was to put aside ideology and partisan politics and deal with everyone individually. I had no choice but to be absolutely fair and impartial with all, regardless of party. I never wanted to exercise my authority the way Lyndon Johnson did, twisting various arms and saying, "Vote this way." I've always thought the best way to lead people is to listen to what they have to say and to try to persuade them directly. But on certain highly charged issues, like abortion or the death penalty, you have to allow your colleagues the freedom to vote their conscience.

That legislature turned out to be one of the most productive in New Jersey history. With the balance so close, legislation was evaluated much more often on its merits than on whether it was favored by one party or the other. In other words, if a Republican or a Democrat wanted a bill passed, he had to cross the aisle to look for support. Working with the Cahill administration, the legislature put in place several laws that put New Jersey in the forefront on progressive issues. We passed laws to protect the coastal area and saltwater wetlands. We increased aid to city schools, and for the first time required disclosure of campaign contributions. And we changed the way political business was conducted, ending the system of having important votes taken in secret and opening the party caucuses to the press. I have always felt that government operates best in the sunshine. The first time I declared the caucus open, every statehouse reporter attended; the second time, half of them came; and the third time, just one or two. The press discovered that once the veil of secrecy was lifted, the caucuses were just plain boring.

In 1973, the Republican party was shaken to its core by the Watergate scandal. The party in New Jersey did not escape. As I walked along a street of my hometown in October 1973, a local lawyer approached me. "You know," he said, "you've been the best legislator we ever had in Trenton. But I'm going to vote against you this time, and I'm going to do it to send a message to that fellow Nixon." State legislators can swim in a pretty small pond, but national currents can drown us. I won in 1973, but by my smallest margin. We were left with only fourteen Republican seats out of the eighty in the state Assembly, and I was reduced to being the leader of a tiny, weak minority. The time of Watergate was very difficult for anyone who cared about the Republican party.

The next year, several state party leaders asked me to think about leaving the assembly. Congressman Peter Frelinghuysen was retiring and his congressional district included a portion of my legislative district. The party leaders argued that I was the only one who could keep the district from going Democratic in what was sure to be a poor Republican year. The idea had little appeal to me. Politics had certainly become more than a part-time pastime, but I was not sure that Congress was the place for me. From my childhood, I knew the pressures that Washington could put on a family. My two sons were about six years old and my wife was pregnant with our daughter, Alexandria, and I wanted to spend a lot of time with them. Yet I felt that loyalty was what the party needed in such difficult times. I talked it over with my father, who urged me to run. So, somewhat reluctantly, I decided to enter what looked like an uncontested primary election. Or so things appeared until another Republican announced that she would like to take a shot at Congress.

Later, Millicent Fenwick would gain a national reputation as the "conscience of Congress." Her pipe-smoking habit, wit, and devotion to the public trust would lead Gary Trudeau to create a *Doonesbury* character, Lacy Davenport, after her. She would become, after Tip O'Neill, perhaps the second-best-known member of Congress. In 1974, however, only the people of Somerset County appreciated Millicent's charm. After representing the county in the legislature she had been appointed to head the state Division of Consumer Affairs under Governor Cahill. When Democratic governor Brendan Byrne took over, he announced that Mrs. Fenwick, a Republican, would not keep her job. So she announced for Congress. Her decision didn't surprise me. She was probably the only seventy-year-old person I have ever known with unquenchable ambition.

It was a tough race to get into. Millicent and I had been friends and had worked closely together in the state legislature. I enjoyed her company, always thinking of her as the kind of person who should be in politics. And she had a big advantage over me, having represented almost half of the congressional district as an assemblywoman, while I had represented less than a tenth of it. Moreover, her position at Community Affairs gave her much greater name recognition. She enjoyed a two-to-one lead in the polls. As if this weren't enough, Millicent and I agreed on most of the major issues, although I was the more conservative on government spending. I spent my time going around to club meetings, selling my case to small groups of voters. I was able to recruit a number of talented young people, Tony Cicatiello, Jim Barry, Dean Gallo, and Mark Harroff, all of whom would play a role in future campaigns and end up going on to successful careers in their own right.

Millicent's base of support was too much for me to overcome. On election night I fell 72 votes short out of some 30,000 cast. To reporters she said, as only she can, that her only regret was "that nice young Tom Kean had to lose." I didn't feel down, but I did feel sorry for my young staff, which had devoted so much time and energy to the race. I did feel good for my family. Deep inside I knew that I didn't really want to go to Washington. And I had a hunch that someday I would look at the loss as being good for my career. It turned out that I was right.

I went back to the assembly, but found myself bored. After wielding power as speaker it was quite a letdown to be back in the minority. Some people enjoy being the loyal opposition. I don't. I like the creative side of government. With so few Republicans to support me in the assembly, none of my ideas saw the light of day. I was savvy enough to realize that the fallout from Watergate was going to plague my party for several years. I had been in the assembly eight years and I knew I was getting stale. I made plans to go back to business full-time.

☆

About that time an invitation arrived in the mail from President Gerald Ford, inviting Debby and me to a dinner for Egyptian president Anwar Sadat at the White House. I had known Gerry Ford since my father's days in Congress, and always had a lot of respect for him. If you study any history at all, you cannot help but be taken by our country's remarkable capacity to produce the right leaders at the right time. Gerry Ford was just the leader we needed after Watergate. His quiet confidence and unquestioned integrity calmed the country.

Everyone knows that a White House dinner is quite an event. You can't help but be affected by the pomp and ceremony and the knowledge that Lincoln and the Roosevelts walked around in those very rooms. That evening I found myself standing in the receiving line talking to Gregory Peck and Redskins coach George Allen. Debby met Omar Sharif. The evening ended with Sadat joining Pearl Bailey, Henry Kissinger, and the Fords in a not entirely melodious rendition of "Hello Dolly." Sadat was relaxed, warm, and witty, but was entirely serious when talk turned to the future of the Middle East.

After dinner the President sought me out. "Tom," he said, "we hope you will help us out in New Jersey this year." I wasn't quite sure what he meant, but I said of course I would do whatever he needed. You don't say no to the President in the White House. That is how I became Gerry Ford's campaign manager in New Jersey for the 1986 presidential campaign.

The experience was fascinating. I was plugged in to the campaign strategists at the White House, and I had access to the president whenever needed. New Jersey turned out to be one of Ford's favorite states. "Jersey Loves Gerry" became our slogan. Tony Cicatiello took over day-to-day operations of the campaign and I hired Greg Stevens, one of the brightest of the State House press corps, to handle public relations.

I remember one time we took the president to a rally in Atlantic City. In the car on the way I explained to him that casino gambling was a very controversial state issue. I suggested that if he received any questions on it, he should say the matter was a local issue and move on. Just as he got out of the car, a reporter asked him about casino gambling. He replied, "I know this is a state issue, but I have to tell you that I don't think gambling is very healthy for anyone." Always forthright and candid, Gerry Ford later lost Atlantic County.

He was also charming and forceful. The state's ethnic newspapers blasted him after the debate with Jimmy Carter in which he asserted that there was no Soviet domination of Eastern Europe. Knowing these newspapers were important in New Jersey, I wanted to set up a meeting with the editors. His advance staff said no way, there wasn't time. I

invited the editors anyway to a large public event where the president was scheduled to speak. Afterward, I whispered to him that the editors were present and would like a meeting. He told his campaign staff he wasn't leaving until we held it, and I set up some chairs in the basement of an eating establishment. The president won the editors over. After about fifteen minutes they had all changed their minds about Gerry Ford. Most endorsed him the week before the election.

Ford was an utterly fearless campaigner. Once we were driving through the middle of a huge crowd in Union Township. Without saying anything, the president pushed himself up through the hole in the car's roof and started waving to the crowd. The surrounding area was flat and he must have been silhouetted for miles. The Secret Service man with me turned pale. But Ford loved the crowds and was not about to be intimidated.

The work of a Secret Service man is tough and each of them is to be respected. The first presidential visit I ran in the state was scheduled to make its initial stop at a large shopping center in Bergen County. The crowd was huge. I was asked to sit in the car with the president on the way to the next stop. But if you're traveling with the president, you had better stay close to him. The Secret Service forms what it calls a pocket in the crowd for the president. If that pocket moves without you, you are left behind. That time I thought I would be smart. The crowd, some thirty to forty thousand strong, was pressing to see Ford. Rather than wait for the pocket, I decided to make my way to the car so I could be in it waiting for the President after he finished his remarks. Getting to the presidential limousine, I reached for the door handle. At that instant, I heard a deep Texas drawl on the left. "Son, if you touch that car, I'll break your arm." My hand flew back. Thereafter, I always asked the Secret Service before trying anything.

President Ford won the New Jersey primary the same day that Ronald Reagan was sweeping California. I went to the convention as one of Ford's floor managers and held our delegation together, the first time the New Jersey delegation had stayed together since Tom Dewey's 1948 campaign. Our cohesion was a big surprise to the Reagan people, who had expected a split.

The evening President Ford was nominated, he invited a few of his top supporters to meet with him in his suite at the Crown Center in Kansas City. Ten or eleven of us were there. We talked about who should be picked for vice-president. All sorts of names were thrown around. Some pushed for a woman. Anne Armstrong was the woman

Ford seemed most willing to consider. The Southerners were worried. They wanted Ford to be dramatic and open the choice to the convention floor. If that happened, I was pretty sure the choice would be Ronald Reagan. The president was listening intently. Had he decided at that moment, we would have had a Ford-Reagan ticket.

Then a voice from the next room said, "Wait a minute." We turned to see Nelson Rockefeller. He had evidently been listening. He came padding in. I was struck, as always, by how short the vice-president was, especially standing there in his stocking feet. "Mr. President," he said, "you've just been nominated to this nation's highest office for the first time in your own right. You must not allow anyone else to make your first decision." That seemed to end the discussion. We left the president about 2:30 A.M. He had still not made up his mind.

About 6:15 A.M. I got a phone call. President Ford had chosen a relatively obscure Senator, Bob Dole of Kansas, which worried me. The chairman of our delegation, Senator Cliff Case, was one of the Senate liberals. Bob Dole was a conservative. My job was to tell Senator Case the news and make sure his reaction was muted when he talked to the press. Case's reaction surprised me. "Bob Dole is a good man, he has a heart," he said. Millicent Fenwick felt the same way. The New Jersey delegation was unanimous in support of the Ford-Dole ticket.

But looking back on that convention, I can't help but wonder what would have happened if President Ford had let the vice-president be chosen by the convention. I suspect a Ford-Reagan ticket would have been able to slip past Carter-Mondale. And if they won, how would Ronald Reagan's fortunes have changed had he been running for president from the second spot in 1980?

☆

The election over and my stint as a campaign manager behind me, I decided to finally leave the assembly and go back to private life. I had been serving for a decade at what I originally thought might be a two- or four-year position. I felt I had done some good things for the state and I knew that politics had helped me develop personally. I realized it was not going to be easy to walk away from what had become a considerable affection for New Jersey politics. I knew I would find myself reading the newspaper, thinking, "Boy, that is a dumb policy," or, "Why is the state doing that?"

The late 1970s were like a horror movie for many New Jerseyans.

The economy was in terrible shape. Unemployment had been rising through most of the decade and major manufacturing plants were leaving for other states. We seemed incapable of solving our problems. We were returning federal highway funds to Washington because we couldn't come up with state matching funds. Students' test scores declined, and more and more students left for colleges in other states. New Jersey, in short, was stagnating when our neighbors were growing. I still had ideas, particularly in the areas of job creation, environmental protection, and education.

The Republican party also seemed moribund. After Watergate, we were in hiding. When Republicans ran, we talked only to groups with which we felt comfortable. No effort was made to expand our appeal to labor, women, minorities, or ethnic groups. We campaigned in suburbs, never in cities. As a result, our base was shrinking and we were taking a beating among young voters. I wanted people to listen to my ideas. I wanted to shake up the party. So I decided to leave public life with a bang rather than a whimper. In early 1977, I decided to run for governor.

I had no illusions, because I didn't expect to win. A fellow legislator, state senator Ray Bateman, already had a claim on the nomination. Ray had been active in Republican politics for years, he knew all the players in every county, he could raise a lot of money, and, most important, he was the choice of the Republican organization. His record in the state senate had been good and at times outstanding. Republicans were licking their chops to get at the incumbent, Brendan Byrne, who was terribly unpopular. My own pollster, Bob Teeter, said that Byrne got the lowest rating of any incumbent he had ever polled. Ray Bateman, it was widely predicted, would win going away.

I respected Ray and could easily have supported him. If he had approached me and asked me to drop my candidacy, I probably would have. He did not. So I ran, because I thought I had something important to say to the party and to the state. I assembled a cadre of young, energetic, inexperienced campaign workers—the Kiddie Corps, as the State House press corps called them, because none were well known to old political hands. My campaign manager was Tony Cicatiello, by now a close friend from our work together in the Fenwick and Ford campaigns. My press secretary was Greg Stevens, who once again left newspaper work to join me in a campaign, and whose political instincts are first-rate. Tony and Greg are the kind of young people who have the idealism and energy that every campaign needs. You take a chance when you hire them, but I'm willing to do that. Once in a while they make mistakes, which is to be expected. In my case, our Kiddie Corps worked admirably.

These days, of course, anyone seriously seeking office must have a professional political consultant. I approached one whose name had been suggested to me and asked for advice. "If you're serious," he said, "you've got to change a number of things. First, your name: It's spelled Kean and pronounced Kane. How can I do radio ads? Everyone will be looking for Cane or Kane on the ballot. Just pronounce your name Keene for the campaign. Second," he said, "is your teeth. Fix them." I've got a rather prominent gap between my two front incisors which I inherited from my father. "These days," he said, "everyone gets that fixed. See a dentist. He'll close that gap in one appointment. Third, you have an accent." I spent nearly seventeen years in New England between school in Massachusetts and my seven summers running Brantwood Camp in New Hampshire. Some of New England rubbed off. "No one," he went on, "wants a governor of New Jersey with a New Hampshire accent." He said he knew a lady in New York who worked with Broadway actors. "Give her a few weeks and she'll have you talking just like everyone else."

I didn't have to think about the advice very long. If I couldn't run as myself, I didn't want to run. So I kept my name, my teeth, and my accent and hired a new political consultant, the firm of Bailey-Deardourff, with which I had worked on the Ford campaign the previous year.

I didn't have a lot of money. Our contributions were coming mostly in ten- and twenty-dollar checks, while the opposition was well heeled. We decided to spend most of our money early, to convince the organization people that my campaign was serious. Bailey-Deardourff put on a five-minute commercial on both New York and Philadelphia television, advertising my record. The reaction was good and my young campaign staff began to think about the possibility of an upset.

I knew better. The party establishment never wavered in their support of Ray Bateman. I wanted to talk about jobs, what had gone wrong in our schools, and ways to clean up our environment. People weren't listening. The voters, and especially the press, were obsessed with just one issue, a perennial one in New Jersey—the income tax. A few years before, the legislature had passed and Governor Byrne had signed the state's first income tax law, the money going primarily for education.

Both Ray and I had supported various versions of the tax, although neither of us had voted for the final version signed by Governor Byrne. Both of us had said during the campaign that we would support repeal of the Byrne tax. I vividly remember one meeting in Passaic where Ray succumbed to the urging of the antitax crowd, and said he would never allow any income tax during his four year term as governor. I couldn't go that far. I could support changes in the tax to make it more progressive, but to abolish it completely was impossible. How else could we support our schools? Ray's was the popular position, however. I knew right then that I had lost the primary. I also had an inkling that Ray had tied a rock around his neck for the general election.

As election day neared, Ray Bateman continued to build his lead. He was getting contributions of five and ten thousand dollars, while we were still scrambling to get fifty-dollar checks. And we made our share of mistakes. At the recommendation of Bailey-Deardourff, which had done an outstanding job up to that point, we decided to put all of the rest of our money into one final television spot to air on the weekend before the primary. As I went over the proposed script for the spot, I was uneasy. It didn't feel right. But with ten days to go there really wasn't time to make changes. The ad showed me exhorting a group of college students about how it was time to open up government. I was yelling and emotional. The commercial was awful. My wife, Debby, is the best judge of commercials I know. We saw the spot for the first time late one night after a long day of campaigning. She was angry. "That's not you," she said. "If we've put all our money into that, we won't even come close." She was dead right. The commercial showed me being someone I was not. Even my strongest supporters said that that person was not the Tom Kean they were supporting. I learned my lesson: never depend on campaign consultants, no matter how competent. The best commercials are simply you being yourself. So if you don't like a spot, don't use it.

After losing the primary by 45,000 votes, I called Ray Bateman and told him I would provide whatever help I could in the general election campaign. I expected Ray to win, and to serve eight years in office.

That's not the way things turned out. Ray is a good man and would have been a fine governor. But as the summer wore on, his campaign grew disorganized and unfocused. He responded to Governor Byrne's challenge to spell out how he would pay for education with a tax plan that was hastily conceived and ridiculed in the press. In January 1978, Brendan Byrne, a year earlier rated as one of the most unpopular governors in New Jersey history, was sworn in for his second term. I watched the inauguration that day with a certain sadness. Politics had been good to me, but I had served the public for a good ten years and now my service was over.

2

You Are the Governor, Maybe

I<small>N</small> the fall of 1980 I had to make a decision. I had returned to running my real estate firm, but kept busy with a number of other pursuits. Governor Byrne, in a generous and bipartisan move, had appointed me to the part-time position of commissioner of the New Jersey Highway Authority. I also returned to my first love, teaching. I taught a graduate-level course in political science at Rutgers, our state university. I was busy, but not entirely happy or fulfilled. At forty-five, I wasn't really sure what I wanted to do with the rest of my life. My days were fragmented as I divided my time preparing for my class at Rutgers, meeting with the Highway Authority, and working on consolidating my company's real estate holdings. But I had no clear plans, no goal for the next ten years.

As I moved around the state, I was surprised by the number of people who asked, "Are you going to run again?" I said I didn't think so, because I doubted I could win a Republican primary and I knew Debby had not been comfortable with parts of the 1977 campaign. But I didn't want to finally shut the door. So I kept up my political contacts and attended the obligatory affairs.

I also kept in touch with public issues by appearing as a political commentator on New Jersey public television. Once a week, I appeared on the nightly news show with former state treasurer Richard Leone, an intelligent and socially liberal Democrat, to discuss various state and national issues. I enjoyed the medium and discovered the freedom a journalist has to express his views unencumbered by political consider- ations. I liked what I was doing so much that I turned down requests to manage both the Reagan and Bush campaigns in New Jersey. Instead, I hoped to cover the 1980 Republican National Convention in Detroit. Early one summer evening I had dinner with Dick Leone. He too had reached a crossroads. For my part, I told him I was getting bored with real estate and that if I didn't run for governor, I wasn't quite sure what else I was going to do. "You know," Dick said, "I've heard worse reasons for running."

Actually there were several other reasons, both personal and political, for my decision to give the governor's job one more try. New Jersey's fortunes had continued to spiral downward. Governor Brendan Byrne had done some good things for the state. He had overseen the opening of the Meadowlands Sports Complex and was fighting to protect the Pinelands in southern New Jersey, the largest undeveloped piece of land between Washington and Boston. But though he was successful in these areas, he ignored emerging problems in economic development, prison overcrowding, transportation, and education.

The economy was still a basket case, worse than when I ran in 1977. We had lost 400,000 jobs since 1970, and unemployment was rising steadily toward double digits. Meanwhile, many economists pre- dicted that all future economic growth would be limited to the Sunbelt states, with the prognosis for New Jersey and other "Rustbelt" states being permanent recession and continued population decline. To me, this made no sense. New Jersey and the Northeast had the human and other resources to become the nation's economic leader, not its doormat. I felt I had some ideas that could work. What's more, I believed I had the background and experience to translate those ideas into policy. New Jersey needed a leader who understood its full potential.

Still, I wasn't sure I really wanted to be governor. I had been close enough to the job to understand its frustrations and the demands it places on one's personal life. There'd never been enough fire in my belly to make me believe that my election was essential to New Jersey's economic health or the well-being of the democracy. I view politics mostly as an obligation, as one way of paying our country back for the good fortune it has bestowed upon me. I have many other interests— sports and music, to name two. Above all, I love my family and I would rather spend time with them than do anything else. At home, I

can be very lazy. I enjoy puttering around the house on a weekend. Sometimes I like to take a day off from work and just go for a walk in the woods, or spend an evening at the movies with my sons or my daughter. All that is virtually impossible for the governor of a big state like New Jersey.

The final decision came not from within but from without, from a core of dedicated people who over the years had come to believe in me. People like Tony Cicatiello; Carla Squier, a perennial on my assembly campaigns; and Phil Kaltenbacher, my old assembly running mate. Tony was constantly calling me, saying, "Make sure you go to the big political dinner next week. You have to keep a high profile." These supporters told me that I really had to run, that I was the best candidate. When you know that able people who love government for all the right reasons believe in you, it makes it very hard to say no. The fact was that our dedicated band from 1977 was staying together without a great deal of encouragement from the candidate—and that, as a source of motivation, was compelling.

For me, politics has always been people. I remember primary night in 1974. I had just lost to Millicent Fenwick but, as I said, I wasn't feeling bad, because I wasn't sure I wanted to go to Washington. I had made the election close, and for me, that was good enough. Then I saw a woman crying at the headquarters. I knew how hard she had worked. She had taken a leave from her job to go door-to-door and run a bank of telephones. The only reason she did it was that she believed I would make a good congressman. Suddenly I felt terrible. I thought, here are people who have given so much and now I've let them down. Knowing that people care so deeply keeps you going late at night on the campaign trail and it gets you out of bed at five in the morning to be at the factory gates. People are politics, and I was listening to the people who cared about me in 1980.

I was pleased to discover that not only was my original campaign organization intact, but joining it were a new group of supporters. Many simply refused to believe that my mind was anything but made up. Debby was not entirely happy with the idea but in the end, she put aside her reservations. Whatever I wanted to do, she said, was okay with her. The point was, as one friend put it, "If you don't run this year, you'll never get another chance."

So I decided to make one more try. Unlike 1977, when my race had been largely to deliver a message, this time I thought I had a chance to win. Politics is like anything else: the more you do it, the better you become. I had learned a great deal from the 1977 race. I thought that just maybe if we put together a good campaign we could win the primary. But other people's thoughts were running along the same lines. A combination of Governor Byrne's abysmal popularity ratings and New Jersey's public-financing law emboldened twenty-one people—eight Republicans and thirteen Democrats—to enter the primary.

Byrne had been a good governor, but his administration had lurched from one public relations disaster to another. He was accused of using the state helicopter for personal trips. His daughter was found with a state car in Washington, D. C. He traveled to more foreign countries than any governor in the state's history. And all this made the newspapers. He acquired a public-be-damned reputation which impaired his political capital and reduced his leverage in the legislature, one controlled by his own party.

No single event contributed to Governor Byrne's unpopularity as much as the naming of the state's new sports arena for Byrne himself. One reason for New Jersey's identity crisis was that we didn't have a major league sports franchise. Fans rooted for teams located in New York or Philadelphia. In the late 1960s Governor William Cahill, with the able assistance of his state treasurer, Joe McCrane, had floated the idea of building a racetrack and stadium on a patch of swampland in East Rutherford, six miles as the crow flies from the Empire State Building. Revenue from the racetrack would defray the cost of operating the stadium. As leader of the Republicans in the assembly, I was a strong supporter of the idea. It's hard to remember that the Meadowlands, today the most successful sports complex in North America, was once regarded as a risky venture. But back then the country had not yet seen sports franchises move from inner cities to the suburbs. And there was no guarantee that the racetrack would make enough money to pay for the stadium. That uncertainty did not keep Cahill from negotiating with the New York Yankees to become the new stadium's tenants. The talks broke down after New York mayor John Lindsay offered to spend almost $100 million refurbishing Yankee Stadium and the surrounding neighborhood. But while the Yankees said no, the football Giants, who had always wanted a home of their own, were keenly interested. In 1971, when I was speaker, the state legislature approved legislation to build the racetrack and stadium with the Giants as primary occupants.

Then things got interesting. Sensing political fallout from a Giants move, the Rockefeller administration put pressure on New York banks to reject the bonds needed to finance the stadium's construction. My friend Nick Brady, chairman of the investment house of Dillon, Read, went to Governor Cahill and explained that no one would buy the sports complex bonds because they were too risky.

At this point the whole project could easily have collapsed. But for once the powers-that-be in New Jersey worked together. Leading the way was the state's largest newspaper, the *Star Ledger* of Newark. Daily, the *Star Ledger* ran front-page stories on the sports complex's progress. Frequent editorials built public support. Soon the *Ledger* could report that New Jersey banks, along with one of the state's most important corporations, the Prudential Insurance Company of America, would take the risk and back the stadium bonds. Recently elected Brendan Byrne announced he would back those bonds with "the moral authority" of state government.

On September 1, 1976, the Meadowlands racetrack opened its gates to a horde of fervid horseplayers, and in a matter of weeks the Meadowlands established itself among the premier racetracks in the nation. Six weeks later the Giants played their first game at Giants Stadium before a sellout crowd of more than 76,000. The cynics and doubters were proved wrong. The racetrack and stadium were so successful that plans were approved for construction of an indoor arena, adjacent to the football stadium. The 20,000-seat arena opened in 1980 and is today home to the basketball Nets and the hockey Devils.

Once the arena opened, the Meadowlands' commissioners decided to pay tribute to three men who had shepherded the sports complex from the drawing board to completion. The racetrack would be named after former governor Cahill. One of the main feeder roads leading to the stadium would be named after Sonny Werblin, the first head of the Meadowlands. And the arena would be named after Governor Byrne, who was still in office.

Both Governor Cahill and Sonny Werblin declined the honor. Byrne kept quiet, and did nothing to discourage the designation by the commissioners, all of whom he had appointed. So the home of the Nets and Devils became known as the Brendan Byrne Arena, and its namesake, while guaranteeing himself national notoriety, earned the undying enmity of his state's sports fans. The animosity lingers to this day. Seldom do I conduct a town meeting or host a radio show without someone complaining about the name of the arena. Even now, seven years later, there are bills pending in the legislature to get the arena's name changed.

A lesson for public officials is never to name anything for someone still in office. There is plenty of time after they leave to decide whether the honor is deserved. I was reminded of this lesson after I was elected governor, when Senator Harrison Williams went to prison and a reporter asked me what I thought about the recently named Harrison Williams Metropark.

In any case, the crowded primary field produced some ludicrous situations. I would go to a debate with twenty other candidates and have thirty seconds to speak on an issue. It was virtually impossible to get any point across. I eventually decided to skip the mass events, even when they were televised.

As in 1977, I was not the favorite. County leaders, with a few rare exceptions, were uneasy with my candidacy. Most favored Pat Kramer, who had done a fine job as mayor of Paterson, the state's third largest city. The other two contenders were Bo Sullivan, a gregarious business-man who refused public financing so he could spend an unlimited amount of his own money on his campaign, and state senator Jim Wallwork, who proclaimed himself the real conservative in the race. As usual I was the outsider, with only three of twenty-one Republican county chair-men endorsing my candidacy.

I knew I had to do two things to win the primary. First, I had to offer a credible platform on the environment, education, and especially on ways to create new jobs. Second, I had to lay out my ideas without saying anything that would come back to haunt me in the general election. The history of New Jersey's gubernatorial elections, like the history of U. S. presidential campaigns, is replete with candidates who bowed to interest-group pressure to win primaries only to find their positions unsupportable in the general election.

I felt that New Jersey's long-standing economic malaise could be traced to the political philosophy in vogue. In that philosophy, the economy was thought to be a zero-sum game, with many believing we had moved into an era in which economic growth was impossible. So a politician's job was to manage scarce resources. In the 1970s, the advocates of the no-growth philosophy forgot that the best way to fund our social goals, whether they be good schools, a clean environment, or a more comfortable life for the less fortunate, was a constantly expanding economy.

New Jersey elected officials, while not exactly members of the Club of Rome, also forgot about growth. Leaders of both parties viewed the business community as nothing more than a cash cow. For years, politicians concentrated only on ways to slice up the economic pie, not make it bigger. It was a pessimistic view of government and a pessimistic view of life. As I watched the Byrne administration in action, I was reminded of one of the last speeches ever given by Winston Churchill, in which he said: "Some see private enterprise as a predatory target to be shot, others as a cow to be milked, but few are those who see it as a sturdy horse pulling the wagon."

New Jersey was so busy shooting and milking private enterprise that businesses left the state in droves and those that stayed never acquired the clout or organization to fight back. Moreover, the business community didn't help its own cause. Business has a peculiar habit, both at the state level and in Washington, of contributing to every incumbent, regardless of whether he supports or opposes their interests. As a result, legislators vote with impunity against business interests all the time.

New Jersey had a number of onerous taxes that had built up over time. For example, because we taxed assets as well as profits, large urban manufacturing businesses that were just barely surviving had to pay huge taxes on their assets. The taxes invariably helped to drive businesses out of the cities and too often out of the state as well.

Supply-side economics offered an alternative to traditional thinking. I studied it very carefully when it was arcane to most people. My friend Jeff Bell was one of its earliest proponents. One of the darlings of the New Right, Jeff had upset incumbent Cliff Case in a 1978 Republican senatorial primary, only to lose to Bill Bradley in the general election. Jeff helped convince me of the truth of the fundamental proposition that certain tax cuts could help create growth and thus bring more revenues into the public treasury. History validates the concept. Economic growth did occur in the mid-1920s after Treasury Secretary Andrew Mellon's tax cut. It occurred again in the 1960s after John Kennedy's tax cut. I was especially impressed with what had happened after Congress slashed the capital gains tax in half in the late 1970s. Investment, and the tax revenue generated by increased investment, grew substantially. I looked at other states that had cut taxes on business and found corresponding growth: states with high taxes saw business fleeing next door to low-tax states.

I came to believe that supply-side economics makes sense, especially at the state level, where competition for business is fierce. If your neighbors have lower tax rates and lower costs, jobs and investments are going to go to them. In 1979, according to the respected Grant-Thornton study,

New Jersey had the forty-sixth worst manufacturing business climate of all the states, in large part because of our high taxes and our antibusiness attitude. If we could get those taxes down, we could begin to attract new jobs and the tax revenues that came with them.

I put together a platform that called for the elimination or reduction of several state taxes as part of a program to promote economic growth. The New Jersey press corps, conditioned to campaigns in which nothing but taxes was discussed, fastened on the proposal and made it, as far as they were concerned, the centerpiece of my campaign. Supply-side economics was much in the news, and my proposals to revive New Jersey's sagging economy started getting some national attention. The word in Washington was that Tom Kean wanted to administer some conservative medicine to New Jersey's sick economy.

☆

I have always distrusted political labels. For one thing, they are protean. The terms "conservative" and "liberal" have shifted so often over time that they have become almost meaningless. I've seen as much in my own lifetime. Senator Bob Taft, "Mr. Conservative" of the 1940s and early 1950s, would hardly recognize some of the views of Georgia congressman Newt Gingrich. Harry Truman would have similar problems with the likes of Walter Mondale.

Abraham Lincoln defined conservatism as "adherence to the old and tried against the new and untried." In my father's time, a conservative was someone who preached balanced budgets and who favored high tariffs and an isolationist foreign policy. Today, a conservative had better be right on abortion, support the Contras, believe in free trade, and be more than a little interventionist in foreign policy. As a supply-sider, today's conservative does not believe that a balanced budget is sacrosanct.

My own conservatism is really a blend of various traditions. I start with a belief in limited government and a reverence for fiscal discipline. I simply believe it is wrong to spend more money than you raise from taxes. I believe the private sector, in almost every instance, can do things better than the public sector. If you find a program or function that the private sector can perform, you ought to put it into private hands. In general, my political philosophy is that government ought to stay out of people's lives as much as possible. People ought to have the opportunity to help themselves.

But our Judeo-Christian heritage demands that we have the compassion to help those who cannot help themselves: the ill, the infirm, and the elderly. Compassion is a necessary virtue, not a luxury, in a democracy like ours, and government is the only institution that can do what is necessary. What's more, many people, especially the young, do not have the chance to develop their talents and abilities. Maybe these people can't rent a home because they are black or Hispanic. Maybe their local schools are nothing more than warehouses where it is impossible to learn how to read and write. Maybe they grew up without a father. These people deserve a decent chance. Government action is often their only hope.

In fact, giving people a chance is not compassion, but enlightened self-interest. For example, by the turn of the century, one out of three children in our nation's schools will come from a minority background. Many will be raised in poverty. But society needs these people because they are the work force of the future. They can keep our democracy as well as our economy strong and resilient. Government has to provide an opportunity for all Americans by giving them a reasonable start at productive, fulfilling lives. After that, they are on their own.

I have always felt this way. It's moved me to get involved in a number of areas like education, civil rights, and urban policy, where you don't find many Republicans or conservatives. As a result, a great many in my party consider me a moderate or even a liberal, which in the Reagan era means I am in some circles viewed with considerable suspicion. The notion that conservatives shouldn't talk about education or urban policy is nonsense, but I had to convince my friends on the right that I could interest myself in those issues and still deserve their support.

That's where supply-side economics came in. The inclusive theme of growth driven by supply-side economics enabled us to bring into our tent the disparate elements of the Republican party. So I formed a strong coalition including Kean loyalists from 1977, old assembly colleagues, and a large band of articulate supply-side conservatives. Thanks to my record in education and the environment, I also attracted people who described themselves as moderates. To see what was going on, the conservative political columnist Bob Novak came to New Jersey. He wrote that Tom Kean had "ended seventy years of internal Republican strife" between what he called "the liberal, blue-blood aristocracy and the populist right."

Hyperbolic, perhaps, but supply-side economics did enable Republicans, for the first time since the New Deal, to sell themselves as the party of growth and opportunity. Now we could talk about positive themes, instead of always talking about what programs we would cut. Republicans were always saying "Yes, but . . ." Supply-side economics gave us a way to be clearly affirmative and optimistic.

The national prominence of supply-side theory gave my tax-cutting platform the intellectual coherence and credence it might otherwise have lacked. I was helped considerably by the endorsement of several important national Republicans. Jeff Bell endorsed my candidacy. Jack Kemp, Republican congressman from Buffalo, New York, violated one of the first rules of politics and came in to campaign for me during a Republican primary. I have always felt greatly indebted to Jack, who risked political capital to back me, and I continue to admire him for his courage in pursuing his ideas. So, with a campaign based on education, environmental protection, law and order, and, above all, job creation through tax cuts, I started to travel around the state.

Any campaign, however, is only as good as the people it attracts. This time, as before, I attracted the young. Bob Franks, a campaign veteran at the age of thirty, was one of the first to join. His ability to recruit various political makers and shakers proved essential. Al Fasola at thirty-two took over what for me had always been a chore, fund raising. Ken Merin, thirty-four, handled the issues and wrote speeches. And after a number of tries, I was able to convince a young man named Roger Bodman to be my campaign manager. Roger had started with Millicent Fenwick and I had gotten to know him as the staffer with the most astute mind in the ill-fated Bateman campaign of 1977. Since then he had successfully managed Jim Courter to a stunning primary and general election upset for a congressional seat. Congressman Courter also took a political risk by becoming overall chairman of the campaign.

I also thought hard about political consultants. I decided to ask my friends from 1977, Bailey-Deardourff, to do the television and radio. But I wanted more than I thought they could deliver. Watching the Reagan campaign of 1980, I became impressed with a young man named Roger Stone, who had been a Young Republican and an activist since Nixon's day and was assigned New Jersey by the Reagan campaign for the 1980 presidential primary. Before Roger's arrival, the Reagan forces had asked me to be the state campaign manager. I declined, preferring my role on public television. But Roger wouldn't take no for an answer. He called my friends, he hounded me, he had contributors contact me. Calls came to my house and office from both the future president and Nancy Reagan. Even though I thought I had firmly made up my mind, I was almost persuaded to change it. Roger was also making incredible headway in a state which, by past performance, should have gone by default to George Bush. I made a mental note that if I ran again, I wanted Roger to be part of the team. This proved to be one of the wisest decisions I made. The collaboration of my two consultants showed my campaign's broad appeal. Up to that point, Stone worked only for "conservative" candidates and Deardourff worked only for "moderates." In my campaign, they worked together for the first time. That made a statement to the party.

☆

As primary day approached, I was cautiously optimistic, even though the state's newspapers didn't give me much of a chance. I knew a number of things they didn't. First, I knew ours was the best campaign team assembled in New Jersey in my political lifetime. Second, I knew from my appearances that our issues were going over well. And third, unlike 1977, I was getting excellent reaction to Deardourff's television and to Roger Stone's direct-mail pieces.

On primary day I won going away. Something important then happened almost immediately. All seven Republican candidates closed ranks behind me. Bo Sullivan, along with his family, appeared on election night at my headquarters to congratulate me. It must not have been easy for him, but I can't tell you what a lift I got from my opponents' support. Too many campaigns spend the entire first month after a primary trying to put the party together. Bo and the other GOP candidates did that within ten days. However, the joy I felt that night and the next morning was short-lived. The Democratic primary was won by Congressman Jim Florio, perceived at that time to be the strongest possible Democratic candidate. The early polls showed him a good twenty-five points ahead. Nobody, including me, really felt at that point that I would be the state's next governor.

Congressman Florio was well known to the voters. For six years he had represented the city of Camden in Congress. Before that, we had served together briefly in the assembly. I was the speaker, Jim a bright and extremely ambitious member of the minority. In Congress, he had a reputation among his colleagues for doing anything and everything to get his name in the newspapers. In New Jersey, he had few friends but numerous allies. As candidates for governor, we offered the voters a number of contrasts. Jim Florio is in many ways an unreconstructed, 1960s-style liberal. While President Reagan sold his federal budget cuts as a way to cut the waste from the federal government and shift responsibility to the states, Florio opposed each and every budget cut down the line. Jim sincerely believes that in any given circumstance, the public sector will do things just as well as and definitely more fairly than the private sector. He also seems to prefer to have the federal government do the work rather than the states. While I was pitching tax cuts as a way to get the economy moving again, he saw them as nothing more than a giveaway. While I attacked the Byrne administration's record, Jim tried to focus the debate on federal issues. I think Jim Florio convinced himself he was running against Ronald Reagan, not Tom Kean.

On the face of it, that was not a foolish strategy in the summer of 1981. The national economy was slowing as the Federal Reserve tightened the money supply to combat inflation, even while the president's budget cuts promised less revenue to cities and states. It certainly did not look like the right time to be running as a Republican, especially in a Democratic state like New Jersey.

For the general election, I decided again to cut against the grain. Most political strategists, especially Republican strategists, will tell you that the way to beat your opponent is to go to your strength, get out your own vote. By this conventional wisdom, the reason politicians lose elections is that they don't do a good job maximizing the potential of their natural base of support. In a state like New Jersey, the strategy means that Republicans should concentrate on the white-collar suburbs and rural towns and write off the cities and blue-collar communities to the Democrats.

I have always rejected that approach because for every vote you get by going into the enemy's backyard, you're getting two votes, one from him and one for you. You also attract a lot of attention. When I first ran for the assembly I spent most of my time in the blue-collar, Democratic town of Irvington, and I carried it every time I ran. This time I decided to pursue the same strategy in a larger arena. What did I have to lose? I was twenty-five points down in the polls.

So, to the dismay of most party regulars, I spent the summer of 1981 on a campaign tour of New Jersey's thirteen largest cities. I shook hands in places that hadn't seen a working Republican politician in years and didn't quite know how to treat one. I began the campaign in the heart of my opponent's political base, the city of Camden, right across the river from Philadelphia. It was a day I'll never forget. I knew a lot about Newark, the state's largest city. I had represented a part of the city in the state assembly and I had walked its streets the Sunday following the riots in 1967. I thought I had seen everything.

I was wrong. I had not been in Camden in about ten years and I was totally unprepared for what I saw. The city lay in ruins. Children lived in abandoned buildings. Men lolled on trash-strewn street corners. From the so-called center of town the ruin stretched in every direction. There was not, I was told, a new building under construction within the entire city limits. City government was bankrupt, both financially and morally.

As I walked around the city, trailed by television crews and newspaper reporters, throngs of people followed me. Many of them were teenage males who would beg for a job saying, "You are running for office. Hire me!" I was shaken. In politics, it's easy to spend your time talking numbers and concepts and theories. As a concept, economic decline doesn't really mean anything until you have real people come up to you and beg for work. That reaches you. I think of the campaign stops in Camden even today; we've made real progress, but a city like Camden still has a very long way to go.

My campaign strategy was questioned not only privately by Republican insiders, but publicly by editorial writers and columnists. Critics couldn't understand why I was wasting my time in the cities, where the few people who voted were Democrats. I read that Kean just didn't have "fire in his belly"; that I was spending my time making points or "spreading an idealistic message," rather than building a real base of support to win an election. Party leaders complained that I wasn't going to all the party dinners and meetings. They phoned Roger Bodman every day to ask for the usual trappings of a campaign: signs, billboards, T-shirts, buttons. Few felt that our plan to save our money for a final television, radio, and direct-mail blitz made any sense.

I didn't miss an opportunity to hit the traditional Democratic voter, going to every ethnic organization event to which I could get an invitation. I spoke at Polish, Ukrainian, Irish, German, and Scandinavian affairs, and was always amazed when my opponent failed to show. I spoke in union halls, and confronted Florio before the NAACP. Everywhere I went, I challenged him to debate, at one point standing in front of his district office in Camden to dramatize my call.

Nevertheless, everybody thought I was being too nice. Some of my advisers went public with the idea that the only way I could win was to "go negative"—ignore the issues and attack my opponent personally. Florio had been running negative ads against me for some time, accusing me of everything from wanting to cut people's Social Security to planning to open a uranium mine. I never felt comfortable with that approach because I don't think of myself as a negative person. In this case, I also felt that negative ads would simply detract from the real issues I was trying to get across in the campaign.

Yet the criticisms stung. The hardest part of the campaign was having the confidence to ignore the people who were upset and stick to my original strategy.

The most important and yet most difficult thing in politics is to be true to your own instincts. For the practical politician, Shakespeare was right: "To thine own self be true." Why? Because it is in the candidate's best interest. I've seen so many politicians try to be someone they're not. But in the age of television, the public will spot a phony every time.

Ronald Reagan has been a successful politician because he is always Ronald Reagan. In private, he is exactly the same man as in public—the same anecdotes, the same values. Ed Koch doesn't become somebody else when he goes home at night. Neither does Mario Cuomo. Neither does any other real master of the art of politics in our country today. If you try to be someone you're not, the public picks up on it quickly and votes the other way.

The same is true of issues. You'd better believe what you're saying in a campaign because television is an unrelenting critic. Most people are at their best when they are saying what they believe to be true. When they twist things even a little, hoping to win a block of voters, the discomfort usually shows. Eventually the voters look at the face on TV and conclude that "the guy doesn't believe what he is saying." I've seen it happen again and again. The public is much smarter than either politicians or political pundits think.

In the 1981 primary, I was approached by some people from antiabortion groups, who told me they could be very helpful if I would come out publicly on their side. A number of them were friends of mine who wanted to support me and had reason to believe their support in a Republican primary could make the difference. I met with the antiabortion activists. I went to their homes. I watched the films and read the books they gave me. These were good, decent people who believed absolutely in their cause. I liked them as individuals and found that I could support many of their group's positions. In our country, needless abortions are performed, many horribly late in the pregnancy. I would like to see abortions limited, but I simply could not agree to support a Constitutional amendment to deny women the right to an abortion in every instance. So, reluctantly in some cases, the activists worked for one of my opponents. I didn't like losing their support, but had I accepted their case, I would have violated my own integrity, and the voters would have known.

My style of campaigning also came under scrutiny. My opponent was attending fourteen events a day, flying all over the state, and shaking as many hands as humanly possible. I simply couldn't manage that, and some people argued that it proved I was too "laid-back" to handle the job of governor.

My own style on the hustings is plodding and informal. I don't look at campaigning as a chore, where the idea is to see as many people as possible, give a set speech, say the cute line, smile at the camera, and then leave. I try to enjoy myself. I find a joy in campaigning because it gives me the chance to meet and, if I do it right, to develop real contact with thousands of different people.

Keep in mind that a campaign event may be the only time the people there will get to see you. They deserve something personal. If you can't give them that in the half hour allotted by schedule, then maybe they should be given more time. If someone stops you on the way out of an event with a legitimate question, they deserve an answer. That goes for reporters, too. I remember once an aide to a state legislator pointed out that I had given as much time to a reporter for a local weekly as I had to the one from the *New York Times*. I took that as a compliment.

My style of campaigning, of course, is not easy on my staff. I became notorious for being hours late for events scheduled for the end of the day. No watches could be set by "Tom Kean standard time," reporters said. Typical was an event where I met a chatty elderly woman who spent ten minutes telling me about her family and asking me how I would change one of the state's senior-citizen programs. I listened while a campaign aide glared at me, motioning that it was time to move on. Finally, the woman finished and I told her that I enjoyed talking to her and that I hoped she would vote for me on November 4. "Oh, I don't live in New Jersey, I live in Pennsylvania," she said. That's how campaign aides get ulcers.

Most politicians love to talk. I also enjoy listening. Perhaps it's because I was the fifth of six children. Perhaps it was the lonely summers, or the fact that I grew up with few friends my own age. Whatever the reason, I have never had a problem sitting quietly while others talk.

As I said, one of the joys of politics is the people you meet on the campaign trail. In 1981, I got to know a man named Ralph White, a black mechanic from Elizabeth who had moved to New Jersey from the Caribbean. One day he just showed up at headquarters, told the staff he liked what he had read about Tom Kean, and offered to pitch in any way he could. Pitch in he did, working tirelessly night after night. Soon he started showing up at campaign events. I would arrive and Ralph would already be there, handing out bumper stickers, plastering signs on walls, talking to people, always with a smile on his face. Whenever I spoke he sat in the front row and cheered louder than anyone else. He was confident. "Democracy works," he assured me. "You'll win."

I developed a real affection for this exuberant, cheery man. Sometimes he would hop in his car and follow me to the next campaign stop. He would lecture me constantly about democracy, about how lucky we were in America, and the things we needed to do to make the country better and stronger. He never tired of saying that this was the greatest country in the world and that everybody ought to be involved in politics to keep it that way.

After a while, I began to get a little worried about Ralph. I knew he didn't have any money and he was spending a small fortune on gasoline just to follow me around the state. Ralph's boss was an active Democrat, and I learned from someone in the headquarters that Ralph was in trouble at work because he spent too much time helping me.

After the election, I lost track of Ralph for a time. About four months after I had been sworn in as governor, he suddenly appeared in my outer office. One of my new staffers didn't know who he was and was giving him a hard time. I recognized Ralph's voice and rushed out to greet him.

He said, "Governor Kean, I want you to know that I am ready to join the Governor's Club and become one of your major supporters." The Governor's Club is a $500-per-member organization and I knew there was no way Ralph could afford it. I said, "Ralph, that is not necessary, you have done more than enough already." He replied, "Don't worry. I just won a million dollars in the New Jersey lottery. It always hurt my heart that I couldn't help you with money in the past; now I am going to be one of your biggest contributors." Ralph proved that a nice guy will finish first. I've had very few fund-raisers since at which Ralph White, with his splendid smile and his vision of America the Beautiful, hasn't been a full participant.

For me, the best part of the campaign is meeting the thousands of Ralph Whites who are out there—good people who believe in a candidate or an idea and are willing to work unbelievably long hours to support either or both. You see them at rallies, stuffing envelopes at headquarters, or testifying at public hearings, because they know that one man or woman can make a difference. God bless them. Without them I would fear for our democracy. That's why on the campaign trail I will listen to anyone: senior citizens, doormen, the police guarding the event, and especially children. If I leave a place and know that I have left questions unanswered or people unsatisfied, I think about it the rest of the day. It bothers me and affects my performance. That's why I stick to my own pace. I do what I want. If that doesn't go over, the voters will elect someone else. It is as simple as that.

There was one thing I could change, however, and that was the way I dressed. In the assembly I had favored an old tweed jacket. If I had a campaign event to attend, I would slip on an old suit and never think about it. While my habits were perfectly okay in the relaxed atmosphere of the assembly, they did not serve me well as a prospective governor. I remember campaigning at a factory in 1977 when I happened to be wearing a belt Debby had made in honor of my bill saving Sunfish Pond. The belt showed in relief animals and trees near a small pond with a sign reading "No fishing." As I walked past a group of workers, I overheard somebody say, "He seems like a nice guy, but would you vote for a guy who wears a belt that says 'No fishing'?"

This time around, Tony Cicatiello told me to retire my old tweed jacket and buy two new suits. I figured Shakespeare's advice to be true to yourself didn't apply to clothes, so I reluctantly forked over the money.

Of course, even with two new suits, I wasn't exactly a fashion plate. That's why it came as some surprise that the year after I was elected governor I was named one of the ten best-dressed men in the world by a group called the Fashion Foundation of America. I was listed with Prince Charles, Helmut Kohl, Roger Moore, and six other sartorial stars. This I did not expect.

I heard about the award in Washington when I was attending the annual White House dinner for the nation's governors. It's a formal occasion that most governors look forward to. As I dressed in the hotel, one of my aides mentioned something about a best-dressed list, but I thought he was joking. Anyway, because I had packed for the trip myself, my suspenders, black socks, and evening shoes were missing from my suitcase. At six o'clock on a Sunday evening, there was nothing to do but improvise. I polished my black loafers as much as possible, hoped my pants were long enough to hide my socks, buttoned my jacket, and prayed that my pants would stay up without suspenders. In the receiving line at the White House, I found myself standing next to Kit Bond, then governor, and today senator, from Missouri. He congratulated me about the best-dressed list, and then looked down and saw my old black loafers sticking out from under my trousers. I'll never forget the look on his face.

Not only did I change the way I dressed in 1981, I also worked on my speaking style. At the suggestion of Phil Kaltenbacher, I spent two sessions with Dorothy Sarnoff, a former actress in New York, who helps politicians and corporate executives work on their public performances. I had always worried about my speaking, which probably is to be expected for someone who stuttered as badly as I once did. I still suffer from a case of nerves before major speeches. But over the years I had improved, trying to concentrate more on content than delivery. Dorothy Sarnoff's best advice was to tell me simply to talk louder and more forcefully. From my teaching days I had always been soft-spoken and conversational. She convinced me to be more aggressive.

The press observed the new suits and the aggressive speaking style and announced a "new Tom Kean." Some reporters even suggested that my conversion to supply-side economics had affected the way I dressed and spoke. It was by no means that calculated. I was simply trying to look and sound better.

☆

The campaign quickly worked its way through the summer months and into the fall. I lived at fairs, picnics, and clambakes. Throughout, I grew increasingly frustrated by the press corps' preoccupation with the supply-side tax-cut issue, to the exclusion of everything else. If I put out a detailed, twenty-page position paper on education, it would be buried on Page 30 of the newspaper. But if I talked about tax cuts, that was Page 1 news.

My numbers in the polls were moving, but very slowly. In September,

they still showed me over fifteen points behind. That hurt fund-raising as people and organizations looking for a winner gravitated toward my opponent. We were to have one debate before Labor Day. If there was to be a turning point in the campaign, I knew that was it. I wanted to be aggressive in the debate and as it turned out I was, surprising even myself. My performance raised Republican morale and most observers thought I had won. But everyone knew I was still far behind. Somehow I had to focus things. I believed that if I could just get people to listen, I could win.

Part of my problem was the media, which perhaps out of necessity more than anything else, tilts political campaigns toward hyperbole and sensationalization. As a candidate, you are competing for the general public's attention with innumerable other events and people, many of them more exciting and more important to the average person than you are. Fires and murders, movie stars and home team victories, can all make politics come over as dull.

So you find yourself forced to be more sensational than you probably should. If a detailed position paper on education doesn't get attention, you instead call for the resignation of the state's education commissioner. That is conflict, and conflict gets covered. If reporters won't attend a press conference in your campaign headquarters, you hold your next one on the steps of your opponent's office. Politicians today are always looking for gimmicks, not because they have nothing substantive to say, but because they need a way to reach the people.

Political debates today usually don't serve much purpose and they are dreadfully predictable. Television has made the quip and the epi-gram—the so-called sound bite—much more important than a reasoned exposition on a particular subject. Then too, the League of Women Voters has probably done more than any organization to standardize the debates and make them meaningless, thanks to their rules about one-minute statements and forty-second responses. The Lincoln-Douglas debates would have been forgotten had they had to conform to the League's format.

The only meaningful event that occurred during the rest of our debates in this campaign involved the audience. The third debate was held at Glassboro College in South Jersey, deep in the heart of Jim Florio's territory. His campaign staff had decided to pack the audience. Every time he spoke, they would respond with thunderous applause. Every time I tried to say something, I was greeted with boos and jeers.

After a while, I was embarrassed. My campaign manager, Roger Bodman, was furious. We had been led into a trap. The noise level almost kept me from speaking. What we didn't realize was that the important audience was not the one in the auditorium, but the larger audience watching on television. They saw me being interrupted by what was clearly a rude and partisan crowd, a debate being turned into a circus. Jim Florio lost a tremendous opportunity. All he had to say was, "I'm glad you are for me, but give Tom Kean a chance to speak." Instead, he said nothing. His unrelenting competitiveness kept him from stepping in. I suspect the debate was even on substance, but our mail and calls showed I won a big victory because of the sympathy I received from the press and the television audience.

Jim Florio's strategy in the third debate, and in all our other public appearances, was to continue to link my candidacy with the performance of President Reagan. To Florio, the question before the voters was not whether Jim Florio or Tom Kean would be a better governor, but a referendum on a national policy, on "Reaganomics."

In the summer and fall of 1981, the jury was still very much out on Reaganomics. Within six months of his landslide victory, the president had convinced Congress to approve a dazzling array of tax and budget cuts, reversing a forty-year pattern of increased federal control of everything from education to building sewers. Despite his success, the president's popularity was not high. The country and most particularly the Northeast was slowly sliding into the worst economic slump in fifty years. Everyone from senior citizens to students predicted calamity from the federal cuts. Many New Jerseyans who had supported the president in the fall of 1980 had soured on him by the summer of 1981.

Relations between our campaign and the White House had not been great since late June when I had suggested, in response to a question, that Secretary of the Interior James Watt ought to resign. But in August we received word that the president was willing to come to New Jersey to endorse my candidacy. My campaign staff, sensing the volatile political environment and Reagan's sagging numbers in the polls, was somewhat hesitant to accept the offer. I had no doubts. I figured that if the leader of your party, the president of the United States, wants to endorse you, your only questions should be, "When, and how many people can I invite?"

I've always had a real affection for Ronald Reagan. I admired his skillful performance during the 1980 campaign. And aside from my strong reservations on environmental issues, I had supported him through his first year as president. After the Carter administration, Reagan's optimism was overdue. Finally, we had emerged from the bitterness of Vietnam and the disillusionment of Watergate. Many years before, Archibald MacLeish had said: "Loss of faith in the American proposition is a secret sickness which can bring the country down." Ronald Reagan helped cure that sickness. He made us believe in ourselves again. And that, despite the Iran-Contra affair, may still be his greatest legacy.

The president is a warm, down-to-earth human being. I have always enjoyed the time I've been able to spend with him. I remember one campaign stop he made in New Jersey during his 1984 reelection campaign. I was seated in the back of the White House limousine with the president and then chief of staff Jim Baker as we drove to a campaign rally in Atlantic County. What did we talk about? Not the economy. Not the campaign. A fly was buzzing around loose in the car, so we spent our time talking about the best way to catch it. Jim Baker showed us both what he called fly-catching, Texas style. You sort of sneak up on the fly and clasp your hands an inch in front of it. When the fly moves, you bring your hands together. It works every time, he said. I thought to myself, here I am in a car with probably the two most powerful men in the country, and we are spending our time on the theory and practice of catching flies.

On this occasion in 1981, I had more pressing things on my mind—my election. I arranged to meet the president at the Philadelphia airport and fly with him to Parsippany, New Jersey, where he would endorse my candidacy. At the airport, I saw clear evidence of why he is the Great Communicator.

My television consultant, John Deardourff, had arranged for the president to tape a thirty-second commercial backing my campaign. The crew and lights were set up in a room off one of the runways. When the president arrived he was handed the script. He looked it over for a moment, then sat in front of the camera. His first reading of the script was flawless. He asked John how it went and Deardourff said, "That was perfect. Let's go." The president said, "Wait a minute. I thought that was a little slow." Deardourff looked at him and said, "It was off by one half a second, but that is no problem." The president replied, "Let me try one more time." He looked at the camera and did it again, this time in exactly thirty seconds. Deardourff, who had worked with politicians at every level, was flabbergasted by the performance.

The commercial finished, we took off and flew to New Jersey. We landed at Morristown and were driven to the hotel in Parsippany. For me, there was an air of unreality. I was in a presidential motorcade. Beside me, the president of the United States was asking about my family and worrying with me about the course of my campaign. Judging from the crowd along the way, it was clear that New Jerseyans had not turned their back on Ronald Reagan. The man engenders a real happiness in people, and you could see it in their faces as he waved to the crowds.

On the Parsippany podium, the president was his usual articulate, down-to-earth self. He gave me a ringing endorsement. He handled the fact that Florio had been trying to make the president the issue with humor and style. Reagan said, "I've got a secret for Jim Florio. I'm not the one running for governor of this state." The crowd cheered. Referring to another Florio commercial, the President said, "And by the way, I am not going to cut that little old lady's Social Security, either."

A couple of days later I learned that my staff had not been the only people apprehensive about the presidential visit. The White House staff had seen polling data that still had me eight to ten points behind with only a month to go, and had urged the president not to come. "Why be identified with a loser?" they asked. He disagreed, and came. The trip was propitious for both of us. Postelection analysis would show that Congressman Florio had erred in directly attacking a popular president. And my victory, according to some Washington columnists, became an affirmation of public support for the president's strategy of cutting taxes to spur economic growth.

☆

As the campaign rolled into its final weeks, the polls finally began to show Congressman Florio's lead narrowing. I could sense the momentum shifting. The crowds were bigger. People in shopping malls and city streets started to recognize me. It is a wonderful feeling, after months of campaigning in relative obscurity, to know that your face and your messages are finally registering with the voters. The last few weeks of the campaign flew by in a blur of eighteen-hour days. In any campaign you have to save your best stuff for last, when everyone is watching. You have to be aggressive, fit, and "on" at every campaign stop.

I started to feel that we had an outside chance if everything went right. I remember one campaign stop in Jersey City, in the middle of the Democratic bastion of Hudson County. It was held in the Casino in the Park where Democratic fund-raisers had been held through the years. Some things hadn't changed. The crowd was raucous. As I spoke, I saw two fistfights had broken out in the back of the room. But some things had changed. The room was overflowing with about 1,500 of my supporters. Usually you could fit all the Republican voters in Jersey City into a phone booth.

Jim Florio still had his lead in the polls and New Jersey's two-to-one Democratic edge in registration. He continued to duck most joint appearances while spending a lot of television advertising attacking the president. He stuck to that strategy in the last week of the campaign, even as his own polls showed his lead evaporating.

I remember an incident involving Gabe Pressman, a respected journalist and a longtime figure on New York television news. Florio and I were scheduled to debate on WNBC-TV, with Pressman as the moderator. Florio's staff notified the station that he wouldn't attend the debate. Gabe Pressman was not used to being turned down. His staff called mine to say Gabe was enraged, and to let us know that WNBC would go on with the debate, with Pressman, me, and an empty chair to stand in for Congressman Florio. Evidently, Jim Florio realized that an angry Gabe Pressman wouldn't help his campaign. At the last minute he showed up. It was not the way to treat a veteran newsman. Through the entire half hour Pressman glared at Jim. It was no secret to the television audience who Pressman thought should be the next governor of New Jersey.

Pressman wasn't the only reporter Florio turned down. He chose to ignore an invitation from the *New York Times* editorial staff. And he skipped a television show, *The Last Word*, on Channel 5 in New York, that was scheduled for Sunday night, forty-eight hours before the election. I had a half hour with the voters, alone, on a major station. The host made sure to remind the viewers that my opponent wasn't there.

Florio's decision to skip the events helped me. So did the editorial writers. I had spent what many advisers thought was an inordinate amount of time in editorial-board interviews. I enjoyed them. They gave me a chance to explain my positions in detail and show my grasp of state problems. In the last two weeks, I secured nineteen out of twenty-one endorsements, including the *New York Times* and Florio's hometown *Camden Courier-Post*. I don't believe that editorial-page opinions make much of a difference, but in a potentially close race, so many newspaper endorsements must have swayed a number of last-minute voters.

Nevertheless, days before the election, not a single political pundit thought I had gained enough ground to win. Some said that I had made it close, but every newspaper and radio station predicted a Florio victory. My opponent asserted that he would win by 200,000 votes and send a message to Washington, a "punch in the mouth" as he called it, about the country's priorities.

☆

For most Americans, Election Day involves a five- or ten-minute jaunt to the polling place to participate in a ritual that began in ancient Greece. For me, the day brought a tremendous sense of relief. I really couldn't think of anything that I would have done differently. Months of excruciatingly difficult work were over, and my destiny was now in the hands of two million other people. I tried to keep my mind off the outcome by playing tennis.

Our first information in was that the turnout was larger than antici-pated. According to the experts, a large turnout was good for the Demo-crats. I was the only one who had felt throughout the campaign that a large turnout would be good for our side.

By dinner hour, however, things were not looking good. Around six o'clock, WABC-TV reported that, according to their exit polls, inde-pendent voters were breaking two to one in favor of Florio. The commenta-tor said that could mean a landslide for the Democrats. Dinner didn't taste very good. Emotionally, I hoped WABC was wrong, but intellectu-ally, I realized the chances of that were slim. At eight o'clock, the polls closed and I turned on my bedroom television. Debby was in the kitchen. At about six minutes past eight, WCBS-TV announced that Jim Florio was the next governor of New Jersey.

I was shaken, not by the fact that I had lost—I was fully prepared for that—but that our hard work had not even made the race close. I remember wanting to get my concession speech over with. I have never liked obvious losers who keep everybody waiting until eleven o'clock before conceding. Let Jim have a good evening, I thought. So I broke the news to Debby, thanked her for all she had done, and told her I wouldn't have done a thing differently. "We gave it our best," I told her. "We just didn't make it."

We got into our car and started the short drive to election-night headquarters at the Holiday Inn in Livingston. On the way, I scribbled out a short and, I hoped, gracious concession. I don't recall it all but I remember ending it with a story about St. Paul. The great missionary, close to death in one of Nero's jails, wrote one last message to his assistant, Timothy, who was almost like a son to him. "I have fought a good fight, I have finished the course, I have kept the faith," Paul wrote. So I planned to end my political career.

Roger Bodman met me when I arrived at headquarters. I told him I was ready to concede. He asked me to wait. Favorable numbers were coming in from a number of Democratic areas. I folded my concession speech and put it in my pocket. By nine o'clock, WCBS and WABC had withdrawn their predictions and said the race was too close to call.

The lead seesawed back and forth through the night. Closeted with my family and close friends, I could hardly believe the numbers. At 11:00 P.M. I was declared the winner by WNBC, but the station withdrew its prediction twenty minutes later. Tension at headquarters was high. By midnight, lawyers were advising us that we should impound voting machines in Democratic strongholds like Camden and Jersey City. At 3:00 A.M., the Holiday Inn was still jammed with my supporters, but I decided to go home and try to get some sleep. The latest figures showed me ahead, but by less than 500 votes.

I awoke the next morning to find the race still up in the air. The *Star Ledger*, while admitting it was still too close to call, had Congressman Florio ahead by 1,130,732 to 1,130,089, a margin of 643 votes. The *New York Times* headline read, "Democrat to Be Governor in New Jersey." The *Washington Post*'s front page read, "Florio Ahead in Race for Governor."

My opponent and I had campaigned tirelessly up and down the state for ten consecutive months. Together we had spent more than $4 million to convey our message to the voters. We had offered them a clear choice between two competing views of the role of government in their lives. What happened? Two and a half million people had split almost exactly evenly in their opinion of the two candidates.

Wednesday, the day after the election, began with maddening uncertainty and ended on a strong note of optimism. The counties all reported their initial totals and I had taken the lead. The *Star Ledger* reported me up by 121 votes, an unbelievably small margin. One week elapsed before the result could be confirmed. By then, I had an edge of 1,688 votes. On Tuesday, November 10, one week after New Jerseyans voted, I stood in front of the press corps in the State House in Trenton and claimed victory. But the tension still didn't subside. Jim Florio, as was his due, requested an official recount.

The month after a campaign is supposed to be relaxing. If you win, you bask in glory, take a vacation, and begin to assemble a staff. If you lose, you pick up the pieces and move on with your life. Either way, you feel relief. But what happens if you tie? In my case, I sat by the phone at my home in Livingston, waiting for the latest word on the recount. We had a number of concerns. First, the paper ballots, including absentee ballots, had to be recounted by hand. Those votes alone could swing the election to Florio. Second, election officials decided to begin to recount the millions of computer cards used in the electronic voting machines. Hundreds of people sat under bright lights in voting recount headquarters across New Jersey, squinting at tiny computer cards. It would have taken six months to count every computer card. After a couple of weeks it became clear that the hand count mirrored the computer count, and the human recounters were sent home. Finally, both sides tried to locate machines that might have malfunctioned. If a malfunction could be proved, the vote from that machine would have to be thrown out.

The rumor mill was working overtime. We heard stories about bags of hand ballots found in the middle of Newark. Two such bags were opened in court. The reporters leaned forward in anticipation and saw old ballots, broken pencils, and loose papers, but no votes. While both parties kept a close eye on the recount, neither wanted to give the impression that we were trying to unduly influence the decision. The prospect of a new election hung over both camps. Once we almost blundered. Some five hundred lawyers and accountants had volunteered to help monitor the recount operation for me. My staff rented two voting machines from a company in Pennsylvania so they could train these volunteers to read an electronic ballot. Somehow, the county sheriff got word that two voting machines were sitting outside Kean campaign headquarters. He called the attorney general's office, which sent state police down to confiscate the machines. My staff spent the next few hours frantically calling the attorney general to clear up the confusion. We could all imagine the headlines: "Kean Supporters Steal Two Voting Machines."

Through the entire nerve-wracking month, my running margin never slipped below 1,688. As small discrepancies were found in some districts, my margin climbed slightly, once as high as 5,000 votes. But never did it drop below 1,688. Finally, on December 5, the recount was validated. My official victory margin was 1,797 votes. Jim Florio learned from his lawyers that no evidence of fraud had been found, and declined a court challenge. One month after the voters went to the polls, my victory was official.

In retrospect, it was a brilliant campaign. Bodman, Deardourff, and Stone had shown themselves a first-class team. Had the election been held a week earlier, I would have lost. I have no doubt of that. Had it been held a week later, I suspect I would have won by a comfortable margin. As it was, after fourteen years in public life, after ten months of intense campaigning, after one of the closest elections in the history of our country, I was governor of New Jersey.

3
A Rough
First Year

THE verdict on the first year of the Kean administration depends on whom you ask. To most of the people of New Jersey, for whom politics is at best an interesting diversion and at worst a total bore, it was an uninspiring year—one that offered little evidence that things had changed in state government and plenty of evidence that the state's fortunes were continuing to slide. To the State House reporters who followed my every move, mine was a stumbling start for an inexperienced governor surrounded by inexperienced people. While some evidence exists to support both conclusions, I think both miss a larger and deeper point. My first year in office, though not productive to many on the outside, was actually among the most productive I enjoyed as governor. It was the year in which the foundation was laid, at times with great difficulty, for all the successes we would later enjoy. Although I wish we could have laid that foundation more quickly, I never lost confidence that we were on the right track. At times, though, I may have been the only person in New Jersey who believed that.

Any sluggishness at the start was certainly not a result of lack of direction. I knew what I wanted to do as governor. I had studied the office for almost a decade and a half, since serving as speaker of the state assembly. I knew the issues. I knew most of the players: who held power, who had to be on your side on any given issue. During those long nights on the campaign trail, I had thought deeply about where I wanted the state to go. Thematically, I had three priorities.

First, and most important, I knew I had to change the state government's agenda. I had to end the preoccupation with taxes that had in many respects paralyzed New Jersey for more than a decade. State government, like any other organization, has a limit to the amount of energy it can expend. If taxes dominate the political debate, other issues don't really get considered. New Jersey's income tax system had been in place only seven years. Before that, its merits had been debated for twelve years. Yet already people wanted to replace the system completely.

I thought it was time to devote ourselves to other issues that had been ignored by previous administrations, primarily economic development, education, and environmental protection. By economic development, I meant more than the tax cuts that had won so much attention in the campaign, although that was important. I meant to rebuild the physical infrastructure of the state, particularly roads and sewage treatment plants, to strengthen the arts, to attract nascent high-technology industries, and to promote tourism and other promising service-sector industries. I also felt we had neglected a whole series of problems, from prison overcrowding to garbage disposal and toxic-waste cleanup. Already the neglect was turning these problems into crises.

My second priority was to make changes in the people who worked for state government. My most famous predecessor, Woodrow Wilson, hated the expression "machinery of government." "Government is not a machine," he said, "but a living thing, modified to its environment . . . shaped to its functions by the sheer pressure of life." In our state, this "living thing" was barely breathing, staffed by people who had grown complacent. Nobody expected much from them, and New Jerseyans got exactly what they expected. With rare and brilliant exceptions, cabinet members had been picked solely on the basis of campaign connections. They were, as a group, not very creative and had achieved very little outside politics. Meanwhile, good management was not taught or rewarded. Innovation was discouraged, and the rewards of the system accrued to those who went along. Our civil service laws had not been touched since the turn of the century.

It is very hard, but very, very important, to try constantly to infuse government with new people and new ideas. I wanted to change the system, but first I needed to attract hundreds of new people into every agency, from the Office on Aging to the Division of Travel and Tourism. My goal was to get the kind of people who had never before even thought of serving in government. I wanted to hire people from private industry and academia who had never worked on a campaign or made a political contribution.

Finally, I knew I had to change the image of the state itself. States are like people: they need self-confidence. Without it, a state, like a person, is bound to fail. Norman Vincent Peale said that you've got to believe you can do it, and he was right. In New Jersey, just the opposite was the case. New Jersey had always deferred to its larger neighbors. We were, the saying went, "a keg tapped at both ends," or, as Ben Franklin had put it, "a valley of humility between two mountains of conceit." If New Jersey was really going to make it, I had to convince the legislature and the people that anything was possible. New Jersey could be proud. New Jersey could be a leader.

In New Jersey, the governor is the only statewide elected official. I had to make sure the voice of that official was heard in a positive way to make New Jersey proud of itself. Only then would change be possible.

Those were the three overall priorities for the administration. Unlike President Jimmy Carter, I did not feel that I had to know every little detail of every government operation. Even if we had a tennis court at the State House, I wouldn't really care who played on it. As Ben Franklin said at the Constitutional Convention, "If we handle the large issues, the little ones will take care of themselves."

There was no doubt I had the power to effect change. Not many people in New Jersey know that their governor is, without a doubt, the most powerful chief executive in the fifty states. We have no lieutenant governor, attorney general, or fiscal officer elected by the people. In other states, these politicians often have other agendas than the governor's. Even worse, they become potential rivals for the job. That doesn't happen in New Jersey. I appoint everyone. Every official is accountable to me. After the major positions, I make an average of five hundred appointments to other public bodies every year, which can include everything from the seven commissioners of the Sports Authority, which runs the Meadowlands, to a panoply of smaller boards from the Board of Dentistry to the Martin Luther King Commission. The boards may not always seem important to a casual observer, but appointment brings respect to a person within a profession or local community.

Beyond the power of appointment, the governor has other advantages built into New Jersey law. Besides the traditional veto power, I have the power of a line-item veto, which even the president of the United States does not enjoy. I can strike individual items from appropriations bills without vetoing the entire bill, and I can go a step further: I can change language itself within the budget. I use the line-item veto often, finding it is the most flexible way to keep control of state spending. In fact, I vetoed well over a billion dollars of legislative spending during my first four years in office. Most were good programs, but things the state simply could not afford. In short, the line-item veto enables me to be fiscally responsible, and it is one of the main reasons that the state of New Jersey still has a triple-A bond rating. We are now one of only seven states that enjoy the triple-A symbol of fiscal integrity. It is not just a symbol. The rating allows us to borrow more cheaply.

Legislatures by their very nature overspend. Responsible only to specific geographic areas and faced with frequent elections, members tend to talk economy but vote for every spending measure that might conceivably benefit a constituent. I remember an otherwise good assemblyman who served with me for a number of years. One session we were faced with a $20 million spending bill, which was obviously outside the bounds of Governor Cahill's budget. So I asked members not to support the bill on fiscal grounds. When the bill was called, I saw the green light flash next to my friend's name and went across the chamber to confront him. "I was going to vote against it," he told me, "but when I got to my desk there were two letters from my district. Both were in favor. Remember, I'm up for election this fall." So much for fiscal responsibility. If the governor won't say no, no one else will.

Almost every day I silently offer a prayer of thanks to Chief Justice Arthur Vanderbilt and Governor Alfred E. Driscoll, the authors of our 1947 constitution. I have become a strong believer in a constitutionally strong executive. And I believe in using my power in creative ways to obtain our objectives. The legislature has challenged me three times, and each time I have been sustained by the courts. Other governors are always surprised to hear what I can do. My friend John Sununu, the outspoken governor of New Hampshire, has gone so far as to call me The Ayatollah Kean. And George Will has written that the governor of New Jersey is "an American Caesar." The fact is, I have great statutory authority and almost total control over the policy-making apparatus. I am not unhappy about it. A good governor should absolutely dominate the political debate in the state and set its agenda.

But there is a big difference between possessing the power and utilizing it. Running New Jersey state government is an administrative task of enormous proportions. With 70,000 employees and a $10 billion annual budget, New Jersey's government is about the size of Italy's. But unlike chief executives of a lot of Fortune 500 companies, the chief executive of a state is not groomed for the job with years of hands-on experience.

In fact, political leadership is the only important activity I know of for which no preparation is thought necessary. Neither press nor public seems to care that often major candidates for mayor, governor, or even president have no practical administrative experience. A state legislature, or for that matter, the U. S. Congress, is not a great training ground for being a governor or president. Neither furnishes much in the way of administrative experience.

I was lucky. I had at least had some management training. I had run a small business. I had been speaker of the assembly, where I was in charge of a large and diverse staff. But I suspect my best preparation was running Brantwood Camp in Peterborough, New Hampshire, some thirty years ago. Brantwood serves city boys who can't afford to go to summer camp. Most are from New England, but they come from poor neighborhoods up and down the East Coast, including Jersey City. Each summer the camp takes in just under three hundred campers in groups of about seventy at a time. Brantwood stresses not only the value of the outdoors, but also the values expressed in the camp's ideals: honesty, loyalty, cooperation, good sportsmanship and unselfishness. Boys learn and live by ideals far removed from those of the city streets. Each summer four or five hundred boys return for Alumni Day. As I write, some former "poor boys" are trying to raise $100,000 for the institution that made a real difference in their lives.

I had gone to Brantwood reluctantly. Ned Hall, the assistant headmaster of St. Mark's, had been director of the camp for a number of years. A superb teacher, he later served as headmaster of both St. Mark's and the Hill School, but his real love has always been Brantwood. The camp that summer needed shack counselors to volunteer for two-week periods. I didn't want to go, but Ned Hall was impossible to turn down. So as a sixteen-year-old sophomore, I found myself in charge of a shack. The oldest camper was only a few months younger.

It was difficult at first. I remember the night a homesick camper ran away. I was petrified. After all, he was my responsibility. I knocked on the door of headquarters to report the terrible news, only to be told, "Don't worry, we'll get him back and in a couple of days he'll get over his homesickness and be just fine." Sure enough, it worked out just that way.

Everybody worked together. Our motto was "BCF"—"Boys Come First." I was still shy at sixteen and reluctant to make decisions, but when you're in charge of twelve- to fifteen-year-olds from the city, you're forced to make decisions every few minutes. I grew to like making decisions and I grew to love Brantwood. By the fifth summer, I was running the camp. I kept the kitchen going, planned and oversaw the athletic programs and other activities, recruited the counselors, and handled any personal problems the campers might experience. I was responsible for about a hundred people, twenty-four hours a day, and I thrived. For the first time in my life, my confidence really grew. One of the things I learned is that we are much too reluctant to give young people responsibility. Our counselors, young men between sixteen and nineteen, performed their jobs well. We forget all the eighteen-year-old sergeants and second lieutenants in World War II, or that a twenty-six-year-old, Jonathan Dayton, helped write the U. S. Constitution. In general, the more real responsibility we give young people, the better.

A great deal of what I know about being a good governor I learned at Brantwood Camp. Until then, I had never been in daily contact with people who have the kinds of problems that government has to tackle on a daily basis. At Brantwood, you couldn't get involved with the kids without understanding their families and their problems. I got to know teenagers of every color and every economic background, and I made lifelong friends. When I became governor, I resigned from some eleven boards and committees. I stayed on only one: Brantwood Camp. In the summer of 1985, I visited the camp on Alumni Day. I was approached by a young man in his early forties. He reminded me that he had been a camper during my years as a counselor. He told me he was a successful small businessman. "Everyone from my old neighborhood is either dead or in jail," he told me. "I came back today to say thanks to you and this place."

Brantwood was important. Yet even running that camp was like managing a corner grocery store compared to being governor. Even the physical environment of the governor's office was relatively new to me. Though I had served as speaker of the assembly, I had set foot in the inner sanctum of the governor's office only a few times. My staff and I had to master details like how the phones worked before we could even begin to think of larger issues.

That didn't matter to my constituents. A minute after the election was certified, all the problems that I had been complaining about during the campaign suddenly became our problems. Any mistakes and ill-conceived policies, even if they were put in place by my predecessor or even his predecessor, were my responsibility. If a patient was mistreated in a state hospital, it was my fault. If state employees didn't like their latest contract, they blamed Governor Kean. If people in South Jersey didn't want a garbage incinerator in their small town, it was my effigy they burned. It was not entirely comfortable to feel the weight of seven million people moved from someone else's shoulders to your own overnight.

In the less than two months between the time the election was certified in early December and my inauguration in January, I had to take on a bewildering array of responsibilities. I had to write my inaugural address, which would set the tone and direction for my administration. I had to hire my staff, twenty cabinet members, and numerous agency heads. I had to get what was then a $6 billion state budget ready for submission to the legislature. If that was going to pass in anything resembling the form in which I submitted it, I had to make friends with key legislators, a surprising number of whom I discovered had only entered politics recently and had never worked with me. New Jersey state government is about the size of Procter & Gamble, the eleventh largest Fortune 500 company. I wonder how Procter & Gamble would fare if it had to hire all its executives within fifty days.

I found my office flooded with requests from thousands of people who felt that my narrow election was a direct result of their work or the money they had contributed. Every single one of them made the same request: they wanted a personal meeting with the governor. Whether it was a small problem or big, whether they wanted a job or just to say hello, they had to see the governor. My nature had not changed; I wanted to be accessible. Hating to say no to people who wanted to see their governor, I found my schedule packed with meetings from morning to night. The major mistake I made during the first year was cluttering my schedule with too many meetings.

All of this, of course, frustrated me. I knew I had the ideas and the power to pull the state out of its malaise. I felt quite confident that my management style and temperament were particularly suited to the job. Yet I found events dictating my response and determining my agenda. At times I was swimming in a sea of details and succumbing to the same problems that had crippled some of my predecessors.

☆

When I think back to my first inauguration, the whole experience seems almost like a dream. I still was having trouble convincing myself that I had won the election and I was the governor. If somebody looked at me and said, "Governor," I often didn't realize that he meant me. I was also still getting accustomed to the trappings of the office—the car, the driver, and the helicopter, which scares me to this day. Perhaps the biggest adjustment in my personal life was getting used to being accompanied by state police troopers everywhere I went. Since the night of my victory, one trooper has always slept in my home in Livingston. Eventually the troopers set up a trailer next to the driveway outside our house so they could keep a constant eye on me and my family.

It was not easy for my family to accept the fact that total strangers were going to share our lives for the next four years. The situation took some getting used to. For example, I would run out of the house with my daughter and hop in our car for a quick trip to the local store to get the newspaper. I'd look in the rearview mirror as two troopers struggled to get in their car to follow us. But they were only doing their job, and eventually my family and I accepted their presence. I know things were especially hard at first for Debby. No longer could she walk into the hall or kitchen without running into people who weren't members of the family. In the evening, Debby or our housekeeper, Ruby Ryce, prepare dinner not only for our family, but for the trooper on duty.

The troopers make every effort to be unobtrusive. One time Debby and I had gone to spend the weekend at Island Beach State Park on the New Jersey shore. We decided to take a walk along the beach early one evening. The trooper realized it was probably one of the few moments Debby and I had spent alone together for weeks. To give us a little privacy, he decided not to walk with us, but to swim along in the water some distance behind us!

The New Jersey state troopers are wonderful people. What's more, they set a good example for our children. In the years I've been governor, I guess we've had at least fifty troopers assigned to us at one time or another. We have yet to meet one we haven't liked and respected. They also try to perform their work quietly, and do their best to respect our privacy. I have also come to respect their esprit de corps.

Sad to say, I have had to share with them the tragedy of a trooper's death. Knowing them and their families makes the sharing doubly painful. There is no more difficult duty I have than attending the funeral of a young trooper slain in the line of duty. One of the tragedies occurred before I was even sworn in. Phil Lamonico had won the 1979 Trooper of the Year Award for making hundreds of drug arrests along Route 80, a stretch of highway in one of the more desolate parts of northwestern New Jersey. He was respected by everyone on the force. Late one December afternoon in 1981, his body was found beside Route 80. It was a vicious, seemingly unprovoked slaying. He left behind a wife and two young children. One of the largest manhunts in New Jersey history ensued. I told Colonel Clint Pagano, our state police superintendent, that he would have the state's full moral and financial support for as long as it took to catch the murderers. It took five years, but eventually two members of a radical group were caught and charged with the murder. In 1986, one of them was convicted and sent to jail.

Inauguration Day was perfect. The opening event was my favorite of the day, a beautiful Holy Communion service with the bishop presiding. In full regalia, the various leaders of the state's religious community joined the procession. I had chosen the hymns and some of the prayers, all of which had a special meaning for me. Only the flash of bulbs and the click of cameras as we approached the altar to receive the host marred the beauty of the day. I will say that after spending six years at a church school and seven years running a church camp, I believe deeply in the fatherhood of God and the brotherhood of man. I have no problem with the divine inspiration of Holy Scripture. But I sometimes have great trouble with men who lead the church. On this occasion, however, everything, with the exception of the flashbulbs, was perfect.

Trouble waited back in my office. As we readied for the inaugural ceremony, Clint Pagano, the superintendent of the state police, drew me aside. There had been, he informed me, at least three threats on my life. They probably came from cranks, but they had to be taken seriously. He questioned whether we should go ahead with the rest of the day as planned. Police protection would be difficult during the inaugural parade and during my address in the War Memorial building.

I really had no choice. A new governor promising a new day for New Jersey could not spend his first day hiding from the public. So I marched and I spoke, but with some apprehension, especially for my family. For those of my friends who thought that the new governor had gained a little weight, I will admit now that I had made one concession to the state police. As I took the oath of office, I wore a bulletproof vest.

Threats are part of public life today. Even as a leader of the assembly I received them. I remember one night shortly after I voted for the income tax. The Livingston police arrived at the house at approximately 4:00 A.M. and I was asked to get my wife and children out as quickly as possible. Someone who sounded sober had called about a bomb, set to go off at 4:15, planted inside our home. An experience like that makes you think twice about public service. But what would happen to the democracy if people who want to serve got scared off so easily? So you go on. Happily, Inauguration Day went off without incident.

My inaugural address was short. But I think it had flourishes, a paean to New Jersey's diversity and a Kennedyesque parallel structure: "Government is a means to an end, it is not the end itself." I closed with a prayer composed two hundred years ago by our first governor, William Livingston.

The speech matched the tenor of the times, solemn and serious. As I spoke the long shadow of the recession was deepening. New Jersey's unemployment had crossed 8.5 percent and was heading steadily upward. And it was a recession that brought personal suffering and economic dislocation. Even the most optimistic economist was not predicting that things would get much better very fast.

Unlike past recessions, we couldn't look to Washington for help and solutions. In my inaugural address I said, "Neither New Jersey nor any of the other states in the nation can turn to Washington, D. C., casting covetous eyes upon what has always been seen as a limitless supply of funds, there for the asking and the taking. That dependency has become deeply ingrained in our governmental system. But it has given birth to a complacency, a feeling that government at the state level has but to identify a problem, not to solve it."

I felt it was time to replace complacency with aggressive self-reliance. President Reagan had succeeded in shifting the nation's agenda—the states were going to get a lot less money and a lot more responsibility. This didn't bother me much. Philosophically, I have always felt that almost any problem can be best solved at the state and local level. In short, I supported Reagan's agenda. Government in Washington had grown too large, wasteful, and irresponsible, an obvious reality from the perspective of the state and local level. I believed absolutely that there should be less government in Washington, but to me that meant having more government in Trenton. Government's role hadn't changed; its responsibilities, if anything, would be greater than ever. But now states would have the prime responsibility for fulfilling the obligations of government. Other people, especially some partisan Democrats, didn't agree with me. They felt that if they complained loudly enough, the nation would go back to relying on Washington to solve local problems. My inaugural was a sharp warning that such hopes were illusory. We had to set our priorities and find ways to accomplish them on our own, by ourselves.

As I spoke, I recognized faces in the audience: former boys from Brantwood, friends from St. Mark's and Princeton, people from my company and workers from my campaign. People I had looked to for support were now looking to me for leadership. After the swearing in, I returned to my office in the State House and greeted friends. The rest of the day was to be enjoyed. I ended the custom of having inaugural events that simply raised money for the party of the governor. One of my parties raised funds for the renovation of the Governor's Mansion; at another, my friend Bill Cosby regaled guests for the benefit of the arts.

☆

Once the hoopla of Inauguration Week faded, it was time to get to work. Within days I had to confront two of the biggest challenges of my administration: staffing the government and dealing with a stubborn legislature controlled by the Democrats.

I happen to believe that any governor or chief executive is only as good as the people around him. A cliché, but also true. Many times in my career I have seen the most intelligent and astute executive brought down by a second-rate staff or cabinet. A chief executive has to have not only the insight to recruit a talented staff to complement his strengths but the courage to get rid of staff members when circumstances demand it.

Never was that simple truism clearer to me than in December of 1986, when I hosted the winter meeting of the Republican Governors' Association in Parsippany, New Jersey. The Republican Governors were in fine spirits. We had seen our numbers go from 16 to 24 in the '86 elections, even while the Republican Senate was going Democratic. The national press corps had their eye on us as we talked about everything from education to international trade with experts such as economist Martin Feldstein and author David Halberstam. Also, at my invitation, President Nixon had given the Governors a closed-door briefing on foreign policy.

But the national press corps didn't want to hear about trade laws or even President Nixon's view about what was going on in the Soviet Union. They had one thing on their collective mind: the Iran-Contra imbroglio that had broken a few weeks earlier. Toward the end of the four-day conference I received a call from the White House. President Reagan asked if I could bring the Governors to Washington so he could explain to us face to face what had happened. So I boarded a plane with some 20 governors and flew to Washington's National Airport.

The President was joined in the meeting by a number of top officials, including Vice-President Bush and Chief of Staff Don Regan. After the President's initial remarks, he asked for our advice. He obviously wanted to hear how we might handle the problem. Yet the situation was difficult. Most of us thought the President had to make a staff change, but it was awkward to make that point in Don Regan's presence. Nevertheless, some Governors came out and called for Regan's resignation.

Carroll Campbell, the newly-elected Governor of South Carolina, put it best. "Mr. President," he said, "it is not a question of fault. The time comes when circumstances make it impossible for individuals to serve you or the country well. When that happens, it is in your interest, and the country's interest, that they resign."

Normally, a President leaves a White House meeting before the other participants. This time, he lingered at the door. As I walked out of the room he took me by the arm. "Tom," he said, "you've got to understand that it was not Don Regan's fault. I can't make him the scapegoat." I knew exactly what the President was going through. He liked Don Regan. A loyal public servant. Yet Governor Campbell was right. The time had come when Regan could no longer serve the President effectively. Staff is so important. I believe that if Jim Baker and Mike Deaver had stayed in the White House, the Iran affair never would have happened.

Firing staff or cabinet members is terribly difficult. Sometimes a person has been with you for years, and might have worked on your campaign. I have had to fire close advisors on six or seven occasions. These were good people, but they were obviously not suited for their jobs. I always try to let them go with dignity, allowing them to resign or first try to find another position in which they can use their talents.

Other executives have probably made this point, but I believe that when you are firing a close associate it is the one time you have an excuse to lie to the press. After all, a human being's dignity is at stake. Under these circumstances, I think it is all right for the public to know only that a public official resigned rather than was fired.

At any rate, in 1981 I wasn't worried about firing people, but finding the right people to staff my administration. The problem was I didn't have any time. After the election was finally certified, I had only about forty days before the inaugural. Until then I had been unable even to interview prospective staff because there was no certainty I would in fact be the next governor. If I wanted my cabinet intact by inauguration, I had to identify good candidates, interview them, and make offers during a three-week period over the Christmas holidays.

Although I would choose my personal staff immediately because I could not survive without one, I decided to take my time with the cabinet. If I didn't find someone I wanted right away, I would not fill the position even though I knew what I was doing was risky. It meant that a large number of important positions were going to be filled by holdovers from the previous administration. It meant that people who knew they were leaving state government, and whose energy was spent looking for new jobs, would be running sensitive programs. It meant that people would be in highly visible leadership positions whose loyalty to me was questionable at best. But I figured the short-term risk was worth the long-term gain. Months would pass before my entire cabinet was chosen.

My personal staff was a different story. I had the key people picked by Inauguration Day because I felt I had a pretty good understanding of my own strengths and weaknesses. A good governor is five different people: political strategist, communicator, idea man, decision maker, and administrator. I thought I had some of the first four people inside me. The administrator I was not so sure about. But administrative details are important, and if handled badly, can cripple a governor. And I knew I could get in trouble if too many of the small matters ended up on my desk. I wanted one person, a strong administrator, who could run the entire office and free me for other work. I envisioned someone like Sherman Adams in the Eisenhower administration, someone I trusted completely. I looked, but I could not find that person.

I settled on a troika instead. Lew Thurston had been policy director for Republicans in the state senate. He would be my chief of staff, to handle politics and run the office. Gary Stein, an old friend from my army days, and one of the brightest and most able lawyers I knew, would plan policy initiatives and keep an eye on the long-term priorities of the administration. Cary Edwards, a friend and supporter from the legislature, would be my chief counsel.

The troika would stay together for a year and a half. Gary Stein served admirably. He was the steadying influence in the office and the person who ended up handling the crises no one else wanted to touch, like prison overcrowding. Lew Thurston spent hundreds of hours screening prospective staff for the entire administration. After three years, I would appoint Gary to a vacancy on the New Jersey Supreme Court. Lew left to be general manager at the Meadowlands Sports Authority. The only one to stay for the entire four years was Cary Edwards, who would work with a legislature of the opposite party to craft an astounding series of legislative accomplishments.

Cary first ran for the state assembly in the 1977 Republican primary as a "Tom Kean Republican," a questionable proposition in that year, when the party favored my opponent. The fact that he so ran reflected his loyalty to people and ideas in which he believed strongly. The fact that he won reflected his political savvy.

Cary's work habits were legendary. Day after day he would arrive in Trenton about ten in the morning, after more than an hour's commute from his house in North Jersey. All day long and well into the evening he would sit camped in his office outside my door, meeting with an endless stream of lawyers, lobbyists, and legislators. After seven or eight at night, the pace of the meetings would slow and he would get to work on the pile of memoranda that had accumulated on his desk. By ten or eleven, he would leave the office, but he was not done working. Invariably, he would stop and spend a few hours at one of the diners that dot New Jersey's roadways. Young lawyers would do almost anything to get invited to a late-night session, where they could sit over hot turkey sandwiches and hear Cary talk about everything from congressional redistricting to death-penalty legislation.

Cary, one of those rare people who possess almost total recall, has a mastery of facts and detail that is astounding. I have seen many a meeting where the position he argued was tenable at best, and yet he would bury the other side in a pile of facts. Accordingly, his knowledge of every aspect of state policy gave him an upper hand when negotiating with all but the most savvy legislators, which was a great advantage for me and the administration.

In diffusing authority among the troika, I went against everybody's advice. The critics argued that it wouldn't work, that there would be too many disagreements and I would have to make every important decision myself. In many ways, they were right. But for me, the system works as long as you have the right mix of able people. The faces have changed since, but I have kept that arrangement to this day.

In fact, one of the keys to our success has been that as one staffer left, another arrived of unquestioned ability. Chief of Staff Lew Thurston, for example, was replaced by an old friend, Greg Stevens, who ran my reelection campaign. When Greg left for a consulting job in Washington, he was replaced by Ed McGlynn, who kept the office running smoothly. Ditto for Brenda Davis and Mike Cole, my second-term policy chief and chief counsel, who sustained the first-term momentum. An administration can be rocked by staff turnover. Ours has stayed steady throughout.

One more position on my personal staff was important: the press secretary. Only a member of a politician's immediate family should be closer to him than a press secretary. The job may well be the most sensitive in an administration. Every time a crisis occurs, the press secretary gets the call and becomes your voice. His response is your response. I have seen politicians spend days cleaning up after an unfortunate remark by a press secretary. Similarly, I have seen a good press secretary defuse an issue completely before it became embarrassing.

When I was elected to the leadership in the state assembly, the majority party had no press secretary. In fact, neither party in those days had one. I heard that a former reporter for the *Newark News* was working as an aide to Congressman Peter Frelinghuysen in Washington and wanted to come back to New Jersey. I interviewed the candidate in an Elizabeth deli. After five minutes, I knew I had my man. Carl Golden asked only two things of me: first, that he have complete access to me. Access is to a press secretary what a good ear is to a musician: you cannot work without it. Second, he asked me never to put him in a position to lie to the press corps. It is entirely okay to say, "I don't know," or, "I can't tell you that," but once a press secretary has been dishonest with the press, he is finished. Carl has been with me for sixteen years, longer than anyone else. We are very different people. He's a beer drinker; I am not. I tend to dress conservatively; Carl is happiest in jeans and sneakers. On weekends he listens to Willie Nelson and Waylon Jennings, while I prefer Luciano Pavarotti and Placido Domingo.

Nevertheless, Carl has an uncanny ability to anticipate my reaction to various problems as they arise, and I rely on him totally. He does much more than talk to reporters. I check in with him every morning. No policy is developed by the Kean administration without his input, and Carl attends every important meeting.

Very few press secretaries could adapt to my style. I do not hold regular press conferences, but I answer questions at public events, usually two or three times a day. Reporters should be able to question a governor whenever the need arises, because the people of the state learn about government through the press's eyes, ears, and typewriters. That means that every day Carl has to interpret some remark I made about taxes in Newark, or explain to a reporter in Cherry Hill why I am going to appoint a particular person to a board or agency.

The style works for me, and I believe reporters appreciate the access. I've only had one real problem since I began serving as governor. A reporter asked me about an issue after other members of the press had left to file their stories. That is not unusual, but this time the story in the morning newspaper misquoted me badly. It was an important story, but I decided not to ask for a correction or call the editor. Instead, I called the reporter and told him he had made a mistake. At first he denied making the error. Luckily, I had evidence, because an aide had recorded the interview. I had said just the opposite of what appeared in the paper. After hearing about the tape, the reporter admitted his mistake and apologized. I told him I would not ask for a correction, but asked instead that the next time he wrote about the subject, he use my quote correctly. He assured me he would. Within twenty-four hours he wrote another story. To my chagrin, the offending quote appeared verbatim. I pulled him aside the next day. After venting myself a bit, I said to him, "Look, I am not going to hurt your livelihood. You can continue to come to my press conferences. I will always answer your questions. But I will never again answer your questions alone. I don't trust you. From now on, any question you ask must be in the presence of at least one other reporter." As a politician, I've been asked questions by hundreds of reporters. Often I have not liked the resulting story, but there has been no other time when a reporter deliberately misquoted me.

In general, you have to have the presence of mind to tell a reporter that you cannot comment on an issue if you don't have all the details. That will never get you in trouble, as long as you make yourself available once you have the full story.

I remember an episode in November 1986, when I had to be in Washington to testify before a Senate committee. George Bush heard I was in town and invited me to dinner and a movie. He seemed quite worried. Finally it came out. The Iran-Contra scandal was just breaking. He was upset by some of the things he had learned, and confused by others. He felt that nobody in the White House seemed to have a grasp of what had happened. So what worried Bush was that the president had scheduled a press conference for the next evening. Bush told me he had argued strongly against going before the press until all the facts were available. Don Regan and others had convinced the president otherwise. The result is history. The president was confused and it showed. He was to be plagued by that press conference for the next six months.

☆

Carl, Cary, Lew, and Gary were all people whom I had known for some time. All four had played a major supporting role in the campaign and I felt it was important to have the people close to me in top positions at the beginning of the administration. I didn't feel that way about my cabinet; I decided to ignore virtually all political considerations for staffing it and the major positions in each department.

My philosophy was heresy in New Jersey, as it would be among most politicians everywhere. "To the victor belong the spoils" is the slogan used to staff government. A winning candidate is supposed to reward all his supporters with jobs, powerful and otherwise, and punish his opponents by taking away all the jobs their people had. In New Jersey, the county political bosses would supply the new governor with a list of supporters and the governor would find jobs for all of them somewhere in the state bureaucracy.

I couldn't do that. I had felt that a number of the departments, under both Republicans and Democrats, had been staffed by incompetent people who had no right whatever to positions of leadership. Their sole qualification was political support for the winning candidate. Virtually every failed program in the state could be traced to the same evil root: political patronage. This tradition, and the attitudes and practices it bred, was one reason why New Jersey had acquired the reputation as a bastion of corruption. Between 1969 and 1980, for example, more than 160 public officials were indicted in New Jersey and almost half were convicted. They included two congressmen, two secretaries of state, two state treasurers, various legislators, and a nominee for the U. S. Senate. And you had to go back to the early 1950s to find an administration that had not had at least one of its cabinet members indicted.

I came into office unencumbered. The state has a number of very powerful special-interest groups, including the New Jersey Education Association, the AFL-CIO, and the National Rifle Association. None of them had supported me. All had put their money on my opponent, and none felt they owned any part of me.

I had also run without committing any state jobs to anyone, which was unique in New Jersey. In the primary, powerful people had expected commitments in exchange for support. I remember a meeting with one county chairman, who had indicated a month before that I would have his support. He said he urgently needed to see me, we got together, and he told me he wanted to be the next lottery director if I won. I explained that I was making no promises to anyone, but that he would be given a fair shot along with others. He said he believed I would make the best governor, but that another candidate had promised him the lottery job in exchange for support. "Match the offer," he told me, "and I'll stay with you." I didn't, and he backed my opponent.

So I came into office without any political IOUs. Nevertheless, some among my supporters had high expectations. Because I needed help, I asked a group of supporters and friends to act as a screening committee, whose first job would be to look at the various departments and come up with a description of the qualities most needed to fill each cabinet post.

I then broke some new ground in New Jersey and, for all I know, everywhere else. I used my transition money to hire an executive search firm or "headhunter." Only when a candidate had been screened by both the headhunter and the transition committee would I interview them. I talked to two or three people for each position, depending on the number of qualified candidates. No matter what their political background, every potential cabinet member went through the same drill.

We ended up with choices that surprised the press, the public, and certainly the Republican party. Some were easy. Mike Horn was the obvious choice for banking commissioner. But I had never seen Borden Putnam, the vice-president of American Cyanamid, until he applied to head the new Department of Commerce. Nevertheless, it took me about three minutes to decide that he was the right man for the job. Irwin

Kimmelman, former judge and assemblyman, was my pick for attorney general. Two people, Ted Hollander in Higher Education and Bill Fauver in Corrections, were retained from the Byrne administration.

After a number of interviews, it became obvious that Ken Biederman was most qualified to be treasurer. Ken had a brilliant mind, having written the paper that served as the basis for the Ford administration's economic recovery program. He was a conservative economist, but a Democrat by registration. Local Republican officials complained bitterly about my choice for this important post.

I spent the most time on the areas that interested me the most, environmental protection and education. In the eight years of the Byrne administration, the Department of Environmental Protection had been managed by six different administrators, including people who served on a temporary basis. I knew that the position could be the second most difficult job in New Jersey government, because every issue under the department's purview is potentially explosive—from finding a proper storage site for toxic waste to reviewing industrial compliance with our air-pollution laws, the toughest in the nation. The job requires someone who has the intellect to understand real science and the personality to deal with angry and often poorly informed constituents, along with a deep personal commitment to the environment. Also, I wanted a planner. The headhunters stumbled across such a person in Bob Hughey.

I interviewed Bob on a number of occasions. I never questioned his ability, but Bob had a strong independent streak, and I wondered how he would work within an administration. After the first interview we parted, each feeling that it probably wouldn't work out. I was disappointed. So, evidently, was Bob. He called for another interview. We met for a long evening session at my home. The subject of most of our discussions was the New Jersey Pinelands.

The Pinelands is one of the most beautiful parts of New Jersey, a largely undeveloped area located smack in the middle of the southern part of the state. Its quiet beauty has been best captured by noted author and native New Jerseyan John McPhee.

As McPhee put it, this quiet expanse of forest sits incongruously in the geographical epicenter of what is now the world's most expansive megalopolis, from Boston, Massachusetts, to Richmond, Virginia. On a clear night, a light in the pine barrens can be seen by someone standing at the top of the World Trade Center in Manhattan. Encompassing more than one million acres, the Pinelands is almost as large as Yosemite, about the size of Grand Canyon National Park, and larger than Sequoia and Great Smoky national parks.

The soft, sandy floor of the forest is fertile ground for shady pines, juniper trees, blueberries—which the locals call huckleberries—and cranberries. In fact, one third of all the cranberries grown in the United States are grown inside the Pinelands. Yet the forest is valuable not only for what lies above its land but for what lies below it. The loose sand gulps water like a thirsty man in the desert, and below the surface sits an aquifer that contains some of the purist water in the world. The aquifer is the size of a lake 7½ miles deep with a surface of 1,000 square miles.

The Pinelands is a world separate from the rest of New Jersey. The people who inhabit it call themselves Pineys, although they do not like outsiders to use the term. Pineys are in many instances the descendants of outcasts. From Tories running from the Revolutionary War, Hessian soldiers fleeing the Battle of Trenton, wayward Quakers hiding from the eyes of upright neighbors, to Indians escaping from the white man, the vast forest has offered seclusion to people for centuries. The Pinelands residents are fiercely independent, laconic, and laid-back, skeptical of the ways of urban living to the north and west. A few still live without telephones or electricity.

The preservation of the Pinelands faced rising land costs and development. In the early 1960s, a proposal was floated to build a huge supersonic air transport center, bigger than JFK, La Guardia, and Newark airports combined, in the middle of what I regard as a natural treasure. The airport would abut a planned city of 250,000 people connected to the rest of New Jersey by the Garden State Parkway.

The idea, thank God, never made it off the drawing board. But by the early 1970s, the borders of the Pinelands were slowly contracting, as developers from New York and Philadelphia offered huge amounts to private landowners in return for commercial and industrial development. The very character of New Jersey's separate world was in danger. What's more, the millions of gallons of water in the underground aquifer were threatened by haphazard development.

Governor Byrne, in his most important accomplishment, had gotten the legislature to approve a regional planning bill to preserve most of the Pinelands. Although some growth was to be allowed in designated areas, it soon became apparent the plan was in trouble. Most gubernatorial candidates in both parties had proposed major revisions; the Democratic legislature was ready with amendments that would effectively undo the whole program; the congressmen who represented the area were very much for repeal; and the Reagan administration didn't like the whole idea. With the active opposition of the secretary of the interior, James Watt, the plan seemed doomed.

Bob Hughey and I talked long into the evening. He had real doubts about the Pinelands and the new preservation program. I told him that the Kean administration was going to support it, without major modification, saying that protection of the Pinelands was very important, not just for southern New Jersey but for the entire state. I could support modifications to help farmers, but nothing that would destroy the original planning concept. Bob decided to come on board and make the Pinelands his first priority. He agreed that once administration policy was set, he would support it, or resign.

Developing our policy took a lot of work. We talked and listened to legislators, congressmen, and representatives of the Reagan administration. Bob and I also spent time with people from local government and spokesmen for the farming community. Eventually, I appointed leaders of the farmers and local government to the commission that regulated development. It turned out that many of the opposition groups had just wanted somebody to listen, so gradually the issue started to move our way. Congressmen stepped back. The Department of the Interior began to work with us. The anti-Pinelands group lost its majority in the legislature. Today not all problems are solved, but I can assure people with certainty that this unique and fragile area will be preserved not only for us, but for our children. Bob Hughey deserves tremendous credit for what happened. Once he overcame his initial reservations, he became my most effective advocate for the program.

As I've said, a great many of my Republican supporters, especially the county chairmen and old-line politicians, were upset by my apolitical method of staffing the administration. My response was very simple. I argued that I needed the best possible people around me at a very difficult time in the state's history and a very uncertain time for the Republican party. I reminded them that my success was going to mean their success. If I was a good governor, with an administration free of scandal and able to handle the big problems facing the state, then our party would grow and might even be able to shake its seemingly eternal status as the minority party. If I fell on my face, so would the Republican party. I reminded them that it had been over thirty years since a Republican had been reelected in New Jersey. If local Republicans wanted to preserve that rare bird, a Republican governor, they would have to swallow their objections and let me appoint a cabinet of unquestioned competence.

This is not to say I didn't want an administration that would be based on Republican principles. I did. I told every prospective cabinet officer about my philosophy of government and my positions on the major issues that would come before their department. I made it clear that if any disagreements arose on those issues, they could confront me with them, but once a final decision was made, they were to be team players. If they couldn't do that, they could not sit in the cabinet.

Even though we hired people carefully, we still made some mistakes. The most visible was my appointment of a new education commissioner. During the campaign I had singled out only a few members of the Byrne administration for direct criticism, most pointedly the state education commissioner. I had been a teacher and chairman of the education committee in the assembly, and I cared deeply about education. The precipitous drop in SAT scores during the Byrne years was a tragedy. During the campaign I said that one of my first moves in office would be to replace the education commissioner. He quit before I got the chance. So the press and education community eagerly awaited my choice of a successor.

I had told my steering committee that I wanted them to keep an eye on qualified women and minority candidates for various cabinet positions. At that time, it was rare to see a black or a woman in a position of authority in New Jersey state government, and I wanted to change that. Although I didn't believe that minority or women candidates should be given preferential treatment, I did want to go beyond the old-boy network and find the talented women and minority candidates who I knew were out there.

The screening committee found a black professional educator serving as second-in-command in another state. He had impressive credentials for the job. He had been a teacher in a New Jersey school. I never like the idea of administrators who had never stood in front of a classroom. He had also served as a high school principal and superintendent. Everyone who worked with him gave him the highest marks. I spent time with him and was impressed.

Both the press and professional educators greeted the nomination enthusiastically. The black community was surprised and elated. A South Jersey newspaper, the *Courier-Post*, summarized general sentiment with a favorable editorial, "The Ideal Man to Lead Education Reform." The state's two most powerful education lobbies, the New Jersey Education Association and the New Jersey School Boards Association, also endorsed the selection.

Everything was going smoothly, and it appeared that I had found a star for the cabinet. Then, as so often happens in politics, things turned upside down overnight. Bob Braun, an enterprising reporter for the *Star Ledger*, the state's most influential newspaper, found a copy of the candidate's doctoral thesis that he had written for an experimental program at Fairleigh Dickinson University almost ten years before. The reporter discovered that my nominee had copied more than 40 pages of the 120-page dissertation word for word, without proper notation, from other published and unpublished sources.

The incident illustrates the volatility of public service. One minute you can be up, basking in the public adulation, the next minute you are down, your character questioned publicly and your career in jeopardy. It is good to remember that if you think you have something to hide, you probably should never get into public life in the first place.

The story became front-page news. A few people came to the candidate's defense, arguing that if the university had not caught the dubious scholarship then it shouldn't concern us, or that the academic standards of the 1960s were less stringent than now. The press turned and called for his scalp. The *Courier-Post*, which had waxed enthusiastic only weeks before, now opined, "A Disqualifying Blow to Education Choice."

The entire incident was very painful to me. As an educator myself, I knew that integrity and credibility were crucial in scholarship. I knew that to appoint a commissioner who admitted to shoddy scholarship would send the wrong signal to schoolchildren across the state. On the other hand, I knew I was dealing with a good, kind, and able man, whose professional career had been exemplary. I cringed to see him forced to endure public humiliation for a mistake he had made nine years earlier. I also hated to see the state's black community denied their first major cabinet post. But I knew in the end I had no choice. Eventually the nomination was withdrawn at the nominee's request. It had been a blunder for the administration, although I still have no idea how it could have been averted.

I turned to another man who had been impressive in our interviews. Saul Cooperman was to prove a brilliant choice for education commissioner. His leadership in education reform was to bring New Jersey

national renown. I do remember, however, the night I called to tell him he was my choice. He was out at a meeting and his wife, Paulette, answered the phone. I identified myself as Tom Kean and asked to speak to Saul. It took me five minutes to convince Paulette to leave the message. It seems a friend, knowing Saul was a candidate for the job, had been calling pretending he was me. Finally, Saul called back, accepted, and said he was absolutely delighted.

For the most part, the system of staffing the government with people of demonstrated competence worked splendidly. It was not complete until I had been in office some four months. But we ended up with the most competent cabinet New Jersey government has ever seen, leaders who would set about to professionalize state government in just four years. And finally, one year into my second term, I was able to sign legislation reforming the entire civil service system, the first change in that archaic system since William Howard Taft occupied the White House.

☆

Even as I was staffing my administration, I had to turn my attention to more hostile forces: the leadership of the legislature.

If my ten years in the state assembly had taught me anything, it was that a legislature can hamstring a governor. Given the power he possesses, a New Jersey governor might be tempted to go it alone, but that's not smart. A stubborn legislature can not only bottle up your legislative agenda, it can cut funding for important programs or harass your top officials. Life is much easier when the governor and the legislature are working together, so I figured it was absolutely essential that I forge some working relationship with the Democrats who controlled the assembly and the senate.

It was not going to be easy, I knew, because the Democrats were not happy about losing control of the governor's office for the first time in eight years and only the second time since the 1950s. Moreover, with an election margin of a scant 1,700 votes, I could hardly claim a mandate from the people.

But I wasn't really worried. The best legislature I had ever served in had been divided between the parties, and as Republican leader, I had never had a problem crossing the aisle to look for support. Unless we worked together there would be no solutions, and that I felt would be motivation enough for future cooperation. Democrats, I thought, would be willing to put aside differences to move ahead with me. I was wrong.

The Democrats were led in the Assembly by Alan Karcher. As assembly speaker, Karcher was the titular head of the Democratic party, responsible for formulating strategy both politically and legislatively. Because of his wit and intellect, Karcher had earned the reputation as the state's most colorful Democrat: bombastic and volatile, always ready with a memorable riposte to any question. So Karcher was the man reporters turned to first when they wanted to know what the Democratic party thought of a Tom Kean proposal.

I like Alan Karcher. Much about him is truly admirable. He has an exceptional grasp of the details of public policy. He is not one who sees public service as a way of somehow furthering his private interests. He believes very deeply in certain principles, especially an expanded role for government in caring for society's downtrodden. Thoughtful, he is not averse to changing his mind on an issue if the facts undercut his initial position. He has enormous potential, and yet it has never been realized. His Achilles' heel, and it is a rather large and sore one, is that he is a completely politic animal. He loves the parry and thrust of the legislative process; if he were a boxer, he would be Jack Johnson, constantly on the attack. Given a choice between a wise compromise and a good public scrap, he will take the scrap every time. Given the choice between solving a problem and creating a partisan issue, Alan will choose the latter and try to squeeze every bit of advantage out of it. He could become one of our state's finest public servants, but his love for political infighting keeps getting in his way.

During my first term, I was the constant target of Karcher's criticisms. Some of them were fair and expected, like his objections to my budget priorities or my insistence on low income-tax rates. Other harangues were of dubious significance and sometimes bordered on the ludicrous; among them, his suggestion that somehow I was in office to enrich my family.

The Democrats concluded early on that the best strategy was not compromise and conciliation, but confrontation. Having read the polls, they knew that only 45 percent of the voters supported me. They decided to oppose me publicly on every possible issue, and in four years they hoped to make the case that Tom Kean had been a do-nothing governor. Given the strategy, gridlock was in their best interest, and they began by slowing down the approval of some of my important cabinet positions.

They went on to oppose virtually every one of my initial policy pronounce-ments, culminating in a year-long fight over the budget. I came to feel that if I came up with a cure for the common cold, Karcher and the Democrats would say, "Maybe that's okay, but let's hold two months of hearings on it."

My style, of course, is very different from Karcher's. Given the choice, I prefer compromise and accommodation to public confrontation, because for me there is little to be gained by publicly criticizing and thereby unduly provoking a public official who disagrees with you. After all, on the next issue you may be on the same side. I like to think of myself as a pragmatist and a problem solver, and I feel that one of my skills is the ability to bring people together. The state had a prison crisis, a transportation crisis, and a recurring budget crisis. I had been elected to solve them, and I was totally frustrated by the Democratic party's strategy of letting the problems fester for partisan advantage in the next election.

I decided to stick to my guns, to prepare the solutions and fight to get them implemented. We would try to convince the assembly that there was more to be gained from compromise than confrontation. We lost the early battles, but we won the war.

All along, we had expected a budget deficit. In the campaign, I had argued that we could save up to $100 million by implementing management reforms in state government. My supply-side platform had also been based on the premise that by cutting certain business taxes we could spur growth and thereby increase tax revenues.

To go about doing this, I met with leaders of the business community, who were as tired as I was of annual budget crises, resolved every spring only in the panicked atmosphere of all-night legislative sessions. I told the leaders I wanted to make cuts, that I knew savings could be found, and that where possible I wanted to introduce business methods to the running of state government. They agreed to help, raised $3 million, and lent us some two hundred executives. In return, I gave them full access to every department and agency. But they weren't there to tell professional government workers what to do; if they had done so, the whole plan would have been a failure. Instead, business executives worked side by side with government managers, no corner of state government escaping their attention. Government workers, initially skeptical, came to support our program. In the end, all of us saved the New Jersey taxpayers more than $100 million a year in ongoing expenses. That was splendid, but not the only fruit the program bore. The two hundred executives went back to the private sector with a new respect for the professionalism of the state work force, while state workers recognized that they could learn something from people in the business world.

That was our first big success in public-private partnerships, one of the hallmarks of the Kean administration. But in 1982, neither the tax cut nor management improvement programs had been initiated. Early in my term, my budget experts examined the books and uncovered some disturbing news. The budget deficit was not going to be $100 to $200 million, as had been predicted in a worst-case scenario, but as high as $600 to $700 million. The previous administration had been playing with smoke and mirrors, having used a number of one-time revenue increases, gimmicks really, to raise millions during its last year in office. The one-time measures were not open to us in 1982. Meanwhile, the economy in 1982 was worse than any experts had predicted, increasing the demand for certain expenditures and decreasing revenue from sales and income taxes.

To put our problem another way, our budget deficit was in relative terms about half as large as the federal government's in 1984. But unlike the federal government, the state of New Jersey couldn't go out and borrow money, or simply print it as Washington sometimes does. Our constitution required a balanced budget by the end of the fiscal year in June.

The recession and the budget deficit dominated the news columns of the state's press. Late in May, a compromise that pleased no one was agreed to. We cut about $300 million in expenditures, laid off some state employees, and increased some user fees to close the rest of the gap. But all along, the road was rocky. Before it was over, the assembly would refuse to let me raise the gas tax, I would veto an attempt by the assembly to raise the income tax, and we all would go through acrimonious twenty-four-hour legislative sessions.

It was tough, but I learned some lessons from the experience. Balancing the budget would have been impossible without two things—the constitutional requirement and the line-item veto. I could never have gotten the cuts or the tax increase without the discipline that the constitutional provisions require.

Almost every governor lives with a requirement for a balanced budget and the power of a line-item veto. In New Jersey, without the two, our budget would resemble that of the federal government. We are, I believe, perilously close to fiscal disaster in this country. For too many years federal spending has run amok. Before we go over the edge, I hope we will have the courage and the common sense to pass a sensible balanced-budget requirement, and give the next president the line-item veto he needs.

Governors, meanwhile, are forced to make hard budget choices every day, and every day we veto irresponsible legislative spending. We cut because we have to—which is why governors of both parties have trouble understanding the Washington lament that "we don't know what to cut," and why almost all governors, including me, support a balanced-budget amendment and the line-item veto for the federal government.

☆

I learned another lesson during the 1982 budget crisis. Nothing is "off the record." The way Washington operated, I knew that "off the record" briefings were very much part of the system, and I also knew that both the executive branch and the press used them for their own purposes. When I first learned the extent of the deficit facing our state, I showed the details to only a handful of people, not wanting to publicize the extent of the problem until I could also propose a solution. But because of the impending crisis, I decided to hold an off-the-record briefing with the editors of the state's leading newspapers.

The briefing was scheduled one week before the budget was to be officially presented to the legislature. The idea was to impress upon the editors the dire financial situation we faced, and to ask for support of the newspapers as we worked our way toward a solution.

The letter inviting each of the editors to the briefing contained two important conditions. The first was that only editors could attend—news reporters could not. The second stated quite clearly that everything discussed at the briefing was not to be used in news stories or editorials. Attendance depended upon accepting both conditions. Of course, this kind of press event was not an innovation developed by the Kean administration. Off-the-record get-togethers are held all the time by the White House, and there was no reason for me to believe that the New Jersey press corps would not play by the same ground rules as their colleagues in Washington.

I was wrong. The meeting was well attended by editors from newspapers all across the state, but one of the editors from the *Bergen Record* went back to his newsroom and told a reporter what had been said.

The next day the *Record* ran a story saying that the state faced a huge budget deficit and the new governor was going to ask for a five cent increase in the gasoline tax to close it.

The ensuing damage was enormous. For one thing, the state's other newspapers had been beaten on a major story because they had kept their word. For another, legislators were incensed because the governor hadn't yet briefed them and they had to read about our budget problem in the newspaper. It took months to reestablish goodwill, time that could have been used more productively. As for the papers, many editors wrote to thank me for the briefing, and requested that it be made an annual practice. The editors of the *Bergen Record* eventually wrote to apologize. For my part, I had learned my lesson the hard way. I would never again hold an off-the-record briefing.

I also learned some lessons about the legislature, which in that first year tested me again and again. I remember clearly a state senator who said to me that he might change his mind and cast the vote that would pass my budget, but for one thing: one of his supporters wanted to be a judge. I'd have my budget if his friend got his judgeship. Another senator had an uncle who needed a job. When I said no to both, the legislators took the rebuffs personally. After all, this was the way business had always been done in state government. It took a while for them to understand I would not trade jobs for votes. As soon as they understood that the rule applied to everybody, I had no more trouble. It has been years since a legislator has proposed a similar deal.

Neither will I threaten legislators with political retribution. My strategy as governor is the same one I used as assembly speaker. I try to reason with them, laying out my best arguments and asking them for support. But I never intimate that I might retaliate if they don't see things my way. In the long run, I believe my approach is best. I respect legislators and I want them to respect me.

As governor, I have found that once a legislator gives you his word on an issue, that word is usually good. And because there are very few exceptions to the generalization, it's good to get a commitment of support early. Nothing bugs you more than to sit down with a legislator who finally says, "You're right, I agree, but I can't support you because last month I gave my word to this or that group that I would vote against the bill."

I do remember one dramatic exception to getting there late. I was a legislator myself and we were deciding whether or not New Jersey was to have an income tax. The supporters were only one vote short, and the rumor was that the Byrne administration had made a deal with Ken Gewertz, a South Jersey assemblyman, for that vote. I asked him about the rumor on the floor. "Hell will freeze over before I vote for an income tax," he told me. The very next day he cast the decisive vote and New Jersey got its first income tax. I asked him what happened. "Well," he said, "I came out this morning and there was the Devil himself frozen solid on my doorstep."

While the legislature and the new governor were getting used to each other, not much was accomplished. The press corps, which has a first-one-hundred-days fixation, seemed to agree among themselves that the first one hundred days of Tom Kean were not promising. "Kean's Rocky Honeymoon" was the headline of a feature piece in the *New York Times*.

I didn't see it that way. I don't think you can judge any administration, or any organization for that matter, on its performance during its first one hundred days. It is the rare and exceptional leader who has his agenda set, and his team in place, quickly enough to accomplish anything meaningful that fast. One hundred days for me is nothing more than a mostly useless, journalistic bench mark. I much prefer to see an organization perform like a marathon runner, slow at the start but building to a steady, if not quickening, pace at the end.

I knew we had learned from our mistakes and in them were the seeds for future successes. I was not worried. But neither was I unduly optimistic, because I had a hunch that things were going to get worse before they got better. The economy was still weakening, as daily hundreds more New Jerseyans found themselves out of work. Every cabinet meeting brought word of a new problem, everything seemed to be conspiring against us, and that summer, disaster struck from a totally unexpected quarter.

It all began at a wonderfully named resort, Shangri-La, in Oklahoma, at my first summer meeting of the National Governors' Association. I was just getting to know my fellow governors. The formal agenda of the group is often meaningless or dull, but the private exchanges are often extraordinarily productive. Governors are not rivals; we don't run against each other, and very few of us are especially partisan. We are judged not against each other, but against whether or not we improve the lot of the people of our state.

Governors share things with each other very easily. If I've had success tackling a problem in a particular way, I will talk about it with other governors. Party lines are forgotten, and it's hard to tell Republican governors from Democratic in our sessions. Close friendships often result, and I've treasured mine. I've worked with Jim Hunt and Chuck Robb on education, with Dick Lamm on health care, with Mike Dukakis, Bill Clinton, and Mike Castle on welfare reform. Closer to home, Mario Cuomo and I have worked together on many mutual concerns, Dick Thornburgh was always helpful, and Pete du Pont and Mike Castle are close friends, although Pete is mistaken when he calls the Delaware "his river."

So I was looking forward to the summer meeting in Oklahoma. The first morning there I woke up with a pain in my left leg. As the day went on, it became worse and worse. I could not sit comfortably; walking, though not as painful, was difficult. That night I got little if any sleep. The next morning things were no better. Then I started to worry. I had never experienced pain so intense and I had no idea what was wrong. I called home and asked Debby to schedule a doctor's appointment and hitched a ride home on a National Guard plane.

The doctor delivered a diagnosis that surprised me. He said the problem wasn't with my leg; the pain, he explained, came from my back. I had heard the word "sciatica" before, but had never really known what it meant. It means that pain radiates down a leg because nerves above it are compressed. "Go home," he suggested, "stay off your feet for a week, and see what happens." So I canceled my appointments and took to my bed, but instead of improving, things got worse. It was excruciatingly painful even to get from my bed to the shower. After a week I underwent a CAT scan, which showed a severely herniated disk. So I was put into a hospital for the first time since I was five.

The weeks in the hospital were, without a doubt, the most frustrating and boring of my term as governor. No easy treatment exists for the ailment, and surgery, while possible, can be dangerous. Instead of an operation, I was subjected to a complex form of treatment that included therapy and traction. Whenever I wasn't undergoing treatments, I was flat on my back, wrapped in a corsetlike contraption that was attached to a pulley counterbalanced by a twenty-pound weight. The idea, as I understood it, was that stress had pushed together the vertebrae in my back and the weight would slowly pull them apart again. It was not a comfortable arrangement. My staff took to calling me Governor Stretch, while I told reporters that I would tower over Senator Bill Bradley by the time I got out.

The humor sometimes tended toward the gallows variety. Although no one talked about it much, there was a chance that the therapy would not work and I would be disabled and perhaps immobile for the rest of my term, and possibly the rest of my life. I had fears the way anyone in my condition would. I began to wonder how I could possibly run a state lying on my back.

The pain continued unabated week after week, while I did the best work I could from the hospital. Important documents were delivered to me at least three times a day. I met with key staff and cabinet members. A computer terminal was installed in my hospital room. I participated in a few events by telephone. I even attended the first annual Governor's Ball in my honor via closed-circuit television. But I missed being in the State House and being out and about. Given the human suffering caused by a bad economy, I thought the state needed to see an active, energetic governor. I cringed when I saw headlines such as the one that read "Ailing Governor, Ailing State."

Always there was the pain. Time and time again it worked its way into my thoughts or spoiled my concentration. At night it robbed me of the sleep needed to keep a clear mind during the day. I wondered, if a real crisis arose, would I be able to take everything into account and make the right decision? Up to that time, I had always thought that the medical reports requested of presidential candidates were an invasion of privacy. I don't anymore. Pain can be debilitating and can affect everything you do and don't do. We have a right to know if a person running for president has a serious medical problem.

There was a bright side to the experience: the reaction of my friends and the general public. My injury seemed to tap some deep well of sympathy within them. Lower-back pain is the third most common ailment in the country, affecting nearly 10 million people. Judging from my mail, it looked as if every one of them was intent on telling me just what to do to get better. More than three thousand letters and cards were delivered. Everybody had a cure, while books and pamphlets on back pain arrived by the score. My doctor said that I had secured one of the best back libraries in the state.

The letters and cards did help. Almost all were encouraging. Henry Kissinger wrote to recommend a Wall Street specialist who had cured Nelson Rockefeller. Others swore by individual chiropractors, osteopaths, or acupuncturists. One person recommended jumping up and down on a trampoline; another said the cure was constant foot massages. I received a letter from an Indian medicine man who wrote, "I can cure

your back, and if you don't believe me, call Mrs. Schwarz in Brooklyn."
One woman even offered to pay the airplane fare to send her favorite
back specialist in from Boston. Ed Koch was kind enough to call, offering
his usual commonsense advice. "Tom," he said, "find your most conservative doctor and listen to him." Debby brought me a Walkman, and
when I wasn't working, I listened to music to get my mind off the
pain.

The *New York Times* called for an interview and asked what I was
doing at that very moment. I replied I was listening to opera singer
Richard Tucker, who had died some years before. A few days later I
received a lovely note from Tucker's widow saying how pleased she
was that her husband's voice still brought pleasure. We kept in touch
until her own untimely death a few years later.

After I had been in the hospital about two weeks, the doctors gathered,
I learned later, and agreed that they would probably have to operate.
They thought I was in such pain that I would concur. But suddenly
and almost miraculously the pain began to subside. The doctors saw
an improvement and I was allowed to walk gingerly around the hospital
room. I told my doctors I had had enough of being a bedridden governor,
and within two days I was limping out of the hospital with Debby by
my side. When I flew to the State House a few days later, I was returning
after a six-week absence, one of the longest stretches of time that a
governor has been out of the office in New Jersey history. Back at work,
I found my desk piled high with economic briefings, all containing
bad news. Someone joked that I might soon enough prefer the hospital
room to the governor's office.

The economy was like a bobsled run, all downhill. Unemployment
had crossed 10 percent in September and was heading higher. The
country was in the trough of the most severe recession since the Great
Depression, and New Jersey was bearing a substantial portion of the
damage. The effect on the state budget, meanwhile, was predictable.
The spring budget compromise had helped, but every month our deficit
got larger. Hardly a day went by without Treasurer Ken Biederman
rushing into my office with a new reading on the state's economy. His
myriad charts always showed the same thing: a dramatic slowdown of
the money coming into state coffers.

The next few months brought more economic bad news and more
legislative wrangling. I called special sessions and made proposals, all
seemingly to no avail. That's when I became convinced that some people

in legislative leadership had a political stake in continued economic woe.

For my part, I was willing to meet with anyone who wanted to help. The state's mayors worked with me. Mayors are executives and so had the same view of things I did, seeing the recession that wreaked havoc on the already weakened urban economy. We formed an alliance, Democratic urban mayors with a Republican governor. It was unprecedented, but it worked. Together we lobbied the legislature for a solution to the budget crisis, which arrived with just three days left in the year. It was not what I wanted. Once again I had to cut the budget, and this time I had to okay a tax increase to preserve aid to our schools. But the crisis was ended. Schools and municipalities in particular could now be assured of continued funding. For that to happen, both houses stayed in session for twenty-two hours straight. Senators slept in their chairs. At four in the morning, I slipped away from the governor's office to soothe my back with a dip in the pool at a nearby state police facility. To the surprise of many, the compromise passed, although by a slim margin. At nine in the morning on New Year's Eve I stood in the outer sanctum of the governor's office and signed the bill into law. I had been up for more than thirty hours. But the budget crisis was finally over, after more than nine months of stalemate. The legislation was a classic compromise. No one liked it, but all of us in New Jersey avoided fiscal chaos.

As the first year of the Kean administration ended, people who make a living watching the State House proffered two bits of wisdom. The first was that the state's budget and economic problems were far from over. We might get a reprieve for a while, they said, but the annual budget crisis was going to be a staple of New Jersey government for the foreseeable future. The other bit of wisdom was about my political future. Certain reporters figured that I would be a one-term governor, and speculation had already begun in some quarters about who would challenge me in a Republican primary. It had been a very rough year, no question. The fact was that my popularity rating remained below 50 percent throughout. I know some of the Democrats were thinking I could not repeat my 1,797-vote margin of victory in a 1985 rematch with Jim Florio.

I paid no attention to conventional opinion or the polls. The first year had its rough spots, yes, but in the long and bruising battle over the budget, there appeared distinct signs of an administration beginning to mature. Despite my setbacks, I had grown more comfortable and confident in my dealings with the legislature, and I knew that many of the programs it had rejected would resurface during the years ahead in a more receptive climate. As for the poll numbers, where some saw danger I saw hope. Despite the public battle over the budget, despite the deepest recession in forty years, despite my illness, my popularity had never dropped. Somehow I had managed to get through to a large number of the people and convince them that I was on the right track, that problems were being addressed. Once the economy started to pick up and some of my ideas started to take hold, I thought it would be no time until my administration would be regarded as both progressive and successful. Was I crazy?

4
New Jersey's Renaissance

O_N November 5, 1985, I returned to the Holiday Inn in Livingston to learn the results of another election. Like four years before, I was joined by people who had taken time from their work and families to make a contribution to democracy. Once again the campaign headquarters was festooned with balloons and bunting. A band played rousing music, everything from "For He's a Jolly Good Fellow" to Bruce Springsteen's "Born to Run." In the middle of the room, cordoned off from the noisy crowd, sat the members of the national and local press corps, ready to translate the meaning of what was happening for the general public.

On the surface, things looked pretty much as they had four years before, when I sweated out the night awaiting word on whether I had beaten Jim Florio. Beneath the surface, however, things were much different. Gone was the anxiety among my supporters, replaced by a relaxed confidence, a near cockiness. You wouldn't find drafts of concession speeches anywhere, because for days I had been working on a victory speech. And television networks were not upsetting my stomach with reports of my imminent demise. For weeks they had been predicting a landslide in my favor.

I wasn't quite ready to schedule the victory parade. I've always been a nervous campaigner. I had read the favorable polls and the equally favorable analyses from various pundits. And I had met enough people on the campaign trail to know in my gut that things had changed dramatically since that rough first year. My advisers told me to relax, election day would be a breeze. But when you are the candidate, you are never quite sure. It's sort of like being favored by thirty points in a football game. You think you are going to win. By every indication there is no way you can possibly lose. But until the final whistle blows, you are not willing to declare victory. Maybe my anxiety comes from being a part of so many close elections. Anyhow, as I got dressed after my traditional election-day game of tennis, I was not completely sure how things would go that evening.

By 8:00 P.M. my worries had dissipated. All three networks had projected me the victor over my Democratic opponent, Peter Shapiro, a thirty-three-year-old political wunderkind who was chief executive of my home county and who had not lost an election in nine attempts. I left for the hotel knowing I was to be governor for another four years.

As the evening went on, the dimensions of the victory became apparent. Four years after being elected by the slimmest margin in the state's history, I was on my way to its biggest landslide. I would win with a 70 percent majority, by over 790,000 votes out of almost 2 million cast. In the aftermath of Watergate in 1973, Brendan Byrne had swamped Republican congressman Charlie Sandman by 720,000 votes. My margin of victory would smash that record. It would be even bigger than Ronald Reagan's 670,000-vote margin in New Jersey the year before, with a much larger turnout.

What caught the attention of the national media was not simply the size of my victory, but the diversity of the coalition behind it. Predictably I won, and won big, in the white, affluent towns in Morris, Somerset, and Bergen counties. I carried a strong majority in the rural farm towns scattered across southern New Jersey. But the tidal wave of support washed through some of the staunchest Democratic areas in the entire country. Places like Sayreville, in Middlesex County, where lunch-pail–toting workers come home every evening to listen to the Yankees on their front porches. Or West New York, an incredible ethnic mix of people.

I swept all twenty-one counties in New Jersey, and I won all but three of the 567 towns and cities. Two were small towns of less than five hundred voters in Democratic Camden County. The third was a tiny town called Roosevelt in western Monmouth County. Populated mostly by Hasidic Jews, Roosevelt was created in the 1930s as one of the federal government's experimental New Deal communities. For five hundred dollars, settlers were given land on which to build and the chance to work on cooperative farms and in worker-run factories. Although four decades had passed since the town's creation, the residents stayed loyal to the party of their namesake. I may have lost Roosevelt, but I won in virtually every other place where the descendants of FDR's coalition lived. Most satisfyingly, I swept the so-called Big Six cities— Newark, Jersey City, Paterson, Camden, Trenton, and Elizabeth.

Exit polls conducted by ABC News showed that my support extended across ethnic, age, religious, and ideological lines. I won 60 percent of the black vote and 69 percent of the support of voters in union households. In a state in which Democrats had a two-to-one advantage in voter registration, I won by more than a two-to-one margin. ABC's exit polls indicated that 43 percent of the registered Democrats had cast votes for me.

Surprisingly, the election proved that political coattails had not gone the way of the Nehru jacket, as many pundits believed. After voters pulled the lever for me, they reached down and voted for other Republicans. The 44–36 Democratic majority in the state assembly was overturned. My durable nemesis, Alan Karcher, would no longer be speaker; in fact, he had to struggle to hold onto his own heretofore safe Democratic seat. When the final votes were counted, Republicans held a 50–30 seat advantage in the assembly. Four Republicans were elected in Hudson County, which had not elected a Republican to the legislature since the 1920s.

From the poor inner cities to the fast-growing suburbs to the bucolic country towns, it was a resounding vote of confidence in me and my party. Lost in the sheer size of the victory was any mention of the skepticism that seemed to accompany my every move three years before. Obviously, this affirmation of my leadership was gratifying. It proved that my confidence during that rough first year had not been misplaced. The day after the election, as I flipped through the dailies, I came across my favorite quote in the newspaper that had most often criticized me. Under an editorial entitled "Avalanche," the *Bergen Record* wrote: "Quite simply, it has never been done before. Not by Woodrow Wilson, not by Richard Hughes, not by anybody. Thomas Howard Kean rolled up the biggest landslide since New Jersey began electing Governors. It was, oh, about 400 times the size of his 1981 margin over James Florio. It was a staggering achievement, a tribute to Mr. Kean's remarkable popularity."

What caused this "staggering achievement"? How, in just three short years, did I go from being one of the incumbents most likely to lose in

America to a man who many now argued was the most popular governor in the country? How could a state seemingly plagued with intractable ills feel good enough about the direction in which it was headed to give its incumbent governor such support?

It is not an easy question to answer, because it is hard to measure the collective fortune of a state as diverse as New Jersey. Some people's lives improve over four years, others' get worse. Searching for objective measures, politicians are often reduced to numbers. In speeches, brochures, and television ads in 1985, I had buried audiences in a blizzard of statistics that I felt proved the fundamental premise of my campaign: a remarkable transformation had taken place in New Jersey.

The most important change occurred in the pocketbook issues. New Jersey had gone from an economic basket case, or "rustbucket," depending on which condemnation you favored, to what the *New York Times* called "a paradigm of economic growth in the modern post-industrial economy." The unemployment rate had plummeted from above 10 percent at the end of my first year in office to 4.4 percent two months before the election. It had dropped from two points above the national average to two points below. New Jersey's business climate, ranked dead last when I first ran for governor, according to the Grant-Thornton study, had risen to twenty-fourth in the country and first in the entire Northeast. Per capita income, a measure of a person's buying power, had risen to third in the country. And the economic boom was not limited to the suburbs, but was felt across the entire state, including the cities. While employment of white males had increased by 7 percent, employment of minority New Jerseyans had risen by 19 percent. Clearly this was a rising tide lifting all boats. Meanwhile, as the economy gained strength, the perennial budget crises vanished. While we spent that first year in office figuring out how to close a $600 million deficit, the fourth year was spent in the much pleasanter task of figuring how to return a hefty surplus to the taxpayers.

The bottom line was clear: more people were working productively and working people were finding more money in their wallets. The burst of economic growth had attracted more than 25,000 new people to New Jersey in the four years of my term, compared to the 119,000 who had fled to places like Texas or Florida during the economic dog days of the 1970s.

To put it another way, New Jerseyans were saying yes to the simple question that President Reagan had repeated in his reelection campaign:

"Are you better off than you were four years ago?" New Jerseyans were quite a bit better off. Not just some people, but virtually all people. The shopkeeper who owned the preppy store in Bernardsville might be taking home more money, but so were the restaurant owner in the middle of Newark, the farmer in Burlington County, and the steamroller operator in North Plainfield.

New Jerseyans felt something positive and important had happened in only three or four years. They obviously thought my leadership had a great deal to do with it, and the result was an electoral landslide of historic proportions, just three years after some had labeled me a one-term governor. But merely charting the numerical measures of the state's progress next to my rising popularity belies the central question. What role did state government play in New Jersey's transformation from laggard to leader? Was I simply lucky to be in the right place at the right time? Or did New Jersey's recent experience offer evidence that strong, active progressive government—Republican government—can be a catalyst for positive change in America of the 1980s?

I think the answer to the last question is yes. Quality political leadership can make a difference and what has happened in New Jersey in the 1980s proves it. I don't mean to imply that a governor can do it alone. You have to understand the history and circumstances of your state and work with them. For example, my predecessors, governors Cahill and Byrne, had already built the Meadowlands, which was to do much for the state's image. Casino gambling, which was to supply 10 percent of the new jobs, was already in place. And the Northeast as a whole was shifting from manufacturing to service industries, creating jobs from Boston, Massachusetts, to Raleigh, North Carolina. New Jersey was ripe for an economic expansion. My job was to put the old problems behind us, marshal our limited resources, and set the right priorities. I did this. And a state that had lagged even in good times emerged as a leader.

☆

Nothing had contributed to New Jersey voters' lack of regard for state government more than its habit of having to respond to crisis after crisis. New Jersey government never anticipated, it only reacted. We had been like a big boxer. From his physique, people expected great things, but when he got hit in the head, his hands went to his head, and when he got hit in the stomach, his hands went there. So he always lost. Even during the confusion of the first year, my message to every cabinet member was ever the same: solve the crises. I told cabinet members I didn't want to hear them talking about problems unless they also had solutions. I told them that unless we could put the crises behind us, we would never be able to plan ahead.

Obviously, reducing crime was a priority. Corporate leaders had told me repeatedly that the main reason they wouldn't move to Newark or Camden was that their employees were afraid of being mugged in the parking lot. I am very conservative when it comes to law and order, and I believe most of the elaborate rehabilitation schemes of the past fifty years have been failures. The best way to reduce crime is to lock criminals up and keep them off the streets for a long time. I've supported mandatory sentences for crimes committed with a gun and for those who peddle drugs in our streets. I believe that judges should have the right to deny bail to violent criminals with prior convictions, if they believe the defendant poses a continuing threat to the public.

Tough laws put pressure on the prison system. When I took office, the prisons were bulging. Prior administrations had simply not seen fit to spend money on prisons. Tough crime laws may be popular, but spending millions to build prisons is not. As a result, federal judges were threatening to release state prisoners before they had served their time. We had to take care of the prison problem before we could even consider strengthening the state's crime laws.

I knew we had to move fast. I sat down with Gary Stein, my director of policy and planning, and came up with a solution. To pay for new prison cells, we siphoned money from the general fund and put a bond issue on the ballot. We raised enough to build two new prisons in Camden and Newark. In all, we added over four thousand new beds to the prison system in less than four years. So I was able to sign new anticrime laws, including a mandatory sentence for people who sell drugs within one thousand feet of a school. By the time I ran for reelection, crime had dropped by 38 percent, a rate of decrease much faster than in the rest of the country. As I write, more than thirty states are under court order to release prisoners. New Jersey is not, and we plan to keep it that way. We are asking the public for additional money to create even more prison space. I want the message to be clear that anyone convicted of a crime in New Jersey will serve their full sentence.

Prisons were not the only construction problem that had been neglected. The roads and highways had been ignored for over three decades.

I'll never forget the day my commissioner of transportation, John Sheridan, came into my office and told me that if something was not done right away, we were going to have to close some roads and bridges. The state hadn't been spending anything on maintenance, never mind new construction. The cost of repairing all our roads, Sheridan told me, would be more than $2 billion. I got the bad news in the middle of the first-year budget crisis, when I was trying to find $300 million to pay for the Transportation Department's normal operating budget.

I know that nothing puts a person to sleep faster than talking about infrastructure. Although dull, infrastructure is vital. America is literally falling apart. Bridges are collapsing. Even the most conservative spenders estimate that we will have to double our investment in roads and sewers. Several studies have estimated that the costs could soar into the trillions.

But Washington won't pay for it anymore. So we came up with the idea of an infrastructure bank. We put available money in a pool, from which the state or towns could borrow. When the loans were repaid, the pool of money would be available for new projects. It was cheaper for towns to get low-interest loans for an entire project than to get federal grants for half a project, when the rest had to be paid for by borrowing money at high interest rates in the bond market.

The first time I proposed the infrastructure bank, the Democrats defeated it in an all-night session. I've learned that sometimes in politics a good idea will fail, but if it has merit, repackage it and bring it up again. So a year later, I modified it a bit and this time I called it the Transportation Trust. And I confronted the Democratic leadership with a powerful lobbying coalition.

Labor and business in New Jersey had never been confused with Astaire and Rogers. Instead, the antagonists usually ended up punching it out in the corner. This time I convinced them they had the same goals. Organized labor had hungered for construction jobs for decades. Business leaders knew that good roads were essential if we were going to create new jobs. So, for one of the few times in New Jersey's history, pin-striped bankers lobbied with rugged union members for a piece of legislation. The Democrats in the assembly were still convinced that if I wanted something, they should oppose it. For a while it looked as if the program would be defeated again. I remember holding one press conference at which I explained that things looked bleak for the trust fund. The leader of one of the construction unions, Richie Tissiere, responded with some colorful language seldom heard in the governor's office. He assured me that the Democrats would never forget it if they killed the bill. He and some other labor leaders left my office and marched down the hall to the Democratic caucus. I don't know what they said. One of them told me later that I wouldn't want to hear the exact language. But whatever it was, within hours I received word that a few Democratic votes had changed. The trust fund would pass after all.

The Transportation Trust Fund was the economic shot in the arm we needed. Now I could assure companies thinking about a move to New Jersey that we could finish a road, improve an intersection, or fix a traffic circle. In all, we spent more than $3 billion in just over three years on the most massive construction program in the state's history. In the process, we created 38,000 construction jobs and thousands of other jobs in related industries.

One of those new jobs was taken by Eddie Isabella, a construction worker in Kearny. Eddie does what his father did, the tough work on road construction crews, digging trenches and pouring concrete. Eddie is very good at his work, but that didn't matter in the 1970s. The construction industry had shut down. Eddie could find work only, as he put it, in "dribs and drabs." As a result, he was having a tough time paying the bills, and he had no money to save for his three young daughters' education. He was scared when he thought about the future, and about leaving the line of work that had given his dad a comfortable and happy life.

All that changed with the Transportation Trust Fund. Now Eddie works not only five days a week, but Saturdays too. He bought a beautiful new home, a new car, and he's putting away money for his daughters' education. So the fund is building more than new roads, it's building new lives. If you multiply Eddie Isabella's story at least 38,000 times, you get an idea of why organized labor fought so hard for the program. Since the fund was put in place, membership in the carpenters, operating engineers, and construction workers unions has at least tripled.

To me, the Transportation Trust Fund is government at its best—a fiscally responsible program putting people to work to create opportunity for other people. Sam Ehrenhalt, who monitors the Northeastern economy for the federal government, has said that the trust fund was the primary impetus behind New Jersey's economic boom. Now we've created other revolving-loan funds to buy land for parks and recreation and to help towns build sewage-treatment plants and garbage incinerators.

Building prisons and roads was an important first steps to reducing crime and creating jobs. But burglaries and unemployment don't compare with public concern over toxic waste. Our most difficult problem was finding some way to deal with this crisis. Like a lot of older states in the Northeast, New Jersey was dotted with lagoons of chemicals, leaking landfills, and graveyards of barrels that were going to require expensive cleanup. This was unexplored territory, and no one knew what to do. When I took office, the state's Department of Environmental Protection had attempted only one cleanup. It resulted in a fiery explosion.

My first decision was to face the problem head-on. I wanted every dangerous site identified and put on the cleanup list under the recently enacted federal Superfund law. Once a site was on the list, we qualified for federal money to help with the cleanup. In the short term, our strategy didn't do much for the state's image. The Garden State became the Toxic State in many minds, because we were uncovering a new waste site every month. But I knew we had to solve our short-term toxic waste problems if we were going to improve the state's long-term image. I believed people were intelligent enough to respect a state that recognized a problem and was dealing with it.

By the time I ran for reelection, we led the nation in the number of sites on the Superfund list, in the number of remedial studies conducted, and in the amount of engineering and construction under way. The *New York Times* could report that "New Jersey's approach to toxic waste cleanup is a model for the rest of the nation." Bill Ruckelshaus, the former administrator of the federal Environmental Protection Agency (EPA), said that in toxic waste cleanup New Jersey was "light-years ahead of the rest of the country." Our program was so successful that we were able to lend the EPA money to keep the federal program running when Superfund lapsed early in 1986. Our image suffered early from our aggressive program. But within two decades, New Jersey will be able to say that we are the first state in the nation to really clean up toxic wastes.

Those were the kinds of crises we faced. Once we found solutions, we could turn our attention to other priorities. Knowing that prisoners weren't going to be released in the streets, that motorists weren't disappearing into potholes, and that entire communities weren't being ravaged by toxic waste, we could begin to plan and deal with problems before they arose. We could be ambitious and creative.

The environment again provides a perfect example for what I mean. Having the nation's most aggressive cleanup program still wouldn't solve the toxic waste problem, because, as I said, new sites kept cropping up. An old factory would be sold and the new owner would walk out back and discover ten or eleven rotting drums or an old lagoon filled with oozing chemicals. The question was, how do we make sure that polluters pay for the cleanup? In most cases, government cleaned the site, then sued to have the responsible parties reimburse us. But many times it was hard to pinpoint the original polluter, who might have gone out of business years before.

We had to switch from reacting to problems to preventing them. So in 1983, I signed a law which requires that anyone who sells property in New Jersey has to certify that the property is clean of all hazardous materials. The law has had a dramatic effect. For example, Texaco was required to sell its huge Eagle Point Refinery in South Jersey to meet federal antitrust standards in the Getty merger. Our environmental technicians investigated and found abandoned landfills and oil spills on the refinery site. Before the huge merger could be finally approved, Texaco had to agree to pay for a $4 million cleanup. By the summer of 1987, this law, the Environmental Cleanup Responsibility Act (ECRA), had been responsible for almost three hundred cleanups, at a total cost of $100 million. Some, like the Texaco cleanup, were large engineering efforts. Others required nothing more than washing oil off a garage floor. Every dollar polluters spent was a dollar that taxpayers didn't have to cough up.

ECRA was just one example of New Jersey's environmental leadership. I signed the strictest "right-to-know" law in the country, giving workers information about the hazardous chemicals in the workplace. I signed the first law requiring government to inspect how safely industries produce certain chemicals, so we could prevent a tragedy like the one in Bhopal, India. The law turned out to be a model for federal legislation. I ordered a survey of exposure to radon, the naturally occurring radioactive gas that has been linked in some studies to lung cancer. And in my second term I signed the nation's first mandatory statewide recycling law.

This leadership has not always been easy. For four years I fought for a bill to protect the state's 300,000 acres of fresh-water wetlands from uncontrolled development. Year after year the builders were able to muster enough support to defeat the bill in the legislature. While the legislature dallied, thousands of acres were lost to the bulldozers. I realized that the builders had nothing to lose if no wetlands protection bill were passed. In frustration, I had my second-term chief counsel,

Mike Cole, draw up an executive order using my emergency powers to immediately halt development in the wetlands and surrounding areas until a strong wetlands protection bill was signed. Some said it was unconstitutional. Mike Cole assured me I was on sound legal footing. The executive order sat on my desk for weeks, while I checked with legislative leaders to see if there were any signs of progress. They said no, the builders were too strong. So I released the executive order, stopping projects up and down the state. Some legislators called me a dictator and the builders' lobby brought suit. But despite the noise, the legislative climate changed immediately. Within three weeks I had a strong wetlands protection bill on my desk for signature.

I'm proud of our environmental record. In 1987, the Washington-based Fund for Renewable Energy and the Environment surveyed state environmental programs. The survey asserted that the nation's environmental future was being written in the states, not in Washington. New Jersey was ranked third overall, and first in hazardous waste management and garbage disposal.

I made environmental protection an issue in my reelection campaign. My success gives me a chance to explode a couple of myths on politics and the environment. The first myth is that Republicans and environmentalists make strange bedfellows. The Reagan years, and particularly the lingering memories of James Watt, have left many people with the idea that the term "Republican environmentalist" is an oxymoron, like nuclear survival.

Nothing could be further from the truth. Historically, Republicans have been the strongest proponents of protecting the environment. Only recently have we lost our mantle. When Republicans argue the point, we like to quote Theodore Roosevelt, who created the Department of the Interior and the national parks system. We Republicans use Teddy to prove we like trees the way Democrats use Harry Truman to prove they will defend the country. But Teddy Roosevelt and his trusted adviser Gifford Pinchot were not the last Republicans to fight for clean water, air, and open space. Richard Nixon's administration created the EPA. Presidents Nixon and Ford, working with a Democratic Congress, put in place almost the entire structure of national environmental laws we rely on today, including the Clean Air Act, the Clean Water Act, the Resource Conservation and Recovery Act (RCRA), and the Coastal Zone Management Act. Today environmental issues are just as important as they were fifteen years ago. Problems like toxic waste, garbage disposal,

and protection of our wetlands are not limited to the crowded Northeast—
they are problems everywhere. Polls show a large majority of voters
supporting more environmental protection, not less. Republicans would
be smart to take heed.

New issues like radon or air toxics require new ideas where conservative
thinking can play a large role. In New Jersey, we have privatized the
construction and operation of resource recovery facilities. Government
monitors the health standards, while the private sector builds the facilities
more cheaply. We are also experimenting with user fees, to reduce
government costs and force the regulated community to pay directly
for regulation. Builders, for example, support the wetlands permitting
program. Now we are experimenting with fees and tax incentives to
encourage private industry to reduce toxic waste at the source. These
approaches rely heavily on the private sector and on a market economy
to achieve the socially desirable goals of clean air and clean water.

I believe we are going to have to do a better job of setting environmental
priorities. So far we have responded to one environmental crisis after
another. News about the latest health threat is treated like rumors that
Liz Taylor is about to get married again: no big deal. People ask, "Is
there anything we can eat, drink, or do without some risk?"

We need to tell people as precisely as possible what threat a particular
pollutant poses. And we need a capability to rank risks so that, for
example, we can tell whether it is more dangerous to breathe a certain
level of radon gas or drink water with tiny amounts of a certain chemical
in it. Scientists call these kinds of rankings risk assessments, and they
are the next frontier of environmental protection. With the information,
we can begin to determine whether spending billions to clean up Superfund sites will do more to protect people's health than remodeling thousands of basements to reduce exposure to radon gas. We have started a
risk-assessment program in New Jersey, trying to harness science and
technology, which have in the past inadvertently given us harmful by-
products, and put these forces to work protecting human health.

One final point, but an important one. New Jersey has enacted
some of the nation's strictest environmental laws even as our economy
boomed. So much for those who say clean water and new jobs are
incompatible. Tension will always exist between the two goals, no question. For example, many builders and real estate agents in New Jersey
will argue that ECRA has sometimes needlessly slowed the sale of a
piece of property. But I think we can put up with the inconvenience

of slightly slower real estate transactions, and the added cost of cleanup and regulatory programs, in order to bequeath clean air and water to our children. Past generations ducked the problems, and future generations may have no way to reverse the damage. It's up to us. A state like New Jersey has a vibrant economy and the toughest environmental laws in the country, which proves for me that jobs in the future will migrate to those states and regions that have done whatever is necessary to protect their environment.

☆

To kick-start the economy, and to protect the environment, we used the same approach. We put the crises behind us, then began to use a combination of incentives and investments to improve New Jersey's business climate. With the budget crisis nothing more than a memory and the economy picking up steam, I was able to return to my supply-side ways and sign five separate tax cuts. In addition, we brought labor and management together to repay a $600 million unemployment insurance debt to the federal government, saving every worker $42 a year.

One of those tax cuts brought me particular pleasure. For years, New Jersey's inheritance tax had been among the highest in the nation. With bankers and lawyers advising older wealthier residents not to die in New Jersey, we were losing more money from people moving their residences to states like Florida and New Hampshire than we were collecting from the inheritance taxes paid by people who stayed. And the tax wasn't just hurting the idle rich. Farmers, small businesses, widowers left with a small estate, anyone who had built a nest egg was affected. I have always believed that it makes no sense to penalize someone for working hard. Why shouldn't they be allowed to pass their hard-earned savings on to their children? We repealed the inheritance tax and gave older people a reason to stay.

Our tax cuts sent an unmistakable signal: New Jersey rewards those who create wealth. We welcomed new businesses and entrepreneurs. The result was a migration of new jobs into the state. From 1982 until I ran for reelection in 1985, the rate of new jobs in New Jersey increased faster than in all but six other states. During the 1970s, by contrast, new jobs grew slower here than in forty-two other states.

We used tax incentives to rebuild our cities, by creating urban enterprise zones. Businesses that located in ten of the most depressed urban neighborhoods got a tax break. An old lumberyard in Trenton, for example, attracted few customers during the weekends when commuters didn't come into town. But now because the same lumberyard charges half the sales tax of its suburban competitors, weekends find the parking lot chock-full of cars. People drive from Pennsylvania, ten miles away, to buy things at lower prices. In all, our enterprise zones are expected to create 18,000 city jobs by 1989. These private-sector jobs are being created in areas that haven't seen hope in years. One is the Camden neighborhood in which I launched my 1981 campaign.

But if the 1980s have taught governors anything, it is that economic growth requires more than low taxes. Many of the low-tax states in the South learned the lesson the hard way, as businesses began to migrate north in search of better roads, more skilled labor, and a better quality of life in general. To keep jobs, you have to keep taxes as low as possible. But you also have to invest, and you have to invest wisely.

Let me give you just one example of what I mean. Have you ever marveled at how wind over and under the wings of a huge airplane can lift it into the sky? That doesn't just happen. It often takes years of engineering effort, and millions of dollars, to test the shape of the wing under all kinds of conditions. In the past, such tests have been conducted in wind tunnels. But the conditions in them are difficult to control and the results are sometimes inaccurate, costing airplane manufacturers millions.

Now a Princeton University engineer has a solution to the problem. Dr. Daniel Nosenchuck has helped design a supercomputer that can simulate the effects of airflow and turbulence on surfaces. Dr. Nosenchuck, who won an Emmy for creating the mushroom clouds in the television special "The Day After," hopes his invention can dramatically reduce the cost of building an airplane or even a space station. The question is, how do we get Dr. Nosenchuck's invention from the laboratory to the marketplace? Japan is great at this; we are not. We win the Nobel Prizes for research. The Japanese take our ideas and win the race to the sales counter. Why? Because brilliant scientists like Dr. Nosenchuck may be whizzes around supercomputers, but they get lost among venture capitalists. They need some help.

That's where state government comes in. In 1983, I convinced New Jersey voters to approve a $90 million bond issue to invest in high-technology jobs. We didn't want the state selling supercomputers; instead, we wanted to be a catalyst to spur private industry and bring business and academia together. When Dr. Nosenchuck stepped out of the computer lab with his invention, he got in touch with Ed Cohen, the executive director of our state Science and Technology Commission. Dr. Cohen is, in some respects, a marriage broker in high technology. He matches scientists like Dr. Nosenchuck with suitors from the private sector. In this case, he found a company from Tinton Falls, New Jersey, called Concurrent Computer, that specializes in building and selling multiprocessing computers. Following Dr. Cohen's advice, Dr. Nosenchuck transferred his technology to Concurrent. Now the National Aeronautics and Space Administration (NASA) is also working with Concurrent to find possible uses of the computer for its space shuttle. Within five years, at least one hundred new jobs will be brought to New Jersey. At the same time, the bond-issue money is being used to build public/ private research centers in emerging fields like biotechnology, hazardous waste disposal, and industrial ceramics. This is not a small, showcase operation. In all, the Science and Technology Commission has helped create 2,500 new jobs in four years. The National Science Foundation picked it as a model of how to stimulate private industry through government investment in technology.

Ours is one small example of the sort of investment states have to make if we are going to protect American jobs in the next century. And that investment cannot be limited to roads and education. Even now, governors are spending money to promote international trade and tourism. In New Jersey, I've invested heavily in the arts, not only because I believe that a state can't be great without interest in painting, music, and theater, but because every dollar we spend on the arts brings four dollars into local economies. Understand that I am not saying we need an industrial policy, where state governments pick winners and losers in the economy. That doesn't work. What I want instead is government to serve as a catalyst in projects where a relatively small investment will create a large number of private-sector jobs.

I cannot write about New Jersey's economic renaissance without bringing up the rivalry between New Jersey and New York. A number of the new jobs now found in New Jersey came across the river from Manhattan. Every year since 1984, more than seventy businesses have moved from New York to New Jersey, including ADT, the world's largest electronic security firm; Peat, Marwick, Main, the nation's second-largest accounting firm; and Hertz, the largest car rental company. You don't have to be an economist to figure out why. Our taxes are lower, and rents and land in New Jersey are on average less than half the cost in

Manhattan. Finally, electrical power costs half what it does in New York.

The business climate is especially good along the Hudson waterfront. In the 1970s, the waterfront was a ramshackle collection of rotting docks and abandoned rail yards. By 1985, it was probably the most valuable piece of undeveloped real estate on the East Coast. Blessed with a stunning view of the Manhattan skyline, along with low rents, the waterfront has turned into the Gold Coast—a developer's dream. I have an office along the waterfront, and from it we work with developers to build the infrastructure that can handle the $10 billion in new investment expected by the turn of the century. We hope it will create 100,000 new jobs.

The exodus of jobs from New York to New Jersey only added to the long-simmering friction between the two neighbors. It started in Colonial days when we almost went to war over interstate commerce. Recently, public officials in both states have skirmished over the construction of the proposed Westway highway; the location of the Statue of Liberty; New York's tendency to drop garbage accidentally into New Jersey's waters; and New Jersey's alleged use of federal urban development grants to lure jobs from New York City. Now, some in Manhattan see me as the Pied Piper, luring jobs across the river. I remember walking down 57th Street one weekday afternoon, on my way to my monthly call-in radio program on WMCA radio. A motorist stuck in traffic rolled down his window and yelled, "Governor Kean, what company are you taking back with you this time?"

Our congressional delegations sometimes fight like junkyard dogs, but the outbursts have never affected my relations with New York's most prominent public officials, Ed Koch and Mario Cuomo. Both are warm, intelligent men, public servants in the best sense of the word. Mario Cuomo is perhaps the most thoughtful man in public life today, and the first to suggest that I put my thoughts down in book form. He has a dry wit and is an excellent judge of character. I remember once we discussed a politician who, according to the media, had undergone a personality change for the better. I believed the media reports; Mario didn't. I asked why. He told me a story about a wasp and a frog on the bank of a river. The wasp asked the frog if he would carry him on his back to the other side. "I'd be crazy," replied the frog. "You'd sting me and I'd drown." "No," said the wasp, "I've got a broken wing. If I sting you, we'll both drown." Off they went with the frog swimming and the wasp on his back. In midstream, the wasp stung. As they were going down, the frog said, "Why did you do it? We are both going to die." "I don't know," replied the wasp, "I guess it's just my nature." People can't remake themselves, Mario said. In the case we were talking about, he was right.

Ed Koch is a character. To me, he is New York City, and I treasure our friendship and enjoy his company. I have marched beside him in parades and seen him draw strength from the crowd. Arms outstretched, yelling greetings, he reacts to everything, even the occasional boo. Ironically, he grew up in Newark, while I was born in Manhattan, my mother's family home. I believe we understand each other.

On a few occasions, I have been privileged to be his guest for dinner at Gracie Mansion. At Koch dinners I have joined Norman Mailer, Bill Buckley, and Jeane Kirkpatrick, and their conversation is not light. After initial introductions, Ed will bring up the most controversial subject in the news that day. Then he will go around the table, asking each guest for his or her views. As you might imagine, Ed Koch usually has the last word.

The man brings out something special in people. I had dinner with him and David Garth, the political consultant, at a New York restaurant a week after Koch's minor stroke in the summer of 1987. He had chosen not to diet that evening. Everybody in the restaurant, from patrons to the chef, came by to wish him well. As we were leaving he asked, "How am I doing?" The entire restaurant broke out in applause. I marveled at the love affair New Yorkers have with this special man.

Mayor Koch, Governor Cuomo, and I all realize that interstate sniping is counterproductive. Northern New Jersey depends on a bustling, vibrant Manhattan for its survival, and New York's cultural attractions and tourist industry only benefit when New Jersey is doing well. New York had some problems in the 1970s, and they spilled over into New Jersey. Today, our strong economies feed off each other, which is why I use every opportunity I get to enhance cooperation, whether by signing an agreement with Governor Cuomo to recoup the tax on products sold through the mail, or investing $5 billion through the Port Authority in a joint effort to repair the ports, bridges, tunnels, and trains that connect the two states. New York and New Jersey will grow together or we will perish together. The sooner both states realize that, the better off the whole region will be.

☆

The news that New Jersey was for the first time outperforming its neighbor economically, obviously helped the incumbent governor. People realized that government could be a catalyst for growth, not an impediment. As they saw the tangible results of our programs, their opinion of state government changed. In 1980, a statewide poll found that only 34 percent of New Jerseyans considered state government to be good or excellent. By the time I ran for reelection, that percentage had soared to 62 percent.

The strong economy filled state coffers and gave us the money to attack the most difficult problems. In my second term, I unveiled the REACH program, probably the most ambitious welfare reform program in the country. We will require every able-bodied welfare recipient, including women with young children, to work or go to school. In turn, the state pays for day care, transportation, and health-care benefits for a year. This is not a cheap program. But if we can reduce welfare rolls by 15 percent, we can save money and, more important, save a lot of urban poor from dead-end lives.

We also tried to prove that government cannot only promote opportunity, but be compassionate as well. We invested millions to guarantee that every pregnant woman, regardless of income, has access to a doctor. We were also the first state to make sure that no one would be turned away from a hospital because they could not pay or had no insurance. We paid for the program through a surcharge on regular hospital bills. A wealthy society has a responsibility to care for the less fortunate. No constituent has ever complained to me that New Jersey is spending too much on pregnant women or senior citizens.

☆

The substantive accomplishments were important. But something else was going on, something not as tangible as a new road or a clean toxic waste site. The state's attitude had changed. My reelection campaign slogan was not "Bringing Jobs to New Jersey" or "Keeping New Jersey Clean," although both were to me important accomplishments. It was simply "Building Pride in New Jersey." Instilling a sense of pride among our state's citizens was probably my most important accomplishment. As I said, once you feel good about yourself, your state, or your country, anything is possible. If you have doubts, things are much more difficult. As a leader, you don't necessarily have to do everything yourself, but you do have to convince others that they can do things on their own.

For years in New Jersey, we laughed sheepishly at New Jersey jokes, not having the courage to fight back. We didn't think we had good colleges, so we exported almost half our children to colleges in other states. We didn't think we could support an arts community, so theater lovers drove across the river to Broadway. We didn't even think we could have our own sports team, so northern New Jerseyans rooted for the Giants, Knicks, Yankees, and Mets while people in southern New Jersey followed the Phillies, 76ers, and Eagles.

I knew it didn't have to be this way. The raw material for pride was there, but the governor had to become a cheerleader. I had to convince people both inside and outside the state that New Jersey was a great place to live and work. I always believed that, because my affection for New Jersey runs deep. When I was growing up I never lived in New Jersey for long periods of time, but I always called New Jersey home. In school, whether in Washington or Massachusetts, or at camp in New Hampshire, I defended my state and was especially sensitive to the jokes and the misconceptions.

When I became involved in politics, I desperately wanted others to stand up for New Jersey, a tiny state that has more diversity than most countries. I wondered how I could let the world know about it, and how I could make New Jerseyans themselves appreciate it.

Building pride is like putting together a mosaic: every piece is essential and related to every other. Once the first year was over, I could finally move around the state. To be able to do that, I was helped immeasurably by my new chief of staff, Greg Stevens. After working for me in the 1977 campaign, Greg had never returned to journalism, and instead pursued a career in politics. He had worked for Senator Bill Cohen before becoming the top aide to Representative Olympia Snowe of Maine. He was a good administrator and savvy political tactician.

I persuaded Greg to return to New Jersey at the end of my first year in office. I knew I was still spending too much time handling the details of governing. I needed someone to whom I could delegate decisions and trust that they would be handled satisfactorily. I hired Greg first as director of communications. I watched him carefully, and he earned my respect immediately. Soon I promoted him to chief of staff. Every day for the next three years, while I was out on the road listening to the people of New Jersey, Greg stayed in the office handling the details of administration. He, more than anyone else, was the architect of my landslide victory.

Communication is vital in government. I needed to hear what was on my constituents' minds and I needed to get the message out about our substantive accomplishments. So I started appearing on a series of radio call-in shows. Eventually, the Strauss family at WMCA in New York gave me the opportunity to host a radio program once a month, linked to a network of eight New Jersey stations. I still do the show out of WHWH in Princeton. I also started a monthly cable TV show with the members of my cabinet, and began to chair old-fashioned town meetings across the state. Town meetings are a little like walking a tightrope. You never know what is going to happen. I've been asked everything from how I would retire the national debt to what I was going to do to protect prostitutes from harassment.

Everywhere I went I talked about New Jersey's solutions to old problems. I pointed out ways in which New Jersey was doing better than its neighbors. I illustrated my points with stories from New Jersey's past and I laid out our potential for the future. Again and again I asked, "Why shouldn't we be number one? Why can't New Jersey be the best?" People were quick to respond. More and more I heard my thoughts echoed by others.

If you are going to influence people's attitudes in the 1980s, you have to use television. In my second year in office, I decided to appear in television advertisements promoting tourism. This was a radical decision at the time, before chief executives like Lee Iacocca began to appear on the screen touting their companies. Usually companies and states hired actors to make their pitch to consumers.

I thought I could be much more effective than a paid actor. We chose a new tourism slogan, "New Jersey and You: Perfect Together." At first, some thought it was silly. In fact, it turned out to be perfect. The slogan immediately became identified with the state.

The television ads were intended for three audiences. The obvious one was potential vacationers, some in the state, but most outside New Jersey. According to some analysts, tourism is now New Jersey's single biggest industry, responsible for 215,000 jobs. So money spent on the advertising campaign was first of all an investment in jobs. Second, the campaign was aimed at businessmen and women who might locate their companies in the state. They needed to see the good things we had to offer. Third, "New Jersey and You: Perfect Together" was intended to reinforce our own belief about ourselves.

We recruited celebrities to appear with me in the ads. Bill Cosby was the first. He doesn't live here but he does vacation in New Jersey. I asked him as a friend and he readily accepted. He is not only one of the world's funniest men but also one of the nicest. On top of that, his is the most recognizable face in American television. His ad is still our most successful.

Brooke Shields also said she would help. She was a student at Princeton and a lifelong resident of New Jersey. Like Bill Cosby, she refused to be paid. She impressed me tremendously. I knew she was a busy student. As sometimes happens, there were all sorts of technical problems on the shoot. Brooke didn't make a mistake, yet scene after scene had to be reshot. Through it all she remained calm and kept her sense of humor. By dinner, the crew was still not finished. My part was, Brooke's was not. I knew she had a rehearsal for the Princeton Triangle show that evening, and I heard her tell the crew that she would be back at 10:00 P.M. She wanted to make it right for her state. Brooke did, and we used the commercial for the next three years. I know everybody who saw it envied the governor of New Jersey.

The tourism campaign worked better than we imagined. The number of visitors to New Jersey jumped by a higher percentage than in any other state. We moved from seventh in the nation in annual visitors to fifth by the time I ran for reelection. Not bad for a state that is fifth smallest in square miles. By 1986, we were attracting 54 million visitors to the state every year, generating more than $12 billion in economic activity, as much as the J. C. Penney Company sells in one year. But the campaign clearly did more than bring people to New Jersey. Hardly a day goes by when I am not approached by a constituent who asks me to say, "New Jersey and You: Perfect Together." The slogan has become a mantra, a shorthand way of saying the jokesters are wrong: New Jersey is a good place to live.

☆

I still avail myself of every opportunity to remind people of New Jersey's pride. One unexpected chance occurred during the 1984 presidential campaign. Gary Hart had emerged from nowhere to challenge Walter Mondale for the Democratic nomination. Senator Hart, after leaving New Jersey, was campaigning in Bel Air, California, when he made a rather unbecoming remark. He told reporters that his wife, Lee, had a better job in his campaign. "The good news for her is she campaigns in California and I campaign in New Jersey," Hart said. His wife then said that while campaigning in California she had gotten to hold a koala bear. Senator Hart responded, "I won't tell you what I got to hold—samples from a toxic waste dump."

This was precisely the kind of wisecrack that we had shrugged off in the past. As I watched the Hart quip on the evening news, I saw that the New York stations didn't seem to be making a big deal out of it. Later that evening, I got a call from an old friend who was playing a major role in the Mondale campaign. He asked me if I had heard Hart's comment, and said he was calling to "rev me up." I told him I didn't need any "revving up." Anybody running for president shouldn't be making nasty little jokes about a state he hoped to carry. Of course, people say things they regret when they are tired and in the heat of a campaign. No one knows that better than someone who has run for public office. But I thought an apology was due.

The next day I publicly requested one. Immediately the TV stations and the newspapers became more interested in Hart's comment. I expected Hart to react quickly, say he made a mistake, and that would be the end of the issue. My friend from the Mondale campaign thought differently. "We have been watching Gary," he said. "He will never admit he is wrong. His ego won't allow it." Sure enough, Hart never apologized. As the primary approached, I reminded New Jersey voters of that fact. I felt that a man who wants to be president of the United States ought to have the strength of character to admit a mistake. Eventually, Hart lost the New Jersey primary badly. A Philadelphia TV station reported that two out of the three people interviewed leaving the polling place mentioned Hart's comment as one reason they voted against him.

The cheerleading became my trademark. People began to make jokes about it. In the winter of 1986, the comedian Joe Piscopo, who was raised in New Jersey, put together a one-hour television comedy special. He asked me to take part, and I readily agreed. The skit featured Joe and Eddie Murphy playing two cops in "New Jersey Vice." The two pulled me and my limousine over. While Joe warned me that I was in trouble because "he was real tight with the governor of New Jersey," Eddie went through my wallet and discovered I was in fact the governor. As the two slinked away, I yelled after them, "Drive safely, we have the best highway system in the East. We have seventy-two airports, two hundred and sixty-two farms, we are fourth in the nation in wine production."

It wasn't as if I had a lot to do with some of the things I was bragging about. The casinos in Atlantic City, for example, were already open and had added a certain luster to the state before I became governor. Bruce Springsteen wasn't hurting the state's image either. His songs made music lovers as far away as Sweden and Japan understand what

As a young boy I was shy, sometimes lonely and never quite sure of my place in the world. I wanted to grow up to be a school teacher.

As an Assemblyman in 1975, I am talking to Senator Raymond Bateman about a speech given by Governor Brendan Byrne. *(The Star Ledger)*

Every summer I return to Brantwood Camp in New Hampshire, where I worked for seven years. Coming to know the disadvantaged for the first time, I also learned how to manage people.

My father, President Ford, and me. I ran the President's New Jersey re-election campaign in 1976, a godsend because I was starting to get bored in the Assembly.

During my first campaign for Governor in 1977. I knew in my heart I had no chance of winning. (*Thomas A. Houser*)

My family—Debby, Tom, Alex and Reed. Because I was raised in a political family, I have always tried to draw a line between family life and public life. It really bothers me to see spouses and children dragged into the spotlight.

Since I was a child, I have always felt at home in the outdoors. Because Republicans love clean air and water as much as Democrats, I think it is wrong that my party fails to make environmental protection much of a priority. *(Joseph Moore)*

Ronald Reagan is a master of politics because he is the same in public as he is in private. I have admired him for a long time. *(Joseph Moore)*

Above: I arrive at the Trenton State House for my first day of work as Governor. *(The Star Ledger)* Below: The irrepressible Ming Hsu and I welcome Samsung executives to New Jersey. An Asian spearheads our state's drive to sell products abroad. *(Joseph Moore)*

Above: During my re-election campaign, I wore a hard hat to rally some union members supporting me. *(The Star Ledger)* Below: My friend, Joe Rodriquez, the son of an immigrant who literally swam ashore to America, is sworn in as a federal judge. *(UPI)*

Above: Coretta Scott King, Len Coleman and I attend a civil rights rally. A Republican can win in the black community by stressing education, economic development, and anti-crime programs that appeal to all voters. *(Joseph Moore)* Below: This country's greatest challenge is fundamental reform of our schools. Success or failure will largely determine our future.

it meant to grow up in Asbury Park. Meanwhile, Bill Bradley's work in Congress meant that New Jersey had a politician in Washington who was in the news for competence, not corruption. And suddenly New Jersey had a playground, with the Meadowlands now world-famous. The Giants and the Nets were New Jersey's teams, and they were entertaining crowds in the Meadowlands before I took office. I was able to add the Devils and later the Jets. To get the Jets, I got to know a splendid human being named Leon Hess.

Conversations with the Jets began behind the scenes shortly after I was elected. My main negotiator was the new chairman of the Meadowlands, Jon Hanson, to whom Phil Kaltenbacher had introduced me a year before my first election. Jon was a successful investor and a good organizer who had never been involved in politics. He apparently saw something in me he liked and became very active because in 1981 he was my biggest fund raiser. After the election I realized the Meadowlands needed a savvy business leader if the facility were going to continue to prosper. Hanson was the man and I asked him to become chairman of the authority.

Leon Hess, the owner of the Jets, let Jon Hanson know he was interested in the Meadowlands. The Jets were attracted not so much by what New Jersey had to offer, but by what New York hadn't and wouldn't. Shea Stadium was a mess. There wasn't enough parking, the stands were dirty, and the rest rooms didn't work. Hess had repeatedly complained to the city. Time after time they had ignored him.

Leon Hess is from New Jersey and a self-made millionaire. I had never met him, but we had a number of mutual friends. Everyone who knew him said that he was a man of the highest integrity. All he wanted was what was best for the Jets and their fans. And when he gave his word, he meant it.

Jon Hanson kept me abreast of his discussions with Leon. Then one afternoon I got a call in my office. Jon and Leon were sitting in a restaurant near the Meadowlands. Hanson told me he needed my okay to offer Hess a few more concessions. I balked at one of them, and Hanson took my message back to the table. A couple of minutes later, I got another call. "This isn't working," said Hanson. "I want you to talk to Leon yourself."

We talked for an hour. While we spoke, the Democratic leadership waited outside my door for a scheduled meeting. About halfway through my talk with Leon, the Democrats got mad and left. Later, I had to call each of them and apologize. The negotiations were secret; I couldn't tell the Democrats that I was doing my best to bring another football team to the Meadowlands.

I began with Leon by discussing mutual friends. Then he expressed his worries. He told me he wanted the option to change his mind and stay at Shea Stadium if New York should meet his conditions. Almost sadly, he said, "New York moves so slowly, I can guarantee you they are not going to meet my conditions on time." I told him I would be happier if he signed a long-term lease, so he could never move back to New York. He said I had him over a barrel, but that he wanted an escape clause in case New York came through. I told him I respected his wishes. I knew he was a man of his word, and I would treat him that way. We agreed to a two-year lease with a clause that he would indemnify the state if he decided to leave when the lease expired. When I hung up the phone we had a deal. Leon Hess took a lot of flak from the New York media for leaving Shea Stadium, all of it undeserved. If New York had negotiated with the Jets in good faith in the first place, they might still be there. Instead, the team plays in New Jersey. I have grown to respect Leon Hess more and more since that conversation. He is a man who does things right. I hope one day he wears another Super Bowl ring, because I can't think of anyone who deserves it more.

New Jersey's other team wears more recent Super Bowl rings. In a way, the Giants' ascent from perennial loser to Super Bowl champion is a metaphor for New Jersey during the 1980s. I have been friends with Giant officials for several years. I've rooted hard for the team, and remember the years of frustration.

By 1985, the Giants were winning, and winning big, on their way to the NFC championship when they played the Bears in Chicago. I had attended almost all of the Giants' home games that season. I had visited the locker room and had become friends with some of the players. While I wasn't able to fly to Chicago for the championship game, my staff had scheduled me to drive to the airport Sunday night and greet the Giants if they beat the Bears in the playoff.

The Giants did not win. They lost badly. As I watched the game I figured there was now even more reason to go to the airport. If you really support a team, you ought to be there when they lose, not just when they win. I went to the airport and waited in the drizzling rain with about ten fans from the metropolitan area. When the plane finally landed, the Giants slumped off. We cheered heartily. I don't think the players knew the governor was among the faithful. The Giants' owner, Wellington Mara, did recognize me. He thanked me for being there.

I forgot about the homecoming until after the Giants won the Super Bowl the following year, by which time I had grown quite close to the team. I had participated in charity drives with some players, especially George Martin, who has a heart as big as his helmet. Debby and I attended the Super Bowl in California. While there I had one of those experiences that I had dreamed about since I was ten years old. The winners invited me into the locker room. The next day I was the only non-Giant to fly back on the champions' plane.

Then a controversy broke out about whether the victory parade should be held in Manhattan or New Jersey. Mayor Koch and the American Express Company offered to host a tickertape parade down Broadway. The Giants said, "No, thank you." They told the press that Governor Kean had been the only public official to greet them the year before when they were losers. Now that they were winners, they would hold the victory parade on their home field in New Jersey. We got our hands on every snowplow we could find and cleared tons of snow out of the Meadowlands. We ordered fifty thousand kazoos and held a victory party for the players: it was New Jersey's day. Mayor Koch retained his sense of humor about the incident. Later that winter at the annual Inner Circle dinner, the mayor got onstage to respond to the press's tweaking of his administration. He opened by bantering with the comedian David Brenner about all the mistakes he had made that year. When he talked about the Giants, I sneaked up behind him, Harry Carson-like, and dumped a bucket of Gatorade® on his head. It brought down the house.

The Jets and the Giants have made a big difference. New Jersey is a big-league state, and that means we ought to be a home for big-league teams. Although the economic benefits are obvious, the teams mean more than that. They are proof that New Jersey belongs with California, New York, and Texas.

We do grow frustrated when Pat Summerall and company begin football broadcasts by saying, "Here we are in New York City," when they are actually six miles west of Manhattan. So in the fall of 1986 we wrote "New Jersey Meadowlands" right across the fifty-yard line. As the players crisscross the field, it becomes a little harder for CBS to welcome viewers to Manhattan.

Painting the words "New Jersey" on the field was not a big thing.

But thousands of little gestures fostered my reputation as New Jersey's salesman and the state's reputation as a leader began to grow. I remember when a reporter for a local newspaper wrote a column on one of my annual "State of the State" speeches. The reporter laid out all my grandiloquent claims about New Jersey and said I was getting ridiculously hyperbolic; no state could be that wonderful. Now, if that is my only crime, I plead guilty. If the governor is not going to brag about the state, no one else will.

The American people do not need political leaders who talk constantly about problems and limits. Politicians must acknowledge that, yes, troubles we have. But we must constantly remind people of our capacity and will to solve every problem. I think I have been able to do that in New Jersey. And if it worked here, it can work anywhere.

☆

Pride, combined with substantive accomplishments, helps explain how I went from the closest election to the biggest landslide in just a few short years. But there was one more factor. I have always believed that most people really don't mind even if you oppose them on a major issue. A few activists may never vote for you, but most voters look beyond individual issues. They want to know whether you are competent and have competent people around you, whether you are honest, and whether you put their interests above your own political ambitions. They want to know that you empathize with their concerns. In short, they want to approve the character and style of your leadership.

Millicent Fenwick gave me that advice. She told me about the first time she got involved in politics. Franklin Roosevelt was running against Wendell Willkie, and she was working for Willkie. It was toward the end of the Depression and life was still hard. One day Millicent saw a woman walking along a country road near her home carrying a couple of suitcases. She stopped to offer her a lift. As they talked, Millicent decided to make the case for Willkie. She explained Willkie's views on foreign policy and on the New Deal. As time passed she saw her passenger nod her head a number of times. "Ah," she thought, "I've made a convert." When they reached their destination, the woman said, "I agree with everything you've said. Mr. Willkie is right on all those issues, but I think I'm going to vote for Mr. Roosevelt. I've got a feeling that he understands my problem and that in the end he'll do the right thing." People do get a "feeling" about a public official. They may disagree with you on all sorts of issues, but if they believe overall you're trying to do the right thing, they'll support you again and again.

How do they get those "feelings"? Well, day to day, governing can be pretty dull business. You make hundreds of small decisions and the cumulative effect of them determines if you are pushing your state forward or holding it back. Even when an important issue arises, you should have time to explore your options fully. It is the prudent way to do business, but it doesn't draw much attention.

The drama takes place during those rare occasions when something outside your control—like fate or Mother Nature—conspires to force you to act without pausing for the kind of introspection that a sound decision usually requires. Those exigencies can descend upon leaders at any level. Any office holder, from school board chair to president, can probably tell you of times when they felt their mettle as a leader was tested.

Once when I was in the assembly, I was chairing the education committee, and had scheduled a hearing on sex education. We planned to hear testimony from the New Jersey Education Association, the school boards, and maybe the Parent Teacher Association. As was common practice, we opened the hearings to any citizens who wanted to speak their minds. Such hearings were not usually occasions for drama.

This one was different. Midway through the hearing I noticed a commotion at the back of the room. Representatives of the American Nazi Party had arrived in full uniform, demanding to be heard. Obviously they thought they could get press coverage. Some on the committee suggested I deny them their moment at the witness table. "Why give them the chance to spread venom?" they argued. I knew that was exactly what the Nazis expected. Once they were denied the chance to speak, they would demonstrate in the back of the room. New York and Philadelphia television would cover them. I surprised the group and let them speak. They went on for about ten minutes. It was the same old drivel, with touches of not so subtle anti-Semitism. I didn't confront them. I asked no questions. Obviously, they were surprised: first, at being allowed to testify, and second, at not being confronted. There was really no story. The newspapers that mentioned the Nazis' appearance at all buried it well toward the back. Meanwhile, not one TV station picked it up. Later, a Jewish group complained to me. They were offended that I had allowed the Nazis to testify. I explained that even Nazis have First Amendment rights. Moreover, to try to shut them up would have created what the Nazis wanted. Representatives of that one organization did not agree, but other Jewish leaders did. More important, I knew I had done the right thing.

☆

The confrontation with the Nazis took place in the state assembly. When you become a governor or a big-city mayor or a national politician, the drama of such moments is heightened. Your reaction to a particular situation is immediately transmitted to many by radio, television, and newspapers. People who may never pay close attention to politics suddenly focus on you. Their opinion on your style of leadership is formed during crises.

The best example of what I mean occurred in Philadelphia. Mayor Wilson Goode, a decent, compassionate man, is still trying to shake a reputation for incompetence resulting from a bad decision about how to evict a terrorist group called MOVE from a row house. As an executive, you must understand that if a crisis is not handled responsibly, you are the one who takes the blame. You are where the buck stops.

The most potentially serious crisis of my years as governor occurred in June 1983. I was finally feeling good about the progress we were making. The turmoil of the first year was behind us and my team was finally in place. The economy was beginning to rebound and the worry lines on my budget director's face had disappeared. I was out among the people. The press was becoming more familiar with my style and I was gaining leverage with the Democratic legislature.

At the time, you couldn't pick up a paper without reading about the health threat posed by dioxin, one of the deadliest chemicals ever produced by man. In the spring of 1983, the Environmental Protection Agency had been forced to buy Times Beach, a little town in Missouri where high levels of dioxin were found.

DEP commissioner Bob Hughey had taken my warnings about crisis management to heart. After reading the stories about dioxin in Times Beach, he dusted off an old federal survey of eleven New Jersey companies that manufactured dioxin-related products. His department began to visit the manufacturing sites, many now abandoned, and test the soil for any traces of the chemical. The very first site they visited was an abandoned pesticide plant near the Passaic River in the Ironbound section of Newark. Late in April 1983, DEP technicians walked in and around the plant and removed sixteen shovelfuls of dirt. The results out of the laboratory were startling. The amount of dioxin in the dirt was so high that the test couldn't measure it. EPA scientists were called immediately. The next day they tested the dirt, using higher calibrations. The preliminary results indicated that dioxin levels in the soil were more than two times the level found at Times Beach.

I was told of the EPA's finding that evening, and I knew this could become a dangerous situation. The plant was located not more than a hundred yards from a densely populated neighborhood, in the center of the state's largest city. While the lab technicians worked, I set about to determine the best way to respond to the crisis. I began to put together an executive order, saying that high concentrations of dioxin had been discovered at the factory site and that we did not know if the chemical was in the river and surrounding neighborhood. I planned to call for immediate testing of the entire area and to offer free shelter for any residents who wished to leave their homes immediately. As a precaution, I decided that I was going to ask a local open-air food market to close until the final tests were obtained. I was relieved to learn that dioxin is not dangerous when confined—only when it is airborne. I held the executive order awaiting confirmation of the initial findings.

The next day I released the executive order. It turned out to be not just a New Jersey story, as newspapers from Texas to Florida speculated about the "new Times Beach." But the neighborhood around the plant reacted with restraint. People there did have many questions and wanted answers fast. But it would take a couple of days to get them.

Soon, however, wild rumors began to circulate in the neighborhood. Some people had heard they couldn't drink the water, others that they should burn all their clothes. I dispatched scientists from the DEP and doctors from the Department of Health, but that wasn't enough to calm people. I decided to visit the Ironbound section myself, even as several staff members counseled otherwise. They said that the tests were not complete and that I might be attacked by the kind of outside agitators who are always attracted to an environmental crisis. I rejected my aides' advice. One of a governor's responsibilities is to be on the scene when something bad happens. If a house is destroyed in a tornado or a strange chemical found down the street, people need to be assured that the governor is doing everything possible to help. You can't assure them by issuing press releases from the state capital.

I went to the Ironbound neighborhood and walked from house to house, knocking on doors and telling people what I knew. I found that I recognized a number of the residents. One was a friend of my father, another had worked in my campaign. Most were older people, and many had lived in that neighborhood all their lives. They were good, hardworking New Jersey citizens who appreciated that I had come to talk to them personally. I got several startled looks as people peered out of their front doors at the governor, followed by a sea of television cameras and reporters, but everyone I talked to was rational and cooperative. The people of the Ironbound handled the media onslaught with dignity. Not all of them were happy, but even the critics appreciated that I was there in person. One old gentleman called out to me, "Get right into the dioxin with everyone else, Governor Kean. Just don't breathe too deep."

Five days later the final test results came in. Tiny traces of dioxin had been found at three places outside the factory, but overall the contamination was limited to the factory site. This was very good news. I scheduled a press conference with Mayor Kenneth Gibson at City Hall in Newark. When it was over, I felt I really needed to talk to the people again, so I went back to the neighborhood.

I stopped at a number of houses, but found few people at home. I went to the only place I could find a crowd, a local bar called Lisbon At Night. I'll never forget the hours I spent there. The room was sweltering, packed not only with patrons but with members of the media. The bar was shaped like a horseshoe. I joined the bartender inside and started to field questions from people with tense faces. Some parents, hearing I was in the bar, brought their children. I explained that the threat was not as great as first feared, and they would be able to stay in their homes. We believed there was a good chance that no health threat existed. As I answered questions, I could feel people grow a little more confident, a little less worried. By the end of the two hours, my shirt was soaked with sweat but the tension was gone. Before I left, I bought the house a round of beer and we toasted each other.

The dioxin crisis had been diffused. We spotted the problem, then acted. And by acting responsibly, we prevented panic. News reports were unanimous in praise for the way the Kean administration handled the incident. For almost three days the people of New Jersey had focused on my action. It was clear that they liked what they saw. Some columnists trace the beginnings of my rise in popularity to that night in the bar.

☆

The dioxin incident was big news in New Jersey and across the country. Two months later I made another decision that got the attention of people in Paterson and Peoria—and Moscow. The decision stemmed from the Soviet Union's shooting down Korean Air Flight 007. Like everyone else, I was appalled by an act of cold-blooded mass murder and by Moscow's refusal at first to acknowledge responsibility and to apologize.

The next day I got a call from officials at the Port Authority of New York and New Jersey. They told me that Soviet ambassador Andrei Gromyko was scheduled to attend a general session of the United Nations in Manhattan and his plane was scheduled to land at Kennedy Airport, which is run by the Port Authority. Port Authority officials warned me of the possibility of a major demonstration at Kennedy.

Of course I believe that governors should not normally have a foreign policy role, but we do represent the people of our state. In this instance, nobody had come up with a way, other than diplomatic protest, to demonstrate our indignation. I thought about it a bit, and concluded that it would be totally callous to welcome Ambassador Gromyko at the very airport from which Flight 007 had originated. Any form of welcome would insult the memory of 269 innocent victims. I also was not sure we could guarantee security for Gromyko and his fellow diplomats if they landed either at Kennedy or at Newark Airport in New Jersey.

As it turned out, New York governor Mario Cuomo had been thinking along exactly the same lines. So we decided to instruct the Port Authority to deny landing rights to the Soviet airliner at both Kennedy and Newark. If the Russians wanted to touch down, they would have to use a military base. In the face of murder of innocent civilians, we were saying no to business-as-usual. The reaction was loud and immediate. Ambassador Gromyko was insulted, decided not to come to the UN session, and suggested that his country would pull out of the United Nations if similar actions were to follow. But if Gromyko was angry, New Jerseyans and New Yorkers loved the decision, knowing that a small cooperative gesture had made clear how they felt.

A few pundits, of course, did not share the public's reaction. The *New York Times* said Governor Cuomo and I suffered from "Glen Cove's Disease," after the town on Long Island that had prohibited Russian Embassy workers from swimming off a local beach. The sickness, according to the *Times*, was "a hallucinatory disorder that causes local politicians to imagine themselves President or Secretary of State." And liberal columnist Richard Cohen opined, "Kean and Cuomo should have kept their airports open and their mouths shut." Surprisingly, neither Secretary of State George Schultz nor any of his aides called us, although one anonymous State Department source did call the action "preposterous."

The day after I made the decision, I was invited to appear on ABC's *Nightline* with Ambassador Jeane Kirkpatrick and Vladimir Posner, a correspondent from Radio Moscow. A big fan of Jeane Kirkpatrick, I admire her intellect and candor. But if Jeane is a beacon of light in American foreign policy, Vladimir Posner is something of a one-man industry in the Soviet Union. The Soviets haul out the articulate Richard Burton look-alike whenever they want to put the best face on something. Jeanne's feelings about Posner quickly became evident. Jeane explained to me that Posner had emigrated to the Soviet Union from Manhattan. "We used to have a word for that," she whispered, "traitor."

When you're on television, you usually try to keep your answers short. So when Koppel asked me why the airports were closed, I replied in less than twenty seconds. To rebut, Posner took more than a minute. During a commercial break, Jeane leaned over again and said, "The Soviets try to monopolize time the same way they try to monopolize space." For the rest of the show, I didn't even try to cut my answers short. The story doesn't end here. A year later I was at the Republican Convention in Dallas when Debby and I were invited to dine with former New Jersey senator Nick Brady and his wife and Secretary of State George Schultz and his wife. Although I had met the Schultzes before, I didn't know them well. We had a wonderful evening, talking about vacation plans, children, anything but politics. But as things wound down, George Schultz took me aside and said, "Listen, Tom, Ambassador Gromyko is planning on visiting the UN soon. You wouldn't close the airports again, would you?" "No," I said, "not unless they shoot down another plane."

☆

I had a great deal going for me when I decided to run for re-election. There were a number of substantive accomplishments I could point to. The state was feeling much better about itself. The voters had become comfortable with my style of leadership.

On top of it all, the Republican party organization was solidly behind my candidacy for the first time in my career, which was the good news. The sad news for me was the Democratic party's choice to be my opponent. Congressman Jim Florio read the polls and backed out. His decision was a great disappointment to me. I longed for a rematch, to prove that people who had voted by party labels in 1981 would vote for performance four years later. Instead, the Democrats nominated a friend, Essex County executive Peter Shapiro. Peter is young, bright, and in some ways not a traditional Democrat. He questioned tenets of the welfare state that Florio took for granted, and he had a more realistic view of the responsibilities of government. He had also been a good administrator, and it was hard to campaign against a friend. As things turned out, both of us stayed on the high road, and I stuck to my policy of never running a negative commercial.

The Kean campaign strategy was simply to take our record of achievement to Democratic constituencies. In front of labor groups, I hailed the Transportation Trust Fund. Black audiences applauded me for choosing to divest state funds from South Africa and for appointing record numbers of blacks to state government and the judiciary. Hispanics were pleased by the emphasis we had placed on cities.

Campaigning as an incumbent, I obviously never felt the obscurity that a challenger invariably lives with. Everywhere I went, I was met by enthusiastic crowds. Groups that had strongly opposed individual policies even saw fit to endorse me. Two campaign events stick in my mind. One sunny October morning, organized labor held a campaign rally for me in front of the State House in Trenton. Eleven years earlier, twenty thousand angry laborers had marched on Trenton to complain to Governor Byrne that they had no work. But that day, thousands had returned to say thank you to me for putting them back on the job. Altogether, fifty-two labor unions endorsed my reelection campaign. On another fall afternoon, I spoke to a gathering of black clergymen at the Quality Inn in Newark. Several times they interrupted my speech with applause, once with a standing ovation. If the clergymen felt that good about me, I knew their parishioners couldn't be far behind.

The earliest polls had showed me up by more than thirty points. As the campaign began to pick up steam in October, it became clear that the lead was not eroding, as everyone predicted. Instead, I was holding Democratic voters and, most surprisingly, making serious inroads into the black community.

Peter Shapiro was probably the best candidate the Democrats could have offered, but he erred in his choices of issues. The polls showed that, after the economy, the next important issue was the environment. He decided to focus his entire campaign on criticizing our strategy to clean up toxic waste. It didn't work. Editorial writers almost unanimously sided with me. Some were even critical that Peter had chosen to play fast and loose with the facts on such an emotional issue. He had mistakenly taken us on where our armor was strongest. Never breaking through on toxic waste, Peter had no way to convince people, even Democrats, that they should vote out the Kean administration.

As November approached, I increasingly began to tie my campaign to the campaigns of the state assembly candidates. For the first time since Watergate, I thought we had the opportunity to take control of that body. If you are a popular executive, you have a responsibility to try to pass your popularity on to the rest of the party. It is a risky strategy, and you can make some enemies by getting involved in local races. But if you are going to build your party, you have to take that chance.

I ignored my opponent and spent the last thirty days of the campaign in swing assembly districts. We decided to spend almost a million dollars that had originally been budgeted for my campaign in those districts. I made an issue out of Democratic obstructionism on important issues, and Speaker Alan Karcher became the symbol for all that was wrong in the legislature. One of my staffers told me, "You know, if Alan Karcher did not exist, we would have had to invent him."

On election night the numbers proved without question that the campaign strategy had worked. Voters of all backgrounds and ideologies said yes to effective government. My victory proved that the political party that promotes opportunity will be given opportunity by the voters. The election was especially gratifying in that it justified several ideas I had about government that I had developed over a lifetime.

Whether we are a state or a country, we need not be satisfied with the status quo or with what others believe has to happen. To many people, New Jersey had always been a corrupt backwater. That is what non–New Jerseyans thought, and that is what too many New Jerseyans believed as well. If you asked almost any pundit, the state's future was as cloudy as the smoke belching from an old factory along the Turnpike. Well, things didn't turn out that way. Today New Jersey is a success story. Our people are proud again and the future looks bright. I believe now, as I have always believed, that good leadership can bring out the best in people.

The problems in this world have partly been created by people. Thus for me, there is no problem that people cannot solve. I really believe that. Whether it is something as basic as building a road promised for years, as complex as improving a business climate, or as slippery as turning around a state's self-image, a problem can be attacked and solved by people of goodwill. Government, the institution that Edmund Burke called "a contrivance of human wisdom to provide for human wants," has a central role. I disagree strongly with anybody who sees government as only an obstacle in the way of social and environmental good. But it must never be allowed to become an institution growing simply to serve itself. I've always liked the way Henry Clay put it: "Government is a trust, and the officers of the government are trustees; and both the trust and the trustees are created for the benefit of the people."

Government in America has gotten a bad rap lately, a result of the misguided notion of both its ardent supporters and its vehement detractors. The supporters believe, wrongly, that government should somehow guarantee each of us a secure and comfortable life, protect us from every threat and risk, and provide us with every want and need. That is not only unrealistic, but dangerous, because, to paraphrase Barry Goldwater, a government big enough to give us everything is big enough to take everything away. I want to add that a government that big would by its very weight destroy the private enterprise that makes democracy possible.

The detractors argue, on the other hand, that government by its very nature is bumbling, corrupt, and inefficient, and ought to be either ignored or cut back—way back. That too is wrong. Certain desirable goals will always exist in society for which government must take the responsibility—educating our children, for example, or providing some level of care for the indigent. Government cannot by itself create new jobs for the unemployed. But it can and should help set the climate that allows private industry to create growth.

My point is quite simply that the system works. Democratic government is neither speedy nor terribly efficient. It is, as everybody knows, often slow, cumbersome, and awkward. But it can solve problems and solve them well. That is what has happened in New Jersey in the 1980s. One at a time, we identified the roadblocks in the way of our reaching our real potential as a state. One by one, we removed the roadblocks. The results are there for all to see.

5

Public Life/
Private Life

THE actress Debra Winger once dated and sometimes shared the Governor's Mansion with Robert Kerry, governor of Nebraska. After the relationship cooled, Winger was asked about the difference between her profession and Governor Kerry's work. She said: "When you are a movie star, all you owe the public is your next movie. But if you are a politician, you owe them every detail of your personal life."

I don't think the average American appreciates the pressure the public puts on the private lives of public officials. Most of us take for granted coming home from work in the evening and leaving behind whatever identity we assumed during the day. A governor cannot, because he is always on stage. Whether you shop at the local drugstore for toothpaste or spend the evening at the movies, you can never get away from the trappings and responsibilities of the office. People recognize you, they ask for autographs, the more aggressive may decide to brief you on some problem in their community. This is not always a problem. If you like people as much as I do, what some may regard as harassment is often a pleasure. But the scrutiny is constant and there is never an escape.

What does trouble me is the ever more pervasive notion that the behavior of a politician's spouse, children, and close relatives is automatic fodder for public consumption. Even basic, everyday decisions, like choosing where to live or where to vacation, now become front page news.

I have spent some time thinking about whether it is possible to maintain a separate, private identity and still hold high public office. I have asked myself more than a few times if a normal person can maintain that special allegiance to a spouse and family and still serve 7 million constituents. This question has haunted me ever since I first decided to run for public office more than twenty years ago. I say haunted because I was raised in a family where politics was what my father did. In fact, politics in our family has always been a sort of disease of the blood.

My ancestors helped settle South Carolina in the early 1700s. John Kean represented his state in the Continental Congress, where he was the first member to propose the abolition of slavery. Later, early in this century, both my grandfather and his brother were U. S. senators. Meanwhile, other political families—the Roosevelts, Stuyvesants, Fishes, Livingstons, and Winthrops—are all cousins of the Keans.

Accordingly, political history sometimes becomes very much alive for the Keans. As a little boy, for example, my father sat on Teddy Roosevelt's knee in the White House and later saw him at Sagamore Hill. My father also very clearly remembered his aunt who had been a nurse in the Civil War and who once dined with Lincoln at the White House. My mother grew up in Hyde Park, and her mother was a good friend of FDR's mother. The Kean family home, Liberty Hall, was built for the first governor of New Jersey, William Livingston, and has since hosted many of the nation's leaders.

As a young man I heard stories about many of the country's leaders, people whom other children may have just read about in the papers or history books. I remember my father telling me a story told to him by his grandfather, about Daniel Webster, who once spent the night at Liberty Hall. The town had been preparing for weeks to hear the great orator speak. Webster arrived at the Kean home quite drunk, and my great-grandfather and other local worthies feared that he was incapable of handling the evening. Nevertheless, they loaded him into the carriage and headed for the engagement. On the way he pulled a new bottle of whiskey out of his coat, only adding to worries that he might fall off the platform. When Webster got onstage, whiskey bottle still in hand, the hand wringing stopped. For a full hour the audience sat spellbound, as a full-throated and booming Webster held forth on the evils of slavery. When he finished, the story goes, the bottle in Daniel Webster's right hand was drained, but Webster himself was stone-cold sober.

Another story my father told me was about Franklin Roosevelt, who was his cousin and a friend. My father was first elected to Congress in

1938, when the Republicans reasserted themselves after the Democratic landslide of 1936 and won congressional seats all over the country. The large class of freshman Republicans was invited to the White House for a reception with their archenemy, FDR. My father was standing in line with a number of new colleagues when the president, seated across the room, noticed him. "Winthrop," the president bellowed, "you don't know how good it is to see a friendly face." The other Republicans looked at my father as if he had just grown a pair of horns. For years afterward he insisted that the incident cost him a committee assignment.

Growing up in Washington during World War II, I had very few friends my age. Every time I made a good friend, that child's father was transferred, because Washington was a city of transients, the center of the war effort. The school I went to included children of diplomats, refugees, or officers in the various armed services, none of whom stayed in Washington for more than two or three years. When the school year was over and I went back to Livingston for the summer, I knew nobody my own age. July and August were the longest months.

But Washington during those years could be fun for a child. Hardly anybody drove because of gas rationing, and for a dime you could climb on a trolley and go anywhere in the city. If you returned the same morning or afternoon, you could get a transfer and ride home on the same dime. In those days, the city had only a few good restaurants, so when I was lucky enough to be taken to one, I inevitably saw somebody famous: a Cabinet member, a prominent senator, or even a general. I remember clearly going to a place called the Allied Inn, where J. Edgar Hoover usually had lunch. Once the great man even said hello as he passed our table. On a scale of one to ten of hero watch, Hoover rated a ten: he was the one catching Nazi spies.

My oldest sister, Beth, was seriously ill. Because my father was absorbed by his work, my mother turned into a full-time nurse to coax my sister back into good health, and I was left very much to my own devices. I walked all over town. In those days public safety was not the issue it is now; I don't remember my parents worrying that their nine- or ten-year-old was walking alone on the city streets. What did I do? For one thing, I got to be a student of the various statues that dot our capital. Friends of my parents were amazed that I could tell them exactly where to find the statue of the Civil War's most obscure general. I also spent a great deal of time listening and absorbing things; I was in the gallery of Congress to hear the great speeches of Roosevelt and Churchill.

In those days, Washington was very much a Southern town, and it took me a while to get used to that. My early heroes had been Washington and Lincoln, but my classmates talked only of Lee and Jackson. The only Civil War song I had heard in New Jersey was "Marching Through Georgia." In Washington, "Dixie" was often played like the national anthem at sporting events.

But sectional difference was not an important reality in people's lives. Everyone was united in a common cause, doing anything and everything to help the war effort. We saved items from bottle caps to pipe cleaners; recycling was a fact, not an idea—waste was the enemy. I also remember my mother packing Bundles for Britain or knitting sweaters or socks for Allied children. MacArthur, Eisenhower, Bradley, Patton, and, above all, Franklin Roosevelt were the heroes of the day. Meanwhile, air-raid drills were frequent and blackouts were common. Every window had to be equipped with a black shade. If the siren went off at night, no light could shine through. If it did, an air-raid warden would knock at your door and give you a warning. The spirit imbued all. There was no question of the justice of our cause or of the fact that the fate of the world hung in the balance. Everybody in our family tried to contribute in some way. Nazi Germany and imperial Japan, represented by Hitler and Hirohito, were evil and must be defeated, so it was with a special purpose that we sang "Rise Up O Men of God" and "Onward Christian Soldiers" at Sunday church services.

Three members of my family, two brothers and a brother-in-law, were on active duty. The highlight of the day was a letter from one of them from the war zone. Meanwhile, it was all too common for the teacher to announce that so-and-so wouldn't be in class that day because their uncle or brother or father had been killed in combat. Of course, nobody in those days questioned a young man's obligation to serve. My father and Uncle John had both fought heroically in World War I, and my father's Distinguished Service Cross and Croix de Guerre are displayed prominently in our home to this day. My brothers Bob and Hamilton continued the tradition. Bob won the Distinguished Flying Cross in the Battle of the Bulge, and Hamilton was wounded in the same engagement. I remember when my parents received word from the War Department that their son had been seriously wounded—no other details. But that news was followed within twenty-four hours by a letter from Hamilton, assuring my mother that he was all right and resting comfortably in a hospital in Great Britain. My oldest sister Beth and her infant son stayed with us while her husband served on a ship somewhere in the Pacific. Throughout, my mother wrote to each of her sons every day until they came home.

As I grew older I became aware of family traditions, of ancestors who were honored for their signature of the Declaration of Independence or the Constitution, of patriots and heroes from the Revolution and Civil War. But my heroes in those years were not people from the past, but those of the present, especially my brother Bob, who took special pains with his younger brother on his various leaves for active duty.

☆

During my career in politics, some have advised me to play up my family history and to make it a conscious theme in my stump speeches or campaigns. In a country that admires Roosevelt and Kennedy, the argument goes, a patrician background can only help.

I don't feel that way at all. Proud of my heritage, I grew up having the sense that my family had been part of great undertakings in our country's history, and that that somehow set me a bit apart from those who didn't know or didn't care. I also know that I have inherited from my father and grandfather a sense of obligation to the country that has treated my family so well. But in running for political office, I have always felt that having a social pedigree is a burden, and not anything else.

Part of the reason is intensely personal. At political gatherings, candidates for positions like a seat in the state assembly are always introduced with no more than thirty seconds of biographical background. Thus, Phil Kaltenbacher would be introduced as a graduate of the Yale Law School and a young businessman. Another candidate might be introduced as a teacher or a doctor or a chairman of some charity. But when it came to be my turn, I would hear, "Tom Kean, the son of Congressman Robert Winthrop Kean," or, "the grandson of Senator Hamilton Fish Kean," or even, "a descendent of Governor William Livingston." I don't get upset about this anymore, but I used to resent it terribly. It seemed to imply that I had no qualifications for public office other than bloodline, and the practice compelled me, in my earliest campaigns, to begin a speech with an otherwise unnecessary recitation of my own accomplishments.

Now I try to move past an introduction of that sort using humor. I tell the audience a Lincoln story. When young Abe was running for the Illinois state legislature, he found himself facing an opponent of considerable social standing. In one debate, the gentleman dwelt on the fact that his father had been a senator, his grandfather a general, and his uncle a congressman. Responding, Lincoln rose and said simply, "Ladies and gentlemen, I come from a long line of married folk."

Or I tell the story about the Princeton graduate who applied for a job with a leading department store in Philadelphia. Checking his qualifications, the personnel manager wrote to one of his references. Soon enough, he received a lengthy personal reply, detailing the young man's fine social standing and his family background, which dated from Pilgrim stock. The personnel manager replied, "Sir, I appreciate your trouble, but I think you misunderstood our intentions. We want to employ the young man for business purposes, not breeding purposes."

When I first ran for governor, the press loved to dwell on my family background. Many stories began by saying, "Tom Kean was born to be governor," and then recited in detail my lineage, as if capacity for leadership were found in a gene passed from one generation to another. That form of elitism grates on me. All Americans can all be proud of our ancestors, a fact that is unique about our country. I don't know how or why the first Keans came to these shores. But I do know it must have taken great courage to sail to a hostile land, knowing that one out of three probably wouldn't survive the trip. I am proud the first Kean made it.

But I am no prouder than other Americans are of their ancestors who struggled to come here to live and to contribute. The Irish, fleeing the potato famine, and the Eastern Europeans, escaping poverty and persecution as well, who encountered the not often friendly face of the Industrial Revolution in the United States. Or the Asians who came looking for opportunity and instead found prejudice, over which they triumphed by relying on hard work and family. And, of course, no one has it harder than the Americans whose families had no choice at all, but were brought here as slaves. They, more than any other group, have had to endure the harsh struggle for self-respect and self-determination.

We are a unique people, all the descendants of heroes. And our country continues to produce them. I think of a day in the summer of 1986, when I was handing out diplomas at Jersey City State College. As one young man approached the podium, President Maxwell whispered to me that he was one of several "boat people" receiving degrees. I thought what extraordinary people they must be, and how lucky we are to have them in America. To cast off in a small boat and to leave behind everything and everybody familiar; to brave pirates, typhoons, and refugee camps and then to learn a new language and culture and, within a few years, to earn a college degree. It is true that as long as our country attracts such people, we should not fear for our future.

The point is that whether you came to America when my ancestors did, or whether you arrived penniless yesterday, you share the same heritage of independence and courage. And that is what gives us all strength. I think it is repugnant for anyone to suggest that someone who has been here "longer" is somehow "more American." Which, in fact, is what offends me when people talk about the first Keans rather than what Tom Kean has accomplished on his own.

But while some feel my lineage qualifies me for political office, probably more feel it disqualifies me. Why? Because I am regarded as someone so removed from everyday problems that I cannot possibly understand how the average person lives. Political adversaries have frequently tried to cast me in that light. In one of my assembly campaigns an opponent asked, "You've never been poor. How can you possibly understand poverty?" To which I replied, "I have never had cancer, but I understand the desperate need for a cure."

My social background was an issue in the 1981 gubernatorial primary. Bayonne is a blue-collar town in North Jersey. One of my opponents, Bo Sullivan, ran a television advertisement asking the question "Is Tom Kean the kind of guy who would drink a beer in Bayonne?" The implication was, of course, that not only would I not drink a beer, but I had no feel for the hopes, dreams, and worries of Bayonne beer drinkers.

Ironically, the advertisement ran only a week after my wife and I had spent an evening bowling and drinking beer in Bayonne with a few friends. After Bo Sullivan's commercial aired, I didn't tell the press about that night. Instead, I said I was going to beat Bo Sullivan in Bayonne, after which he could buy me a beer. My staff had bumper stickers printed which read, "Tom Kean drinks Bayonne beer." After I won, Bo, former Secretary of Labor Ray Donovan, and I went to Barrett's Tavern on the Bayonne–Jersey City line. With cameras clicking, Bo bought the entire place a round.

Jim Florio took a more indirect approach to my presumed pedigree. He packed his speeches with anecdotes about his immigrant past, never failing to close an appearance by noting that he had been born in Brooklyn, the son of a shipyard worker, and that he had worked his way through college as a night watchman. His television ads played on the same theme and implied that his opponent was privileged and out of touch.

The approach didn't work for Congressman Florio, just as it has never worked for any of my opponents. I have found that if you will be yourself, people will listen to what you have to say. They will of course look at your background or qualifications for office, but they really want to know who you are. Then they will decide whether or not you are the kind of person they will vote for.

☆

Money is another problem. Taken together, my family is wealthy by most definitions. Individually, we are not as well off as some think. My father and mother have more than forty descendants, so any family money has been spread rather thin. Nevertheless, the perception of wealth exists. In the 1981 primary, I deliberately and publicly weighed the pros and cons of accepting public financing. My hesitation forced some of my opponents to ask difficult questions. Would I at some point dump big amounts of personal wealth into a television blitz? My waffling also kept some supporters in the primary loyal to my campaign, the kind of people who might have gone elsewhere if they suspected I was to be badly outspent. It finally kept the press off balance. In fact, had the members of the press simply checked the disclosure form from my last campaign, they would have learned the truth. I didn't have that much money. As it was, at least one of my primary opponents spent an amount on his primary campaign that was very close to my reported net worth. In any case, I honestly believe that had it not been for New Jersey's public financing laws, I might not have received the Republican nomination for governor in 1981.

The matter of financial disclosure is never easy. Most of us believe that how much money we have or don't have is a private matter. The first time I disclosed, I compared the experience to swimming in a cold lake. The anticipatory anxiety is much worse than the actual experience. My advice to prospective candidates is to disclose it all—and all at once, not in stages. One set of news articles will appear. People will say, "Well, I thought the Keans had more money than that," or, "I didn't know they had that much." Then it will be over.

I strongly believe in disclosure for high-level government officials. I do think, however, that indicating sources of income is much more important than detailing amounts. I also feel that in some ways we have gone too far. People who serve on school boards or local town councils perform a real public service. Requiring disclosure at that level can keep too many good people out of government.

You may not know that not just the wealthy object to full disclosure. In an assembly debate on a disclosure law, one of the most articulate spokesmen against the bill was a representative from an urban district. I had never thought of him as having much money and I asked him after the debate why he was so opposed to disclosure. "Look," he said, "I've got two kids in college. They are doing well but it is costing me an arm and a leg. My wife and I have borrowed money—probably a lot more than we should. We owe money. Someday we will be able to pay it back. But in the meantime, the fact that we owe that much money is nobody's business but our own."

Before I leave the issue of money, I also want to say that the high cost of political campaigning, and the system of financing it has bred, is a blight on American politics. When it takes as much as $8 million to win a Senate seat in a state like New Jersey, it will not take long before our Congress begins to resemble the British House of Lords. The problem exists at the local level too. When I first ran for the state assembly, I spent $2,000 on my campaign. In 1987, one candidate spent over $70,000 on a primary bid for an assembly seat. In 1938, I don't believe my father spent more than $200 when he ran for Congress. In 1986, the average congressional race cost $300,000 and an average Senate race, $3 million. These are not numbers an average person can contemplate.

So now nearly everyone has to turn to political action committees (PACs), the proliferation of which I believe historians will regard as one of the most important—and negative— developments in American politics of the 1970s and 1980s. In 1974, there were 608 PACs that doled out more than $8 million; by 1987, there were 4,100 dispensing more than $130 million. So while individual and party contributions doubled, the amount of PAC contributions quadrupled.

That is dangerous for several reasons. First, PAC money favors incumbents, who already enjoy other built-in advantages. Incumbents receive six dollars of PAC money for every dollar a challenger gets, which deters potential challengers, good people in many instances, from even thinking about public office. What's more, PAC money comes with strings attached. Someone who gives you a lot of money naturally expects something in return. When you don't toe a particular line, the PACs can play a not so pleasant or civic-minded kind of hardball.

I once saw a prominent state senator in New Jersey introduce legislation to protect wetlands from overdevelopment. The next day he got a call from someone at the builders' lobby who told him that not only was he going to lose thousands of dollars in campaign contributions, but the lobbyists were going to call other Republican senators and inform them that unless they dissuaded him from pushing the legislation, they too would lose their contributions. With a system like that, even the most independent legislator will find it hard to see the needs of the general public because too many of the special interests are in the way.

The money in politics today threatens to greatly distort the system set up by our Founding Fathers. Several possible solutions have been advanced. One is a constitutional amendment to overturn the Supreme Court's decision in the 1971 case of *Buckley* v. *Valeo,* which defined PAC contributions as a form of free speech. Another solution proposes to limit available television time, by far the most expensive component of campaigns, much as the British do. For me, the most realistic solution is some type of national public financing of congressional elections.

Presently, New Jersey has the most comprehensive public financing laws of any state. Any candidate for governor who can raise $50,000 is entitled to two dollars in state funds for every dollar raised privately, with a cap on the total expenditure allowed. The system is financed by a voluntary checkoff that appears on state tax returns. In 1984, for example, 40 percent of the state's taxpayers checked the public financing box. Individual contributions, including PACs, are limited to $800 because nobody gets bought for $800. While the current system needs some tinkering, it has largely served its intended purpose. Since passage of the law, New Jersey voters have been given a wide choice of candidates for the state's highest office. In my view, only some form of public financing will free Congress from the PACs. It will be expensive, no doubt, but we ought to be willing to pay that price for democracy and the national interest.

☆

The high cost of campaigning is a major reason why many of our ablest people do not run for public office. But cost is not the only reason. An equally large deterrent is the knowledge that if you are elected to a position like New Jersey governor, you will live in a fishbowl, your personal life shared with 7 million people. For many politicians a normal family life becomes exceedingly difficult to enjoy and maintain. So, unable to balance private life with public life, an elected official often sees his marriage and family lose out.

I learned of the dangers early while growing up in Washington. Even as a child, I sensed that Washington social life could be facile and shallow. Too often friendships were based on the shaky foundation of convenient political arrangements. And living in a city absorbed with the pursuit of power, anyone could easily lose touch with the things that really matter in life. Family life was often neglected as a public official or journalist set off to pursue the siren call of career.

But pressures of political life did not affect our family as much as others. My father kept an unbelievably regular schedule when he was in Washington. He left the house promptly at eight every morning and returned at six for his one drink preceding seven o'clock dinner. He worked Saturdays at the Capitol but only for half a day, always returning home for one o'clock lunch. Meanwhile, my mother did everything she possibly could to provide our family the attention and care we all needed. My father was a serious man. He preferred spending time poring over tax codes or the Social Security laws to the Washington social circuit. My mother was much more fun-loving, enjoying the company of people, but she cared little for the parties of pretentious official Washington. Her family was her world. Much to her credit, and to my benefit, she treated the silly side of Washington with a disarming naiveté, which any form of official pomposity richly deserves.

At state dinners my mother did attend, she would invariably end up sitting next to the most important person in the room. If a prominent ambassador or important Cabinet member were a guest, my mother would be seated right at his side. Meanwhile, my father would be relegated to the other end of the table, next to, as he put it, "somebody's wife." He was fond of repeating his cousin Alice Longworth's observation that "Washington is full of fascinating men and the women they married when they were very, very young."

My father would come home after these parties absolutely furious. "What did the ambassador say about the uprising in his country?" he would ask my mother. She would reply, "What uprising? We talked about our children and where we vacationed last summer."

At one party, my mother was introduced to the ambassador from Chile. "You mean that long, thin country?" my mother asked. That summed up how my mother approached life, official and otherwise. My brothers and sisters love to tell the story of the time a man broke into our family home in Livingston. My mother, who was in her late seventies at the time and quite alone, was confronted by a stranger in her bedroom. She asked him what he wanted, and he said he was looking for someone. She asked him to wait in the living room while she went to see if anyone was around. She quickly went downstairs to call the police. As she was hanging up, she saw him coming downstairs. He was stark naked. When the local police arrived some ten or fifteen minutes later, they found the two of them in the living room talking over a cup of coffee. After they had put some clothes on the intruder and taken him away, a policeman asked my mother, "Weren't you afraid?" "No, not really," said my mother. "After all, I could see he wasn't armed." It was typical of my mother that she spent the next few days on the phone making sure the young man was getting proper treatment.

My mother and father both did their best to give our family the place it deserved, especially when the outside world put heavy demands on them. I fear, however, that they were an exception to the usual pattern found in Washington. I saw politicians then and I see them today who drag their family into the spotlight. They display their family in campaign literature, with appearances featuring doting wife, cherubic children, and shaggy dog. The message for public consumption: "I am a good family person. Vote for me." The private situation in the real home is often different. I can't tell you how many families I have seen destroyed by the publicity and hypocrisy. The fact is, a family that is always on cue can never be a real family, which is why there are so many tragedies among political families. Too many of the kids I grew up with developed serious drug and alcohol problems that stemmed from lack of real attention and affection.

I remember vividly a time when I couldn't have been more than ten. A friend had invited me over to play after school. About four in the afternoon, I was introduced to his mother, a beautiful lady, but still lying in bed with a drink in her hand. My friend's father, a famous columnist, was out of town giving a speech. I guess the report card must have just arrived, because as soon as my friend was out of earshot, his mother beckoned me over toward her bed, and said, "You're his friend. Tell me, what is wrong with Johnny?" I knew the answer. I just couldn't say.

The memory has stayed with me. Back in 1967, when I first decided that I would give politics a try, I knew we would face problems ahead. Debby insisted that the needs of the family would come first. I agreed with her. We also agreed that our family life would be completely separated from my public life, so no one in the family would be pressured to campaign or become involved in my career if they did not openly choose to. Finally, we agreed that if a situation arose in which a private decision might affect my public career, the private considerations would always win out.

At times, the understanding that Debby and I have has created consternation among the press and my supporters. Our home is a family sanctuary, and no member of the press has ever been invited to it. Neither has any public function ever been held at our house. Only rarely do I have any sort of meeting there, and then only with people already well known to my family. At first, especially during the 1981 gubernatorial campaign, reporters attributed my reluctance to share my private life to snobbery. It was a tradition for public officials in New Jersey to court reporters at their homes and to make a big deal of their families. But gradually the press corps came to tolerate my unusual ways. Nevertheless, I continue to worry, especially about my children. It is hard to gauge the impact of your public life on a child. Politicians grow thick skins; their children and spouses do not.

There are so many dangers. What does it mean if your father is a celebrity? Do you start to feel that maybe you're different, that you don't have to make it on your own? What do children go through in school when their parent is criticized in the daily paper? How does that affect them? It is so hard to tell what children are thinking, because often they won't talk about what's really on their mind.

It was a little thing, but I remember an incident during my 1981 inauguration. My daughter, Alex, was then in second grade. Debby and I felt her father's inauguration was something she should remember, so we took her out of school for the day. I was so proud of her, because she was completely well behaved during the long church service and the inaugural ceremony. Once, during my inaugural speech, she allowed herself a tiny yawn. An alert photographer caught the moment. The cute picture then made most of the papers. What Debby and I didn't find out until much later was that one of Alex's classmates had brought the picture to school. Alex was embarrassed. She worried for weeks because she thought somehow she had let me down.

Another example: In 1977 I lost the primary to Ray Bateman. Our twin boys, Tom and Reed, were then nine years old and I had just finished ten years in the assembly. That job of course had been part-time; I made my living as head of my real estate corporation. But all Tom and Reed had heard about all their lives, both at home and at school, was my work as a politician. They knew I had lost the primary for governor. Both of them, I found out later, were afraid that I was out of a job. Would the family have to move? Would they have to leave school? Could I find another job? They were relieved when they discovered that I was still "going to the office."

Our children have done very well and for that I credit Debby. Knowing my strange career produces harsh demands, she has devoted herself unselfishly to the children. Whether it is receiving family support at a school sporting event, getting a ride to a friend's house, or just having a parent around when they need someone to talk to, our children have always been able to count on Debby. Meanwhile, her constant presence at home has given me the confidence and luxury to devote more time to the affairs of New Jersey. Crises in the governor's office really don't bother me. I'm an optimist, who lives by the simple belief that all problems can be solved by people of goodwill. Some problems just take longer than others. But if there is something wrong at home, I cannot concentrate on the job. Debby's devotion to our family gives me the peace of mind I need.

Debby does not like the public aspects of being the state's first lady. She would much rather be in the audience listening to a speech than on a platform giving it. In fact, she does not speak in public. She worries terribly about those times when she must appear publicly, even though she always wins rave reviews for her appearance and personality. She loves people and is at ease in small groups, but she dislikes crowds. She has taken time to work behind the scenes, especially on two personal causes: preventing mental retardation and stopping drug abuse. But she prefers to avoid publicity and the limelight.

Once in a great while, a brave staff member or consultant suggests that my campaign or my image would be strengthened if Debby somehow took a more public role. I put that advice in the same file with the suggestion that I should change the pronunciation of my name and close the gap between my teeth. People should be themselves. I think I am. Besides, Debby was not elected, I was, and I am happiest when she is comfortable. When spouses or children are forced into public life, trouble is sure to follow.

☆

The biggest obstacle to a normal family life when you are a governor is simply the weight of your schedule. If you are going to do the job right, you have to be at it almost twenty-four hours a day. Invariably, every day of the week, including weekends, is dominated by the state's business. You have to be on call at every moment: a prison disturbance, a fire, a hurricane, a strike, or any of a hundred other crises can demand your immediate attention.

On the average, I receive from 200 to 250 invitations a week to attend events in New Jersey or elsewhere. Sometimes the number can climb to 500 a week or more. A great many of the invitations are to speak or appear at conventions or festivals. Others are a bit more unusual. I once received a letter from a high school boy whose father had promised to buy him a skateboard if he could convince the governor to visit his house. I did, and the surprised father paid up. I have performed magic tricks with David Copperfield, chanted, "Big smoke, no fire," on a Formica table at the New York Giants training camp, and thrown a fake punch at Michael Spinks. Meanwhile, I have eaten everything from sauerbraten to pirogies to tacos, because New Jersey has only about ten fewer ethnic groups than the United Nations has countries.

I have to turn down almost 95 percent of the invitations I receive. Nevertheless, I am usually on the road almost every day from nine in the morning to at least nine in the evening. I can cut a ribbon at the grand opening of a new office building on the Hudson waterfront at 9:00 A.M., fly by helicopter to Atlantic City for a speech on crime at 11:00 A.M., stop by my office at Trenton for three meetings in the early afternoon, tape a tourism commercial at Giants Stadium at 4:00 P.M., and attend an art reception and a political fund-raiser in the evening. That sort of day has me traveling about 350 miles.

So it is difficult to keep your sanity. To do so, you have to become extremely flexible mentally. You have to be ready to participate in a complex discussion with investment bankers about the future of tax-exempt bonds, then leave to stand next to Spiderman to launch a campaign against child abuse. You have to be somber when delivering a eulogy at the funeral of a public official, and then later that same evening you are expected to be witty, even hilarious, as the honored guest at a political or corporate fund-raiser.

Everywhere you go in New Jersey you are the center of attention. And if you are to grow in the job, you must learn that your every move is watched and your every word weighed. And sometimes you have to be quick. Once I paid a visit to a summer school I created for talented high school juniors interested in the arts. After lunching with the students, I toured the school to take a look at their projects. I was listening intently to a student explain to me the intricacies of sculpture, when I saw her face turn beet red and her eyes nearly pop out of her head. I did not know that she had inadvertently splattered plaster of paris all over my pants. The girl recoiled in terror, fearing that somehow she was going to get in trouble. I had to assure her that the plaster of paris would go well with the color of the egg on my tie.

Even an innocent remark can get you in trouble. I happened to be traveling with Vice-President Bush the day after his debate with Geraldine Ferraro. We were in Hoboken, where George was receiving the endorsement of the International Laborers Association, led by the crusty Teddy Gleason. The real salt of the earth, members of the unions speak the language you would expect dockworkers to speak. We were leaving to get in the car when one of the workers yelled, "How'd you do last night?" The vice-president turned around and said, "I kicked a little ass."

I know George Bush didn't mean anything malicious by the remark, because he is a decent and honorable man. He was simply trying to reply in the same spirit the question had been asked. As he spoke, I noticed a boom mike overhead, dangerously close to the vice-president. When we got in the car, I warned him that the remark might have been recorded. He didn't think it was possible. Later, I pulled aside Bush's press secretary, Pete Teeley, saying, "Your boss doesn't think this is a problem, but this is something you ought to be aware of."

Sure enough, by the next day the remark was all over every major newspaper in the country. George had to spend time answering questions about what he really meant. To me, he didn't mean anything other than what was a fact, that he had beaten Ferraro in the debate. But the way he expressed himself got him in trouble. So always onstage, a politician must understand that his most innocent remark can always be misinterpreted.

One of the things I find most difficult to do is to give a speech at the end of a long day. Often that speech is the third or fourth one on the schedule, and maybe the tenth speech you have delivered in a month on the same subject. But you have to understand that the audience did not hear the first, second, and third speeches of the day, and they have not heard you address the subject. They were invited three months ago to attend the event, and they have been looking forward to hearing their governor. While your speech may be just another one for you, it is by no means just another one for them. In fact, going to the event is probably the only time they will see you in person. The entire impression they have of your abilities as a leader is going to be formed in perhaps ten minutes. You owe it to them, and to yourself, no matter how tired or irritable you may feel, to throw yourself into the speech. And when the audience responds with laughter or applause, it all becomes worthwhile and both you and they benefit.

Anyone who performs before a group feels the same way. I remember years ago attending a benefit performance of a French farce starring Bert Lahr and my brother-in-law's sister, Angela Lansbury. The show was wonderful. I went backstage later to see Angela. She didn't know I was coming to that particular performance. Benefit audiences, my actor friends tell me, are especially tough to please. Because they have usually spent a lot of money to come, they feel they are owed a great performance. In any case, Angela, after hugging me, said, "I knew just where you were sitting. Fourth row on the side." "Did you see me?" I asked. "No" she said, "but I could hear you and your friends laughing. Because of that, I gave a better performance. I always do when there are a couple of 'gypsies' in the audience." I feel that way too. I know I'll give a better speech when I can spot a couple of people in the audience who really seem to be listening to what I have to say.

The other frustrating thing about my schedule is not having the time to sit down and get to know the people you meet. I don't like receiving lines where the most you get are a handshake and a hello. Many of the people on any governor's schedule are doing really interesting things. Incredibly, I find that people will sometimes say things to a governor that they might not say to their closest friend. Unfortunately, there is rarely time for even the most casual banter. The room is usually crowded, a band may be drowning out conversation, and the host or hostess may have me in an armlock rushing to get me to greet as many guests as possible.

I often have trouble hearing people in such circumstances, and have a habit of smiling and nodding. Debby hates it. "How do you know they haven't told you their best friend just died?" she has asked me. She's right. The habit can get you into trouble. I once attended a Hispanic reception in Jersey City. The affair was long and the night was hot, and much of it was conducted in Spanish, a language I do not understand. After it was over I was trying to leave, but my path was blocked by a large gentleman with a glass in his hand who was talking a mile a minute in Spanish. When he finally paused, I smiled and nodded. To my surprise, he said *"Gracias,"* and waved me toward my car. "I think," said my aide, "you just promised to make him secretary of state."

So you come across all kinds of characters in my line of work. Once in a while you worry about guilt by association, because people like to have their picture taken with the governor. There's nothing wrong with that and I always oblige, but you have no idea who the strangers are who approach you and ask that a picture be taken. You just hope that the photo won't show up some day to prove close association with some known criminal. Once I was greeting people at a charitable affair with Bob Hope. The host wanted as many people as possible to get their pictures taken between the Governor and the star. Hope was wonderfully gracious for a long time, but the event went on and on. Finally, he turned to me and said, "Governor, do you know all these people?" I said, "No." "Oh," he said. "I was just wondering how many of them are people out on parole." Bob Hope is just as funny off-stage as he is on. Another time, he cracked me up during an invocation. We were part of a ribbon-cutting event for a new casino. The minister was praying in solemn tones for all the officers and employees of the great organization. Hope then whispered in my ear, "He's praying for management, but the customers are going to need the help."

I took part in still another ceremony to celebrate the success of a furniture store that had received tax breaks as part of our urban enterprise zone program. The proprietor took my picture and said he wanted it for his scrapbook. I then learned that my picture was gracing the front window of his store, beneath a sign that read: "Buy low-priced furniture where all the famous people shop."

☆

It is necessary, of course, to say no to many people's invitations so as to have time to spend with your family. The result will be to make some people angry. But the personal price is steep if you succumb completely to the demands of the public. Again, my rule is that private considerations should always outweigh public ones. Twice during my tenure as governor I have stood for my principle in the face of intense public criticism. Both times, my family benefited and, in the end, that is all that matters.

The first incident happened early in my first term, and involved what I thought would be the prosaic decision of choosing where my family was going to live. For more than twenty years, New Jersey governors have lived in a comfortable old mansion in Princeton called Morven, built by Richard Stockton, one of the signers of the Declaration of Independence.

The New Jersey Historical Society had always coveted Morven. At the end of my predecessor's term in office, the Society agreed to refurbish a rundown, 150-year-old, Greek Revival house down the road in Princeton called Drumthwacket, in return for permission to turn Morven into its headquarters. Drumthwacket, Scottish for "wooded hill," is a huge white mansion with a colonnaded porch, more than 13,000 feet of floor space, and ten-foot ceilings. The mansion was to be ready for the new first family by January 1982.

A couple of things happened. First, it turned out there was no way that Drumthwacket would be ready in time for the new administration. In fact, it would probably not be ready for at least a year. Second, Drumthwacket turned out to be exceedingly costly to renovate, much more than anyone had anticipated. The Historical Society had put almost $2 million into shoring up the walls and the foundation and repairing the heating system. Then it ran out of money. With the few dollars it had left, the Society bought four or five antiques from the nineteeth-century American Empire period and scattered them throughout the house.

The rest of the house was furnished with a hodgepodge of whatever was available, including, among other things, a metal desk in the library, Formica-topped coffee tables, and furniture from the old office of Senator Harrison Williams. It was hard to blame anybody, because the Historical Society had simply run out of money. But it looked awful.

Debby likes and appreciates antiques, having once worked as a guide at Winterthur, the Du Pont Museum in Wilmington, Delaware. We both took one look at the mess and concluded that it just would not do. New Jersey, the center of so much of the nation's history, deserved much more in its Executive Mansion. Why shouldn't we make it into something New Jersey would be proud of? Debby suggested we form a committee to find the best way to furnish the mansion. I agreed. After a couple of meetings, the committee decided that the first thing to do would be to allow the Historical Society to sell whatever pieces they had acquired to get out of debt, then to begin a private fund-raising campaign to furnish the house more tastefully. No one was to hurry. But we wanted to do it right.

One cold January day shortly after the decision was made, I was in Rhode Island attending the winter meeting of the Coalition of Northeast Governors, which had just elected me vice-chairman. I picked up a copy of the *New York Times* to see if my election had made the paper. Instead, I was startled to see a picture of my wife and a large front-page story headlined "Mansion Antiques Are Rejected by Mrs. Kean."

What happened, I suspect, is that a disgruntled Historical Society consultant had alerted the *Times* that the Empire period pieces were being sold. The story concentrated on the value of those pieces, ignoring the rest of the stuff cluttering the place. The reporter interviewed a few noted furniture dealers who argued that American Empire pieces, while controversial and even ugly to the layman, were increasing in value among furniture connoisseurs. The implication was that Debby was a philistine who had exceeded her authority by ordering the furniture sold.

I was furious. Not only had selling the furniture been my decision, but Debby had agreed on her own to try to rescue the project, and turn the mansion into something more presentable. The public flap over her supposed lack of taste in furniture was precisely the kind of thing I had hoped to avoid by keeping my family out of the gubernatorial limelight. To make matters worse, with the *New York Times* breaking the story, New Jersey newspapers felt compelled to run lengthy follow-ups with arcane details about everything from the furniture itself to Mrs. Kean's education.

A flap of this sort has a way of fascinating the press corps. It is sometimes hard to get ten reporters interested in a program to finance road construction, but if the issue is how to furnish a mansion, everyone wants an interview. For at least a month, my office was preoccupied with reporters' questions about Drumthwacket's renovation.

We stayed on course. Debby got help from a number of other governors' wives, especially Ginny Thornburgh, the wife of Pennsylvania's governor. The Drumthwacket Foundation, under the chairmanship of Finn Casperson, agreed to raise private money to furnish the mansion. The Princeton and Newark museums said they would help. As I write, the house is furnished with New Jersey Colonial antiques. Open to the public once a week, the mansion is the scene of numerous public events. Everybody comments on its beauty and the taste with which it is furnished. Debby has done what she promised. New Jersey can be proud.

So we weathered the Empire furniture brouhaha. But another Drumthwacket controversy was brewing when I announced that my family would stay at our home in Livingston, instead of moving into the Princeton mansion. Drumthwacket would be used for public ceremonies and hosting dignitaries. This decision set off another round of criticism. From the tone of some of the newspaper editorials, you would have thought I was a king and not a governor. How could I refuse to live in the mansion that had been renovated for me for $2 million? What about the dignity of the office?

People who were personally close to me, and even many who were not but knew I was trying to maintain a stable family life, knew I had made the right choice, one that successfully drew at least a partial cloak around a big fishbowl. The public was welcome at the State House or at Drumthwacket, both public buildings. But my home, where I continued to pay the bills, was private. Home was for the family. My children could stay in their own schools with their friends; our neighbors would remain our neighbors. My family would be raised in a home and not a museum. The taxpayers would save $80,000 a year in maintenance and staffing costs. Drumthwacket is now well on the way to becoming what Debby wanted it to be, a jewel in the state's crown. And when I go home, even though I may not get there until midnight, I just see my family. Of all the decisions I have made as governor, living at home was the wisest.

The Drumthwacket controversy taught me the rather painful lesson that it is almost impossible to remove your family from the glare of the spotlight. The criticisms aimed toward you can be handled if you are a good politician. But those directed at your family really hurt. Still, I refuse to make compromises where my family is concerned.

The issue of public versus private surfaced again on the related issue of where my family vacations. For a number of years before I became governor, my family vacationed on Fishers Island, New York, a nine-mile-long retreat located twenty-two miles from the northern tip of Long Island. Although I owned land there, we rented a house, and since becoming governor I have done my best to be with the family for two or three summer weekends. In the spring of 1986, we decided to sell the parcel of open land we owned so that we could buy a cottage and ten acres of land. I filed a deed with the local authorities, and then made a public filing with the state, as you must do when you buy land. Months later, an intrepid reporter for the *New York Daily News* stumbled across the deed.

The headline read, "Jersey may be perfect for you, but not for Kean." At issue was not only my choice of a summer home, but our state's tourism campaign. To some members of the press, there was something hypocritical about my telling people to vacation in New Jersey and then purchasing a summer house out of state. I was amazed by the kind of effort the press expended to cover the story. One newspaper went so far as to hire an airplane to fly over the island and take a picture of the property. The photo appeared with a front-page story entitled, "Governor's Out-of-State Hideaway." The only problem was they had taken a picture of the wrong house. Then another reporter wrongly identified two islands as having been purchased by me.

The *Bergen Record* was the funniest. They not only ran a picture of the wrong house, they sent a reporter out to the island. Because there are only a few stores on the island, the young reporter headed to the first one she saw to ask some questions. She ended up standing in line in front of Debby who was buying some coffee. Debby stood beside her at the counter as the reporter asked the owner, "What are the Keans really like?" and, "Do you ever see Mrs. Kean?" The owner said she saw Debby once in a while. As a result, the reporter editorialized, "The people who summer on Fishers Island have refined nesting habits and spurn the stray flocks who intrude on their territory." And the island folk wondered about a paper that would send a reporter to ask questions about a first lady she couldn't recognize standing next to her.

The flap lasted about three days. Such incidents, however, require some perspective and a sense of humor. In this case, the press overlooked two important realities in their haste to pry into my personal life. The first is that I am thoroughly familiar with every possible vacation spot in New Jersey. During the summer, I entertain at the governor's official beach house at the Island Beach State Park on the New Jersey shore. On many weekends I go to sporting events at the Meadowlands, visit craft fairs in the Pinelands, or go to an opera or a play at one of New Jersey's theaters. I have traveled to every corner of the state, eaten at every ethnic festival, and marched in every parade. No one is more qualified to boast of our state's attractions than this governor. My weekends on Fishers Island in no way detracted from what New Jersey had to offer.

The second is that, like any other human being, a governor feels the need once in a while to escape from the problems of work, clear his head, and think a bit about something besides the next crisis. That's why you will find that most governors have places they love to go outside their state. Only in such a place can we take refuge in anonymity. We don't have to sign autographs or offer opinions on why unemployment is up or down. A number of my predecessors have had homes in Florida. On the day the story broke, I received a call from the governor of another state who was vacationing at the Jersey shore. "Should I leave?" he asked.

For some reason the press assumes that governors are not like other human beings, but the general public is a little more understanding. During the entire Fishers Island controversy, I received only three letters of complaint. One was from an admittedly partisan Democrat and the other two from owners of hotels at the shore. The vast majority of my constituents seemed to understand that I had a right to a little privacy.

What can we make of my experience? Is intense scrutiny of public figures necessary? Overdone? Is it draining our political system of good leaders at precisely a time when they are desperately needed? I don't think anyone has definitive answers to these questions. They need to be examined by the elected leaders, the press, and all who care about good government. But I would like to make a few observations.

The 1980s witnessed the emergence of the family as a dominant political issue. Politicians of all sorts have been advised to appeal to the widespread sentiment that the family is in trouble and desperately needs help. Accordingly, as I have said, politicians are expected to display their families while campaigning. Meanwhile, government policies are now evaluated according to whether they will strengthen or weaken the family.

What troubles me is that many public officials seem to ignore their own professed concerns and values. A politician, after waxing eloquent about the virtues of family life, will think nothing about spending weeks or even years away from his own children. And politicians who say mutual respect is the basis of a stable marriage may then force an unwilling spouse to undergo political rigors for which nothing has prepared her.

Hypocrisy is a sure path to trouble. I do not mean, of course, to paint all or even most of my colleagues with the same broad brush.

Many spouses and children enjoy speaking in public and are a willing asset to a politician's image. Their participation should be encouraged. But in those instances when a spouse or child is not "camera ready," a politician must have the courage to give them the freedom to stay out of the hurly-burly of public life.

Our country was founded on the principle that every American should be allowed the pursuit of happiness, a principle that covers public servants. When I took the oath of office, I pledged to uphold and defend the laws of the state of New Jersey faithfully. At no time did I promise to submit the choice of my home or vacation spot to public referendum. Neither did I agree to share my wife and children with 7 million people. People who think that I did or should, misunderstand the role of a leader in a democracy.

In 1985 I came very close to not running for reelection as governor. For months I hesitated. I talked individually with each of my children. I loved the job but I wanted to see more of the family. I longed at times for a "normal" life. There were weeks when, had I been forced at that moment to make a decision, it would have been to retire from public life. My reasons were all personal. My eventual decision to run for another four years may have been the most difficult decision of my governorship.

I know the privacy issue is costing the democracy some fine political talent. Recently I talked to a good friend, a United States senator, who would make a fine president of the United States. He is not running. The reasons he told me have entirely to do with his family and its right to privacy. Families last a lifetime. Long after the cheering throngs have disappeared, the angry phone calls are no longer coming in and the crises have passed, your spouse and children will still be with you. Every American ought to keep that in mind before venturing into the public arena. And it wouldn't hurt if the voters thought about it the next time they judge the private actions of their favorite public servant.

6
The Noblest Profession

Public officials love to be praised, and I'm no exception. Without a need for approval of our fellow man, we probably would be spending our time doing something else. Typical of the letters I savor was one that came in after we unveiled our welfare reform program in the winter of 1987. "Congratulations," a woman wrote. "Your welfare proposal is the most creative I've seen yet. Keep up the wonderful work. New Jersey leads the way again." After I announced another new program, a crackdown on tax cheats, a constituent felt compelled to write, "You just set the Republican party back twenty-five years, and you reminded me that arrogance in political leaders can bring about tyranny!" The fact is, I get thousands of letters of both sorts every month. But my point is that governors very often get full credit or blame when neither is entirely deserved.

The prime mover behind my welfare reform plan, for example, is a man named Drew Altman, our human services commissioner. Our acclaimed transportation trust fund was the work of John Sheridan. Gene McCaffrey, the commissioner of personnel, designed the first reform of our civil service laws in almost ninety years. What I am saying, and I mean it, is that any governor is no better than the people around him.

I have tried very hard to fill my administration with talented people who really care about New Jersey. Many of them have given up lucrative jobs in the private sector to work for the taxpayers' benefit. They really have put aside their own ambitions to help me try to make New Jersey a better place.

For me, three New Jersey officials symbolize the best in public service. The three seem to have little in common; what they do share is important. Each is a member of a racial minority, and each was at one time forced to overcome clear discrimination. Each was fortunate enough to live in a country where opportunity exists, and once having become successful, all of these remarkable people decided to share their success with others less fortunate.

The story of their lives speaks to the strength of democratic society. In ancient Athens, each citizen, upon turning twenty-one, had an obligation to stand in the public square before his family and take an oath, which went: "I will strive unceasingly to quicken the public sense of duty so that we will make this city greater, better, and more beautiful than it was before I took this oath." The three have, in my judgment, accepted the spirit of that oath.

☆

The first story belongs to the head of New Jersey's Division of International Trade, a woman, five foot one-half inch tall, who is the incarnation of sheer energy, named Ming Hsu.

What moves today's international economy wouldn't be recognized by the merchants who sailed from the port of Perth Amboy three hundred years ago. Market quotation machines and telecommunications satellites keep our economy fully part of faraway places. But for the peripatetic Ming Hsu, the essential item of international commerce is nothing more complicated than a suitcase.

Ming Hsu travels the world promoting New Jersey products and services. Ten out of twelve months of the year she is telling consumers in Russia, India, West Germany, the Caribbean, Taiwan, and China about New Jersey computers, chemicals, banks, and food products. And while she's at it, she's convincing foreign companies to bring their factories and their jobs here. Just when many Americans blame Asian countries for our trade woes, an Asian-American is New Jersey's top saleswoman, globetrotting to drum up business for the United States.

The rigors of travel are nothing new for Ming Hsu. She's known them ever since she was six years old, when the Japanese invaded China. Young Ming enjoyed a comfortable life as a member of one of China's leading families. She was the daughter of Chen Chin-men, a member of Chiang Kai-shek's cabinet who later held several important ambassadorial posts. The Japanese invasion in the late 1930s shattered Ming's privileged existence. For the next ten years she was forced to move from town to town, staying one step ahead of the Japanese army. One night as she flew unaccompanied by family out of Hong Kong airport, her plane was strafed by machine-gun fire. Later, she was sent away to a remote village, and she watched with terror as Japanese tanks passed within yards of her hiding place.

Looking back, Ming Hsu says she survived mainly because of a combination of stubborn will and optimism. Both, she adds, were instilled in her by her grandfather, Chu Chih Chien. One of the first prime ministers under the Chinese Republic, Chu Chih Chien was a well-known statesman, diplomat, and patron of the arts, and remains today a folk hero in the People's Republic. Ming recalls her grandfather's simple philosophy: "Life is full of obstacles big and small. Work hard and they will vanish."

In 1944, Ming Hsu was able to leave China when she boarded the U. S. troop transport the *Billy Mitchell* for the trip to America. It was an exciting six-week journey for the young girl, because the ship was packed with people from all over the world. But food was in short supply and the passengers were served only twice a day. At night, all lights on board were turned off. Ming slept in the cramped space of what was once officers' quarters, which had been filled with bunks for the women and children. During the day the passengers practiced climbing into lifeboats, in case the ship was torpedoed. I remember commenting on her ability to climb effortlessly up and down the ladders of the U.S.S. *New Jersey* when we visited the ship in the harbor at Inchon in 1986. She reminded me where and when she learned the skill.

Once during the trip the *Billy Mitchell* stopped at Guadalcanal, and Ming went ashore to meet the members of the First Marine Division. That evening she was invited to dine with the ship's captain. At dinner, Ming met a young marine lieutenant who said that he would soon be back in action. Having seen many die, he said, he didn't think his chances of going home were very good. So he asked Ming to do him a favor. He brought her a rifle. The gun, he explained to the young woman, had killed his best friend just a few days before. He had taken it from the body of a dead Japanese soldier. "You are Chinese," he said. "Only you can understand the hatred I feel. Keep this rifle for the rest of your life." Taken aback, Ming accepted the gift. She didn't want to hurt the marine's feelings, but she naturally felt uncomfortable handling a deadly weapon. A few weeks later the ship landed in San Pedro, California.

As the English-speaking daughter of a high-ranking Chinese official, and the only civilian woman allowed to leave China during the height of War World II, Ming Hsu was somewhat of an instant celebrity in America. She was invited to appear on John Daly's *Report to the Nation* program on CBS radio. With some emotion she told the story about the young soldier. That brought a call from the War Office in Washington. A commander in the navy had heard the story, recognized his son, and wanted to see her. He and his family took Ming to lunch at the opulent Astor Hotel in New York. Ming decided not to tell them of their son's despair of ever again seeing home or family. Instead, she simply assured them that he was in good health and good spirits, given the extreme circumstances. Several months later, Ming received a letter from the young lieutenant, thanking her for seeing his parents. He went on to write that he was grateful that she didn't say anything to his parents about his being dead drunk the night he saw her. Finally, Ming understood where he had found the intestinal fortitude to approach her with his gift.

When Ming Hsu came to America, she planned only to get a good education and then return to China. Immigration quotas for Asians have always been very strict, and she saw no way she could become an American citizen. Ming's plans changed abruptly after Mao Tse-tung took control in China. Her father went to Taiwan with Chiang Kai-shek and her mother and sisters eventually came to America. Her more distant relatives did not fare as well. Several aunts and uncles suffered greatly after Mao took power and then again during the Cultural Revolution.

Once it was clear that America was her home for good, Ming decided to begin a career. It wasn't easy. Ming had done very well in school, winning a Penfield fellowship from New York University for the study of international law and diplomacy. But despite her obvious talents, she couldn't seem to get her career started. She wanted to go to law school, but you had to be a citizen to be admitted to the bar. The Foreign Service was out for the same reason. So was teaching at a state university.

Undaunted, Ming Hsu went to work as a researcher at NBC television. But even there she found her path blocked, this time not because of her nationality but of her gender. She was qualified for the news department but was told they didn't accept women. So she left NBC for the parent company, RCA, with hopes for a job with international flavor. Again she encountered discrimination. The company was willing to fire men in her division and give Ming their responsibilities, but not their title and pay. She tried to apply for a David Sarnoff fellowship to help work toward an MBA, but was told that women were not considered for the award because they were not likely to stay with the company. Talk to Ming Hsu about sex discrimination and you don't hear words of bitterness. "That's just the system," she says, "and you learn to work with it. You learn that you have to work twice as hard to get ahead if you are a woman. You may think that's unfair, but you do it."

Ming Hsu believed that one reason corporate executives were wary of promoting women was the feeling that women could not adapt to a man's world. Throw a woman in a conference with a bunch of men, the common wisdom had it, and she won't know what to talk about outside her area of expertise. So Ming Hsu listened to what the men were talking about, and the talk was very often about politics. She decided to get involved.

Ming and I first met in the late 1960s. She was just getting involved in Republican politics and I was making my way up the ladder in the assembly. We found we liked each other and we shared many ideas. We both went to the 1972 Republican Convention in Miami. The Nixon people had a need for someone to explain the president's China policy to skeptical conservatives. Ming Hsu's energy and eloquence attracted attention. She started to work with party leaders, people like George Bush, Bob Dole, and Bill Brock. At their urging, she crisscrossed the country speaking to women and ethnics about the Republican party.

Her message was simple. "Republican party people always feel comfortable talking with their own kind, business leaders and suburban wives," she recalls. "I said it's time we talked to people we don't feel so comfortable with." The experience taught her a lot about people and it taught her something disturbing about democracy. "I am bothered about how Americans take their voting rights and just about everything else for granted," Ming Hsu says. "Coming from a part of the world where people literally kill each other for a chance to vote, it startled me that Americans refuse to get involved in governing themselves."

In 1978, Ming Hsu was forced to give up her role in national politics when she was named a staff vice-president of RCA, the second female staff vice-president in the company's history. The company's attitude toward women had changed considerably. Ming was a big reason why. All the while, Ming and I kept in touch. She was chairman of an organization called Women For Kean during my 1977 primary race and did some public speaking on my behalf.

When I was finally elected governor in 1981, I looked for every possible way to get the economy moving. New Jersey was bleeding jobs like a hemophiliac, losing manufacturing jobs to Korea and Taiwan. Unlike some other states, ours was not seen as an attractive place for foreign investment.

We needed an advocate, someone who could spread the word about our great location, our transportation network, and all the other incentives we had to offer business. Leaders of some of our small companies told me of the help other states provided in marketing products to foreign countries. We had some potentially successful businesses that were struggling because they had no way to make contact with lucrative markets halfway around the globe.

I thought of my old friend Ming Hsu. I knew she had always been interested in government, but I felt that her high salary at RCA would keep her from ever coming to head the new Division of International Trade. Nevertheless, I asked my transition team to approach Ming about leaving RCA. Despite her high salary, Ming told them that she was growing frustrated with the rigid corporate environment. She liked the freedom and responsibility that the new position offered. What's more, she had always longed to do something useful for her state and country. I was surprised when she said yes.

It wasn't long before Ming began to bring jobs to New Jersey. Before she came on board, Lucky Goldstar, the huge Korean electronics firm, had thought about opening a manufacturing operation in the United States. The company looked at New Jersey but decided instead to move to Huntsville, Alabama. Ming concluded that Lucky Goldstar had headed south not on the merits, but because New Jersey didn't develop an effective sales pitch.

When rumors started that Samsung Electronics, Korea's largest firm, was looking at the United States, Ming called on the company management in both Korea and the United States. She made the point that although labor costs were lower in the South and West, New Jersey, with its highly educated work force and physical infrastructure already in place, offered a better business climate over the long run. She convinced

Samsung that an American manufacturing operation would help calm the protectionist sentiment growing in this country and could open markets in other countries, especially China, which had been closed to Korean-based manufacturers.

In the spring of 1984, Samsung announced it was setting up its first manufacturing operation in the United States, in Ledgewood, New Jersey. More than 350 New Jerseyans now run a highly automated production facility. Samsung's decision sent a signal to other Korean companies, many not as large or prestigious as Samsung, that it made sense to come to New Jersey. Lucky Goldstar, Daewoo, a textiles and electronic appliance producer, and Hyundai, the auto maker, all now have American headquarters within the state.

I was able to see Ming's work firsthand in the fall of 1986, when I led a foreign trade mission to Korea and China. Her contacts amaze me. Everywhere she goes she is greeted by old friends. The American ambassador to Korea greeted her with a hug. The consul general in Hong Kong spent hours with her trading stories about their old days together in Shanghai. In China, she and the vice-mayor of Beijing turned out to have been neighbors whose families had both been ravaged by the Japanese. She is particularly close with the "old Asia hands," Americans and Europeans who have worked in Asia for decades. Asian-Americans do not occupy high positions in most American companies or in the American government. Ming Hsu's success in both fields is noted throughout Asia.

Since 1981, Ming Hsu has entered New Jersey in more than thirty trade shows. As a direct result, our companies have generated over 7,000 leads and over $60 million in sales. One manufacturer of electronic billboards, for example, had never thought about the overseas market. Ming Hsu took him to a trade show in Hannover, West Germany. A year later, that firm had distributors throughout Western Europe. The number of foreign companies in New Jersey has more than doubled since Ming Hsu decided to work for state government. With $9.5 billion in foreign investment, New Jersey now stands fourth in the nation. More than 140,000 New Jerseyans work in factories or offices run by foreign firms.

But she's still not satisfied. Like most corporate executives, Ming Hsu often finds that government moves slower than a snail's pace, and she is sometimes frustrated by bureaucratic inertia. But with her contagious optimism, she says that is just part of the challenge. She blames many problems she has encountered on the peculiar American attitude toward public service. "Americans, especially in the corporate world, have this sort of hands-off attitude toward government," she says. "They think that government work is somehow beneath them. It's so different in the Far East. If you are successful in China or Korea, the greatest honor is to have a member of your family serve in government. Even in Britain it is different. The best graduates of Eton, Cambridge, Oxford, and other prestigious institutions have always wanted to go into the foreign service or other government careers. That's just not true here," she says, "and I think it hurts our country very much."

Ming touches on a cultural problem that I think has become endemic to our society and helps explain our country's overall sluggish economic performance. More and more of our best and brightest students, the new Ming Hsus, are choosing careers in finance or law or working as consultants. They transfer wealth through paper transactions but do nothing to create it. Jobs in manufacturing or production are seen as less prestigious or lucrative and are not as popular. We have seen very few genuinely creative and practical ideas to spur productivity, precisely because government and industry no longer attract the brighter graduates of our best schools. In the automobile industry, the emphasis on "bean counters" over people who can actually build cars has almost brought down entire companies.

Some politicians believe the answer to our problems is to punish the Japanese or Koreans for their success. But bashing them will do nothing to improve our own productivity. In my judgment, high tariffs will act like cocaine on the economy: there will be an immediate high but the long range effect could be fatal. There's no easy answer to our problem. We need to compete more aggressively in manufacturing, and part of that means attracting bright people away from today's glamour professions like risk arbitrage and mergers and acquisitions. Here the Wall Street crash of 1987 may have a silver lining. We also need to market American products in other countries more aggressively. We're doing that in my state, and a great deal of New Jersey's success is due to the hard work and perseverance of a descendant of one of China's most prestigious families.

☆

If Ming Hsu's clients are entrepreneurs with big plans for the future, Len Coleman's clients are people whose plans are rarely bright or secure.

Len is the commissioner of the New Jersey Department of Community Affairs, and in that job this tall, strikingly handsome man is responsible for the welfare of the people we too often forget: the homeless, the old, and the poor.

Twenty years ago, Len Coleman wasn't looking for new ways to help the less fortunate. Instead, he was looking toward a future in professional football. Len was one of the most talented football players and all-around athletes the state of New Jersey has ever produced. His Montclair High School football team won the state championship in his senior year. In that season, it seemed the player's every move was dramatic. In one game, he fumbled three times in the first half only to redeem himself by scoring the winning touchdown with two seconds left in the game. In another game, he led his team to two scores in the final five minutes, for a one-point victory. In the big game against his school's archrival, he dislocated his shoulder in the first period and was told to sit out for the rest of the game. Disconsolate and desperate to play, he went into the stands to talk to his father, who had himself been a stellar amateur football player and probably would have played pro football had not the color barriers existed. "If you understand the consequences and are ready to take the risk, get back in there," his father told him. The coach acquiesced. At halftime the trainer taped Len's shoulder to his waist and, feeling somewhat like a mummy, he charged back into the fray and scored the tying touchdown as his team went on to win the state championship.

Honors and offers rolled in for the young athlete. That year the New Jersey all-state football team had a backfield that was a recruiter's dream. At quarterback was a fellow named Joe Theisman from South River High; the fullback from Passaic was Jack Tatum, later a hard-nosed defensive back with the Oakland Raiders. One halfback was Franco Harris from Rancocas Valley High, who was headed to stardom at Penn State and four Super Bowl rings. The other halfback was Len Coleman. *Scholastic* magazine picked only Len Coleman from the illustrious contingent for its All-American team.

Naturally, Len was recruited by a number of major colleges, and in the spring of his senior year he traveled the country visiting campuses. He went to Ohio State, Michigan, Syracuse, and Penn State. With Jack Tatum, he spent a weekend in South Bend, Indiana, taking a look at what the Fighting Irish of Notre Dame had to offer. The attention he received was exhilarating. But beneath the smiles Len felt the sting of discrimination. After touring the football facilities, Tatum and Len were invited to a party. When they arrived they found only black people. The white players had been driven to a separate party on the other side of the campus.

This was not the first time a Coleman had encountered racism in a supposedly friendly place. Len's dad was blessed not only with great athletic ability but with a mellifluous voice as well. He was part of a choir, the Bordentown Quartet, that went to Princeton University to sing once in the 1920s. The elder Coleman was delighted to learn that free tickets were available to an afternoon alumni baseball game. Mr. Coleman was sitting in the stands, enjoying the game, when a Princeton alumnus rose and looked in his direction. "If that nigger isn't out of here in five minutes, I'm leaving," the man yelled. Mr. Coleman was humiliated and angry. As he left the stadium, he swore quietly to himself that he would live to see the day when his son would attend Princeton.

Mr. Coleman's wish came true when Len, after much deliberation, chose Princeton University as the place to showcase his athletic talents. The decision was not an easy one. The lure of big-time college football at the Ohio States and Michigans was strong. There, Len was sure to gain the attention of the professional scouts. Princeton, which offered no athletic scholarships, was certainly not a football school. But Len's mother and father had taught him that education was the key to the way up. Len had confidence that his football talents would catch the eye of pro scouts, even at an Ivy League school. At Princeton he could double up: advance his athletic career and earn a good education.

When Len entered college in 1967, Princeton was not the racially integrated school it is today. In fact, the school's composition had changed only slightly from when I was there. I remember a year in which only one black was enrolled in the entire undergraduate body. When Len arrived some fifteen years later, Princeton remained very much a Southern school. Because the university was eager to improve its image, Len had been heavily recruited. Only one black had ever made it through four years on the football team. University officials were hoping that Len Coleman would help change things.

It is never easy being a trailblazer, as Len soon discovered. In his freshman year he showed great potential on the practice field and it was clear to most observers that this was no average Ivy League athlete. Despite his exploits in practice, Len found himself relegated to the bench. That did not sit well with the anxious freshman. He thought about quitting and went so far as to deliberately skip a practice. The freshman coach tracked him down and asked him what was wrong. Len told him straight out that he was "pissed off" that he was riding the bench.

The next game was against Columbia. In the second quarter the coach told Len that he was giving him a chance. The first time Len touched the ball he ran 41 yards around the left end for a touchdown. In the third quarter he went 69 yards for another score. In all, he gained 160 yards on just nine carries. The Princeton fans who left the game that day knew there would be plenty of victory celebrations as long as the tall, gangly freshman running back was at the school.

It didn't turn out that way. The week after the Columbia game, Len sat on the bench for all but three plays from scrimmage. The next week the same thing happened. The pattern continued through the season and into his sophomore year when he moved up to the varsity. If Len did get a chance to play, it was only when Princeton was either far ahead or far behind. Even with his meager playing time, he managed to lead the varsity in receiving his sophomore year. Len wasn't the only player who thought his talents were being wasted. Next to Len on the bench sat two other talented players who happened to be black. As the season progressed they became more and more frustrated. It was clear that none of them could break into the starting lineup.

When the season ended, the black players decided to file a formal complaint against the coach. This was 1969, and racial tension was widespread across America. The protest became a cause célèbre on the Princeton campus and received national attention. Opinion was divided. Some thought the players were right to take a stand while others disagreed. One newspaper commented that Princeton had been a great institution for a long time and would continue to be a great institution after the affair was over. The editorial went on to say that it only hoped the players fared as well. Len discovered that a number of "friends" now greeted him with cold stares when he passed them on campus.

A commission was appointed to look into the matter. They concluded that, although no blatant discrimination had taken place, there was a need for greater sensitivity in handling race relations. Meanwhile, the coach who had been the subject of the complaint left, and was replaced by his assistant. Len Coleman felt vindicated, but it was a Pyrrhic victory. The next year he and the two other blacks were not invited out for the varsity football team. If they wanted to play football, they would have to try out for the jayvee squad. It was a turning point in Len's life. Until he decided to join the protest, he knew he was going to be a professional football player. By taking a stand for principle, he had seen that dream disappear. Now he needed to reexamine his life to find something else to replace the direction and motivation that football had provided.

Until the racial incident at Princeton, Len had never really believed that the color of his skin could be a barrier to achievement. He decided from then on it would be his brain, not his athletic ability, that would determine his future. He decided to study hard. Princeton had a great faculty. He would learn from them and develop the ability to serve others. He told himself that one way or another he would help blacks who had not had the good fortune he enjoyed.

He returned to Newark after graduation and got a job teaching fourth grade in an inner-city school, after turning down other jobs at much higher salaries. "I knew I would always survive," he says. Teaching was a wonderful experience. As one of only two male teachers in school, Len became a father or big brother to a great many of the boys, too many of whom were growing up in homes where there was no male present.

Len had always liked politics. He remembers as a boy sitting around the dinner table listening to his family argue the merits of Stevenson and Eisenhower. His parents, unlike most black Americans, had remained loyal to the Republican party after the New Deal. They were believers in what Len calls working-class conservatism. If you worked hard and saved, you would get ahead. They didn't expect a lot of help from government or other institutions. Len told me once how after his grandfather died the family discovered a trunk filled with $11,000 under his bed. His grandfather had lost faith in the banks during the Depression and had never given them a penny since.

In 1972, Len Coleman decided to enroll in the Kennedy School of Government at Harvard. The school had been founded twenty years earlier by Lucius Littauer, a wealthy, conservative congressman from upstate New York. Littauer's philosophy was that "if idiots are going to be running the government in Washington, they might as well be trained idiots."

At the Kennedy School, Len began to think seriously about social change and political philosophy. The discussions often centered on how to make black Americans fully part of our society. He began to explore the rich history of black America. He listened to Paul Robeson and read W. E. B. Du Bois and Malcolm X.

He came under the tutelage of Dr. Marty Kilson, the first black professor of government at Harvard. The son of a minister, Kilson is brash and articulate, a man who loves advancing controversial ideas and defending them. Len today fondly refers to him as an "eccentric pragmatist." Kilson argued that if they were to break through the "client-patron relationship" in which most black Americans find themselves, "they had to know how to pressure the system." Once they exerted pressure and won attention, they could back off and broker a compromise. More than any other person, Dr. Marty Kilson shaped Len Coleman's philosophy of government.

Len's emerging philosophy could be summed up in one word: "opportunity." He believed that black Americans wanted the same things that white Americans wanted. He began to see government as the one force that could level the playing field and give black Americans an equal chance to compete. Instinctively and intellectually, Len Coleman began to feel that government could enter into a social contract with black Americans in which each would take on certain responsibilities in return for improvement of their overall condition.

At Harvard, Len became involved in chapel life. He had been at Princeton while the Vietnam War was winding down. Like a lot of college students, he not only questioned the war itself but had been nagged by guilt over his not fighting at a time when other people his age were getting killed. At the Kennedy School he looked for another way to serve his country and promote our interests abroad. He had always been intrigued by Africa and after graduation he decided to work as a missionary for the Episcopal Church in Kenya.

It was a long way from the quiet classrooms of Harvard to the noisy streets of Nairobi. Len's job was to put the ideas he had learned at Harvard to work on a continent that was struggling to pull itself into the modern world. Historically, the Episcopal Church in Liberia, for example, had been tightly controlled by Americans, with even bishops being appointed by the American church. Len sat on the management team that put together an autonomy plan for the church. This was especially important because in Africa, church and state work closely together and the church is a major institution dealing with issues like health care and education.

The African nations were slowly moving from an archaic health-care system based on curing illnesses after they were diagnosed to one that relied on preventing them before they occurred. Len helped to establish a series of community health centers in Malawi villages that would provide basic medical examinations and preventive health-care education to people who had never been to a doctor.

An Episcopal bishop was looked to for leadership on a number of other matters, including the operation of local school systems. The bishops would turn to Len for advice on management matters. Of course an African community worker's life was filled with a few more dangers than his American counterparts had to face. In Burundi, Len escaped from the country only hours before a coup took place.

Len really loved the experience, and what was originally to be a two-year hitch quickly turned to four. He discovered he was learning things about management and public policy that he would not have learned back home. He concluded that you can't fight social problems in a vacuum. He realized that no single government answer exists to problems like homelessness, illiteracy, and lack of good health care. Africans believe in a holistic approach to things, in the development and care of the total individual, and the four years on that continent added a different perspective to his ideas about the way government should operate.

Upon coming home, Len became head of the Newark Urban Coalition. He put together a job-training program and won a citation from the president. He helped provide private funding for a legal-services program in Newark. He became friends with Congressman Jack Kemp and started advocating tax incentives to attract business to depressed cities.

I first met Len in 1981. He was working for one of my opponents in the Republican primary. I remember thinking he was exactly the kind of person we had been trying to attract to our campaign. When I won the nomination, he came forward and offered to help. You take such offers with a fair amount of skepticism. Usually, that's the last you hear from a person. But Len's offer was genuine and I found him working hard for my election. My staff, as usual, was young and although diligent, had made a few mistakes. In particular, they seemed to be having trouble reaching out to the minority community, not just blacks but Hispanics as well. Len has never been shy about anything. He came right to me with his criticism and with a plan to get me more exposure. I listened and it worked.

In 1981, with a conservative in the White House, black Republicans were scarce. Len took a real chance supporting me. But I noticed that other blacks, both Democrats and Republicans, respected his talents. I soon decided that if I was elected Len would play a leading role in my administration. I was determined that Len not be seen as a token, for his sake and for the sake of the administration. I wanted him to head a department that was not traditionally known for dealing with what were thought of as "black issues," like urban policy or welfare.

He agreed to head the Energy Department, during a time when the energy crisis still was on everyone's minds. We had to decide whether to allow completion of a controversial nuclear reactor called Hope Creek. Len helped negotiate a precedent-setting cost-control agreement for Hope Creek, and put together a state master plan that will serve as our energy blueprint for the next decade.

But his real interest lay elsewhere. After my reelection in 1985 I asked Len if he would take over the Community Affairs Department. At last Len had the opportunity to work with the issues he had studied at the Kennedy School and worked with every day in Africa. The problems facing the homeless and indigent in our inner cities are not unlike those facing the poor in and around Nairobi.

Len wore two hats during my first term in office, one as commissioner of energy and the second as my informal liaison to the black community. Although proud of my record on civil rights, I received a disappointingly small percentage of the black vote in 1981. I desperately wanted to convince blacks that a Republican could listen and respond to their needs.

Len went to work. He was perfect, because he understands black politics and has spent his entire life building bridges between people. He understands the issues that matter to black voters. He also knew firsthand how the government bureaucracy had been used over the years as a subtle instrument of discrimination. In short, Len knew the system: a few blacks on top while the important subcabinet jobs that really make government work remain lily-white. For years Republicans had told black Americans, as he puts it, "to pull yourself up by the bootstraps, but they didn't stop to think that some of us could never afford a pair of boots." Together, Len and I set about to break this stereotype.

Our first step was to become open and accessible to black leaders, not enough of whom knew about my background and commitment to civil rights. They didn't know, for example, that I had helped open the first Northern chapter of the Southern Christian Leadership Conference while I was studying at Columbia, or that I had marched with Dr. King. They saw me as just another rich, insensitive, country-club Republican.

We relied heavily on the existing black organizations, the National Association for the Advancement of Colored People (NAACP), the Urban Leagues, and especially the black churches. The last remains the one cohesive force in many of our inner cities. I learned that if you have an idea that you think might work in the black communities, the first people you want on your side are the black ministers. Len and I spent a lot of time in black churches in Newark, Trenton, and Camden. I discovered that the minority network in New Jersey is very tight. It doesn't take long for word to spread about a new governor who is accessible and willing to listen.

As I talked to black leaders, I couldn't help but conclude that blacks were tired of years of unrequited love for the Democratic party. The leaders enjoyed the attention they were getting from a Republican governor. And they told me it felt good to know that their support was at long last not being taken for granted.

We made a big effort to appoint qualified blacks and other minorities, particularly to seats in the judiciary. Len told me that early in life, black Americans learn there are two reasons why the system is against you. The first is that your school is not in the same league with the suburban schools white children attend. The second is that the court system is run by whites. Every time a black person goes to court, he sees a white person behind the bench dispensing justice. So we appointed a record number of black judges. They were not always liberal; in fact, several were the opposite. But they sent the message that Tom Kean was responsive to the black community and wanted to see black people's rights protected like everyone else's.

You can't deceive yourself and say that just because it is the 1980s, civil rights do not matter to black Americans. Len told me that the first mistake a lot of Republicans make is glossing over the importance of the rights issues. Some in my party argue that you can ignore them and win black support simply by stressing jobs and economic opportunity. Len calls that "Harvard talk. It sounds good in the classroom, but it breaks down in the real world."

Once I established my record on civil rights and my commitment to giving blacks an equal role in the power structure, I found I could sell them on new, conservative approaches to various problems—urban enterprise zones to attract businesses to our inner cities, for example. Minimum-skills tests for graduation from high school, because it is black students who are shortchanged when they cannot read or do simple math. Mandatory sentencing for certain crimes, because black neighborhoods are victimized by vandals and hoodlums. These are all conservative ideas and they play well in the black community. But to get them a fair hearing, you must first push civil rights. I knew this from a lifetime of experience in politics. But Len Coleman helped me sell my case.

In 1985, I astounded the pundits by winning 60 percent of the black vote. It was no longer high school football glory, but Len was still pulling moves that surprised everyone.

Len's potential is unlimited. He is intelligent, telegenic, and ambitious in a way that makes people confident, not wary. And unlike a lot of older black politicians, he is respected both inside and outside the black community. I'll go out on a limb and predict a day when Len Coleman wins very high public office.

☆

As a governor, I rely heavily on lawyers, but like so many other businessmen I am sometimes frustrated by their preoccupation with details and their inability to see the big picture. Like most people, I have gazed at complicated legal documents that take twelve pages to tell you that your car insurance has expired. I have ended a few meetings by quoting Shakespeare: "The first thing we do, let's kill all the lawyers."

The fact is, government could not work without good lawyers. And if you asked me to name one person whose work represents the law at its very best, I would tell you about Joe Rodriguez. Thoughtful, intense, and devoted to high principle, Joe has made a career out of fusing knowledge and respect for the law with social activism. That has lifted him to the pinnacle of his profession, a seat on the federal bench. Along the way he has broadened the rights of millions of Americans.

Joe is the son of immigrants, a fact he has never forgotten. His father, a Cuban, literally swam ashore near Atlantic City one evening in June 1918, a survivor of the U.S.S. *Carolina*, sunk off the coast of New Jersey by German U-boats. His mother, a native Puerto Rican, arrived in America a few years later. They fell in love, married, and became the first Hispanic family to settle in Camden.

Mario Rodriguez studied English in the kitchen of his Camden home. He got a job manufacturing cigars at the American Tobacco Company, where he worked for forty years. Mario's job brought home enough money so that nobody went hungry. The close-knit family became a magnet for other Hispanics moving to South Jersey. When a new family arrived, frightened by the unfamiliar, the Rodriguezes would take them to the doctor's or lawyer's office and explain their problems in English. Joe's mother founded what is now the only Hispanic Catholic church in Camden and his father kept the books for the local civic association. The Rodriguezes were so beloved, and their contribution so appreciated, that more than fifteen years after their tragic death in an automobile accident, the people of Camden still hold an annual ceremony in their memory.

Mario Rodriguez held to a few simple principles which he passed on to his son. "Be proud of your heritage," he told Joe, "but accept the fact that America is your home." He urged his son to make an extra effort to learn the culture and beliefs of the people who had been in this country longer. Above all, he insisted that young Joe master the English language. "Language can be your weapon," he said. "Learn to use it." And he insisted that no matter what career his son chose, he not just be ambitious for himself. "If you go into politics, be in it for others, not for yourself," Joe recalls his father saying. "We are very lucky to have such freedom and liberty. In return, we must share our gift with others who are not so fortunate."

When Joe began practicing law, there were only a few Hispanic lawyers in the state. With his father's words in mind, Joe began to get involved in legal and social organizations that had previously shut their doors to Hispanics. He acquired a reputation as a knowledgeable, savvy lawyer and won respect in his profession and the local community.

I first heard about Joe in 1971, when I was the young majority leader of the state assembly. Camden was rocked by three days of violence stemming from the alleged beating of a young Hispanic by city police officers. The city was in turmoil, with many Hispanics, including Joe's parents, taking to the streets to protest. They demanded justice. They loudly asserted that they were tired of a white establishment in the city that was racist and ignored their rights. Joe Rodriguez was one of the few people who was trusted by both sides in the conflict, and he was asked to mediate. Acting as an emissary between the Hispanic protesters and the mayor's office, he helped reduce tension and open city government to influence from the Hispanic community.

His trial by fire won Joe recognition throughout the state. In 1972, I was assembly speaker when Governor Cahill picked him to be the first Hispanic to head the state Board of Higher Education. In 1973, Governor Cahill named him to an even tougher job, director of the State Commission of Investigation (SCI).

The SCI was created by the legislature out of frustration. It was intended to be an agency that could investigate corruption inside and outside of government. Sponsoring the bill to create the commission in the assembly, I remember leading off the debate by saying that I hoped this finally would be an agency with the independence to attack organized crime and government corruption.

Joe was not shy in exercising this newly vested power. In fact, he moved with a speed and vigor unanticipated by the fledgling Byrne administration. He started a controversial investigation into the possible corruption that could grow out of the state's new casino industry in Atlantic City. He focused public attention not only on organized crime's potential role in the casinos themselves, but on businesses that relied on the casinos for their survival. He brought attention to the activities of one reputed mobster, and had his life threatened because of it. He probed corruption in municipal government and investigated state-run boarding homes, fraudulent charities, and abuse of the state Medicaid system. Even political heavyweights found there was no way they could slow the commission or its energetic chairman. Many of us cheered, but those accused of wrongdoing fought back with criticism. Joe stood his ground, arguing that the purpose of the SCI was not to be popular, but to do what was right.

When his tenure at SCI was over, Joe was elected president of the state bar association, the first Hispanic elected to that post. It was the ultimate symbol of his professional colleagues' respect for his integrity and ability.

His father would have been very proud of him. By the end of the 1970s, Joe had been at the center of a series of landmark cases that expanded the rights of individuals, not just in New Jersey but across the country. He brought the first suit to force suburbs to make more housing available to the poor. In the wake of the Karen Anne Quinlan case, he helped establish rules to govern the termination of a person's life-support system. He helped expand liability protection for millions of homeowners. He was part of the legal team that won a suit for a young boy who had been scalded in an improperly constructed bath tub.

I had met Joe and admired his work, but we had never really talked until I ran for governor in 1981. Shortly after I won the nomination, two mutual friends independently suggested that Joe and I get together. Both felt that he and I shared the same beliefs.

I agreed to the meeting out of respect for Joe. I wanted to get to know the man but foresaw no possible political advantage. Joe Rodriguez was a lifelong Democrat. His hometown was Camden, the center of Jim Florio's congressional district. Besides, it was early in the campaign and nobody gave me much of a chance. My best poll had me a good fifteen points behind Florio, so it would certainly not help Joe politically to support me.

When Joe and I met, I liked him immediately. And as we talked I realized that we shared a common vision for our state. Gradually, I got a glimmer of hope. I heard him say that Florio had done nothing to earn the support of the Hispanic community in the state. "In politics as in all else you should have to earn your support," he said. Just maybe, I thought, he and his friends will stay neutral.

A few days later I got a call. Joe promised to give me a public endorsement. That meant more to me than an article in the newspaper, because when Joe believes in something, he works for it.

His friends thought he was crazy. But for me and my campaign it was a real boost to gain the endorsement of a highly respected leader of a significant ethnic group. If a man like Joe could demonstrate independence because he believed in me, then it should be possible to persuade others. From that moment on, I believed I could confound the pollsters and win.

After the election, I wanted to make Joe a part of state government, not as a reward for his support, but because we shared common beliefs and because I knew his talents and integrity would contribute greatly to my administration. Because of his commitment to public service, I knew it would not be hard to lure him away from his lucrative law practice, as long as I offered the right job. I knew he would be a great governor's counsel or attorney general. I recognized that down the road he would make an able supreme court justice. In fact, he was my second choice a few years later when I appointed the first woman, Marie Garibaldi, to the New Jersey Supreme Court. But the more I talked to Joe, the more I realized that he was perfectly suited for another job, one that is unique to New Jersey state government.

The public advocate's office was created around the same time as the SCI, after the Watergate scandal, when a strong populist feeling swept the country. The public advocate, the people's lawyer, is a cabinet-level post unlike any other. The person in the office has the power to sue other cabinet members if he believes they are failing to carry out state laws or mandates. The advocate's job is, in fact, to give a voice to the voiceless and to stand up for the little guy against very powerful interests, including, at times, government itself. Joe Rodriguez' entire life had been spent preparing himself for that job. To be the public advocate was his definition of public service. I asked him to serve and he readily agreed.

Joe worked with his usual verve and spirit. He sued to keep the ocean beaches open to the poor. He saw to it that casino profits were invested in the local economy of Atlantic City. He sued on behalf of inmates in state institutions. I didn't agree with everything he did. Joe was the first to sue to question the constitutionality of the death penalty law. And I disagreed strongly with Joe's support of the *Mount Laurel* decision as the way to open the suburbs to more low-income housing.

But the more I got to know Joe, the more impressed I became with his respect for the law and for the system. His mental agility was admirable but what really inspired me was his heart. I became convinced that on his heart were inscribed two documents: the Constitution and the Bill of Rights.

I remember once asking him about the early days and whether his fellow Hispanics had criticized him for working within the system. "Of course," he said. "But I tell them to take a look at our flag. That flag means that this country works for everybody, that is the way it was set up, and you know what, my life proves it. You can always complain that you don't get what you are entitled to, but that is the easy way out. What's harder, but what really counts, is to work to make the system work for you, too." I concluded that Joe's attitude and respect for the law was just what was needed on the bench of our federal courts. When an opening occurred in the federal district court that covers New Jersey, Joe Rodriguez, despite his party affiliation, was my first choice. I let President Reagan know it. The Justice Department concurred, and Joe's name was submitted to the U.S. Senate.

I had no idea that Joe's nomination would create controversy. A few people in New Jersey on the extreme right wrote to the Senate Judiciary Committee about Joe's nomination. They noted that Joe was a registered Democrat and that as public advocate he had opposed the death penalty. Senators Orrin Hatch, Jeremiah Denton, and John East sent Joe an eight-page set of questions asking for his views on everything from school prayer and abortion to his belief in "the existence of a Supreme Being." As might have been expected, some of the more liberal members of the committee got hold of the questionnaire and released it to the press. Senators cried foul, arguing that ideological litmus tests should play no role in federal court appointments.

I called the chairman of the committee, Strom Thurmond, who said yes, there could be a problem. I was genuinely angered. I knew Joe Rodriguez to be an honorable man who would faithfully uphold the Constitution. He was certainly no ideologue or radical, but a gentleman of common sense, ability, and compassion. I was distressed that his judgeship could become a political football between right and left.

Hearings were held and the committee members saw what I already knew: Joe Rodriguez was an eminently capable and fair jurist. He responded to the conservatives' questions honestly and candidly. Some people would have trimmed their sails to get the post. Not Joe. He said it would be his duty as a judge to follow precedent and the guidance of higher courts and he would be faithful to that obligation.

I felt better when I talked to the conservatives about their impression after the hearing. I remember Orrin Hatch in particular saying, "Now that I have looked into it, this guy sounds like a pretty good man." Strom Thurmond went so far as to say Joe was a great candidate. Joe's nomination was approved unanimously, and I was able to stand by his side while he took the oath of office. Again, Joe had proved in his own way that if you work hard and stick to your guns, the system works. A few months after assuming his post, this immigrant's son was swearing in new Americans in the very same courtroom where his father had taken his oath of citizenship fifty years before. Now Joe's daughter, also a lawyer, is carrying on the responsible fight for social change.

☆

Hsu, Coleman, Rodriguez. Many people in our state have never heard of them. All three struggled to overcome obstacles which in the end strengthened personal character. Joe, Ming, and Len are all successful. They are paid decently for what really is interesting work, though each would earn much, much more in the private sector. Each has given back so much to New Jersey and America.

I strongly believe that everyone in our country owes a debt for the privilege of living in a democracy. Not everyone can be a Joe or Ming or Len, but they can contribute. They can serve on a school board or a PTA. They can help with a charity or work for a worthy candidate. Everybody has an obligation to do something. On this point, my father was right.

And let me make one final point about the three people who serve with me. It is very important that successful members of minority groups be placed in top government jobs. People identify with people like themselves and with their success. It is proof that democracy works, that anyone, regardless of background, can make it, can serve.

The truth is that blacks, Hispanics, and women in business are not that visible. In general, the only people who know about the talents of a particular black or woman corporate vice-president are the people in that company. In government, it is different. When a young Hispanic sees Joe Rodriguez behind that bench, he knows the law works not only for the Anglo, but for him, too. The Chinese community across the country is very aware of Ming Hsu. The highest-ranking Chinese woman in American government is known in Chinatown in San Francisco and in the Chinese community in New York.

That kind of visibility is important. Every group of Americans needs to become convinced that if you want to get involved in government in a democracy you can do it. It is especially important for people who are Hispanic or black. A Len Coleman or a Joe Rodriguez is a great example of what somebody can do, that our system has no cap. Some would say this is only tokenism, but it's not. A symbolic individual matters. It's the reason I push so hard to put black teachers in the schools and colleges and minorities on the bench. Without role models, life is much tougher. Without them, it is much easier to give up and blame the system.

Something else: Too often people view government as an impersonal monolith, staffed by those heartless, dull people called bureaucrats. That's unfair and untrue. Some of the finest people I have ever met have chosen public service as a career. They care very much, even while governors get a lot of credit for their work. When I see the latest poll says that 80 percent of the state's people think I'm doing a good job as governor, I'm grateful. But also responsible are Ming and Joe and Len— and Carl and Greg and Mike and Ed and Brenda—all the fine people who are our government.

And the day people like them shun government we are all in trouble. If you don't have good people in investment banking, well, that's not so good but we will survive. But if you don't attract good people to run the democracy, the system is imperiled. In my state and in our country, we have had times in which public service fell into disrepute. We can't afford another. We've got to make public service something that people aspire to. We've got to make sure that there are many, many good people willing to govern our country two and three decades from now. John Adams said nearly two hundred years ago that "as soon as the public business ceases to be the chief business of the citizen, the nation will fail."

7
Four Decisions

GOVERNORS decide. It's the way we make a living. Painters paint, writers write, sailors sail, but governors make decisions. Being a governor is thus not like being in Congress. Members of Congress are judged by their words and their voting records; governors, by their actions. For a governor, problems cannot be simply debated; they must be solved. Mario Cuomo says it's the difference between prose and poetry. Legislators can do the poetry; we must do the prose. Pete Du Pont made the distinction clearly at my first governors' conference. "When I was in Congress," he said, "I worked six years on a financial-disclosure bill. I believed disclosure was important to restore public confidence in the aftermath of Watergate. Sometimes I got the bill out of committee, but there was always another obstacle that blocked approval. Ten minutes after I was sworn in as governor, I signed an executive order. Everybody disclosed." Another former congressman put it this way: "In Congress, I spent all my time trying to get on the front page. As governor, I spend my time trying to stay off it."

Some of the decisions governors make matter to only a very few people, like an appointment to a professional board or agency. Others can immediately make a difference in the lives of 7 million people, like putting your signature on mandatory seatbelt legislation.

A lot of times we get blamed for things we shouldn't. President Reagan tells the story about the radio comedian he heard who liked to pick on mothers-in-law. "But everyone needs a mother-in-law," the comedian added, "because you can't blame the governor for everything." I remember once when the state public television network, whose board I appoint, decided to discontinue a program called *The Uncle Floyd*

Show. Uncle Floyd was a clown famous for zany antics, mismatched clothing, and bad ventriloquism. His program had a small but devoted band of followers, who were determined to use every source of pressure at their disposal to revive Uncle Floyd's imperiled television· career. My office was flooded with letters asking me to reinstate the clown. People even picketed my house demanding the same thing. The next day I flew to Washington, where Massachusetts governor Mike Dukakis and I were on a national C-Span call-in show. We expected calls on welfare reform, education, or some other national issue. Instead, the third caller getting through asked me if I was going to save Uncle Floyd. Mike Dukakis couldn't believe it. But I explained to the caller that my job did not include second-guessing the programming decisions of the public television station. The fact is that sometimes the issues that governors think important are not always the most important in the minds of our constituents.

Saying that all governors make decisions does not mean we make decisions in the same way. Just as John Updike doesn't write like Saul Bellow, there is a world of difference between the decision-making style of a Tom Kean and a Mario Cuomo. By examining that style closely, I think you can come to know a lot about a governor and a lot about how effective he or she is in the job.

I want to share with you the story of four highly visible decisions I made as governor of New Jersey. Two were made when I was still struggling to find my feet, and the other two after my administration was on the ground and running. Two of the decisions involved appointments of officials to important offices; the two others involved deeply personal, moral questions. Taken together, the four actions should give you an idea of how I approach making any decision and the philosophy that underlies my approach to governing.

☆

Early in my tenure, I was faced with deciding whether to reinstate the state's death penalty. This is one of the most difficult moral issues confronting public officials, especially a governor. The governor is the person who receives the late-night calls from the American Civil Liberties Union (ACLU), or from an attorney for a convicted killer, asking for a stay or commutation. For a governor, the issue means voluntarily taking on life-or-death decisions. So your position had better be thought through.

The death penalty in New Jersey dates from Colonial times, when it was mandatory in all murder cases. Not until the end of the nineteenth century was it amended to allow some discretion based upon the nature of the crime. In the late 1960s, a then-obscure New Jersey superior court judge named Brendan Byrne first overturned the law on procedural grounds. The U.S. Supreme Court upheld that decision several years later. Shortly thereafter, the Supreme Court ruled, in the famous *Furman* case, that the death penalty in thirty-nine states, including New Jersey, constituted "cruel and unusual punishment."

Nevertheless, overturning the death penalty offended the basic sense of justice among many law-abiding citizens, who were growing increasingly afraid to walk their neighborhood streets. More and more, it seemed, the law was tilted toward the criminal, not the decent citizen. As the 1970s went on, support for a new death penalty grew stronger. One incident in particular crystalized New Jersey public opinion. A man ruthlessly shot and killed two police officers after ordering them to undress at gunpoint. A death sentence in the case was denied. Public outrage followed.

Meanwhile, twice during the 1970s, a majority of New Jerseyans voted in nonbinding, public referendums to reinstate the death penalty. Brendan Byrne was by then governor, but his feelings did not shift with public opinion. He twice vetoed new death-penalty laws that had passed the legislature with strong support. Once Governor Byrne left office, it was clear the legislature would not wait long to present his successor with the same difficult question.

In 1967, I was asked about the death penalty at candidate forums during my first run for the assembly. I believed then, as I believe now, that the protection of the physical security of the citizenry is the first duty of a responsible government. Cicero believed that, as did Madison, Hamilton, and Jay when they collaborated to explain the Constitution to former colonists in *The Federalist Papers*. Anyone who takes the responsibility seriously has to take a close look at the death penalty. I did. Early in my political career, I opposed it, on the grounds that one should not take another human life under any circumstances.

My opinion changed in the early 1970s. That was not because of some epiphany, but rather a slow and nagging revulsion at the rising crime rate that was threatening more and more of my constituents. Moreover, the court system was no longer working the way any responsible person would want it to. Rarely is justice in America dispensed quickly and with an even hand. Victims are often treated impersonally, while the criminal is given every courtesy. Criminals are released from prison early, after having learned to become better at their work. The violent are back on the streets to commit even more violent crimes. I felt that because of the obvious shortcomings of the criminal justice system, we needed every possible deterrent, especially to murder, rape, and other outrages.

I know that the deterrent effect of a death penalty is questioned. Rates of violent crime or murder differ little between states that have a death penalty and those that do not. Yet I looked beyond the theories and statistics of criminologists to my own experience. I thought back to conversations I had with city teenagers at Brantwood Camp. These were decent kids, but they lived a tough life. At thirteen or fourteen they had already been on the streets for years, fully schooled in some of life's most unsavory lessons.

One thing they knew a lot about was crime. Some of them had already been arrested. Others had listened as older brothers or friends bragged about holding up liquor stores or busting into the change machines at laundromats. I remember one talk I had about crime with an especially tough kid. He said, "Don't tell me that kids don't know about the law. I know exactly what will happen if I rob a store. I know exactly what penalty I face as a juvenile if I shoot the owner and kill him. I can tell you how I should behave in court, the length of sentence a kid my age usually gets, and the chance of getting convicted. You have to know these things to survive." He then told me a harrowing story of a neighborhood gang that had robbed a drugstore for money and drugs. They made a decision to kill the owner on the spot so there would be no witnesses. This kid's cousin was given the gun and told to pull the trigger. The reason? He was a juvenile with no record. Thus, even if caught he would be subject to less than a year in jail. These street kids knew the odds. First, chances were they would not be caught without a witness. Second, if caught, chances were they would not be convicted. And even on the small chance of conviction, one of them would probably only spend a short time in jail. I asked the kid what he would have done if there had been a death penalty. His answer: "Hell, man, nobody wants to fool with that!"

I decided a death penalty was necessary. The statistics here don't lie; the death penalty is not a deterrent in every case or even most cases of murder. But it might deter some people in a few cases, and that is hard to ignore. Say somebody goes out to rob a store one night in Newark. He knows that if he shoots the owner there will be no witness to his crime. But if for a second in the back of his mind he understands that if he pulls the trigger he may lose his own life, he may not squeeze. So even if the death penalty saves just one innocent life, that is justification enough for having the law on the books. As speaker and later as minority leader, I fought for the death penalty in the assembly. The issue also became a prominent part of the Republican platform during my gubernatorial campaigns.

My support for the death penalty did not exactly make me a maverick in the Republican party, because the overwhelming majority of Republicans supported my position. When the question came up in primary political debates, the candidates responded in pro forma fashion. I remember one debate held in Princeton during the 1981 primary. The moderator asked each Republican candidate to give a one-minute summary of his position on the issue. Down the line we went, from Mayor Pat Kramer to Bo Sullivan to me. All of us somberly said that we were absolutely disgusted at the violent crime rate and that we steadfastly supported the death penalty as one part of the solution.

Last to speak was a long-shot candidate, a colorful fellow from Newark named Tony Imperiale. Tony had been the one independent elected when I won the speakership in the divided legislature back in 1971. He held a black belt in karate, and law and order was his raison d'être. He had risen to prominence in Newark politics after the riots, winning the support of white ethnics by arguing that it was time to get tough with the hippies, radicals, blacks, and other practitioners of civil disobedience. The rugged former policeman struck a responsive chord in many people tired of the violence and chaos. To his supporters, mostly white, Tony was like John Wayne, a symbol of justice and action. To his detractors, mostly black, he was a vigilante.

Obviously, Tony supported the death penalty. When the moderator put the question to Tony, he chose not to simply echo his Republican rivals. Instead, he stared at the studio audience, then pointed toward us and said, "I want you to think hard about which one of us is the toughest on crime. Tonight, when this debate is over, it's going to be dark out. Many of you will have to walk across a dark parking lot to your car. Who would you want walking beside you in case a mugger attacked? Pat Kramer? Tom Kean? I think you want Tony." The audience cracked up.

Once I was elected governor, the legislature wasted no time passing new death-penalty legislation. The new bill incorporated the criteria that had been laid out by the U. S. Supreme Court in its landmark 1972 decision. Murder would now be the only crime that could produce the death penalty; the question of guilt or innocence had to be determined separately from the question of death penalty or imprisonment; the jury had to conclude that the murder in question was especially heinous, and then weigh that against a circumstance like mental illness.

The bill reached my desk late in March, barely three months after I had been sworn in. Bill signings are usually an occasion for hoopla and congratulations, and I usually invite the bill's sponsors and interested citizens to a public ceremony in front of the State House press corps. Various speakers compete to extol the virtues of the legislation and the character of the legislators who helped create it.

The death penalty was different. I signed the bill alone, in the privacy of my office. The signing represented a grave step we were taking as a state. I took no pleasure in it. I felt, instead, that it was something we had to do if we were going to save a few innocent lives.

Public reaction was predictable: support from most people, condemnation from a few, the latter led by the self-proclaimed guardians of the public conscience. Editorial reaction was mixed. Only the reaction from the black community surprised me. Throughout, black elected officials had been almost unanimous in their opposition to the bill. I had expected the same from the black community. Instead, I received widespread support. Blacks, after all, are the people who suffer most from violent crime, a fact politicians sometimes forget. Accordingly, the black community strongly supports tougher laws and stronger enforcement and they will back politicians dedicated to making neighborhoods safer.

As I signed the New Jersey law, my friend Chuck Robb, then governor of Virginia, was going through the pain of deciding the final appeal of an inmate on death row. I thought of the time down the road when that terrible decision would be mine. I knew I would have to make any decision on what I saw as the merits of the case and the record of the trial. After the bill was signed, another five years passed before the New Jersey Supreme Court decided that the new death penalty was constitutional. As I write, I have yet to be faced with Chuck Robb's ordeal. It will come before I leave office, of that I am sure. I am ready.

☆

The death penalty was the first highly visible policy decision of the administration. This decision was followed within a month by another, unexpected one of equally high visibility, but much more enjoyable. I had the rare opportunity to appoint a member of the U.S. Senate.

The circumstances surrounding the appointment were unusual. In February 1980, the press broke the story of a controversial FBI investigation called Abscam, in which a number of public officials were alleged to have accepted bribes from a phony Arab sheikh. Several New Jersey officials were alleged to be involved—which further besmirched the state's already tarnished reputation. Nine months later, the FBI indicted New Jersey's senior senator, Harrison Williams, for allegedly using his position to help the sheikh invest in New Jersey casinos and a titanium mine in Virginia. One year after indictment, Senator Williams was convicted on nine felony counts.

At the time of the indictment, Williams was being mentioned as a possible nominee for governor. The speculation, of course, stopped immediately, and the question became whether the senator would be forced to leave office before his term expired in the fall of 1982.

The related question was, if Senator Williams left, would the choice of his successor fall to a governor from the opposite party? On the day of my inauguration, outgoing governor Byrne carried an envelope with the name of a prominent Democrat in it, in case the senator resigned before Byrne officially left office. Williams did not. The irony was clear to longtime observers of New Jersey politics. Here was the son of Congressman Robert Kean, now in a position to appoint the person to replace the man who had denied his father a Senate seat twenty-three years before.

Senator Williams finally resigned on March 11, 1982, almost a full nine months before the expiration of his term and in the face of almost certain expulsion by his colleagues. Before he resigned, I had made a simple decision not to rush the choice of his successor. I had some people in mind for the job, but I wanted to know everything I could about any possible candidate.

Meanwhile, Republicans were already in the middle of a hotly contested primary to determine who would be the party's Senate candidate for the full term in the fall. The announced contenders were Millicent Fenwick and Jeff Bell, two very talented people whom I liked as friends and admired as public servants. Jeff was one of the two or three people most responsible for convincing me that supply-side economics would work in New Jersey. Millicent and I had been friends since our congressional race eight years before. I felt she had done a great job representing her district and the state in Congress. A number of other close friends of mine were thinking about entering the race for the Senate seat, and might be interested in an interim appointment. Congressman Jim Courter in particular came to mind. He had chaired my campaign in 1981. A Senate appointment might give Jim a leg up if he decided to jump into the race for the full term.

Of course, I had to consider the political implications of any choice I made. I could pick one of the announced candidates for the Senate seat, giving that person an advantage with the voters in the primary and the general election. I could leave the seat open for the three months until the primary election in June and appoint the Republican winner to serve through the summer. The ensuing visibility would still give that Republican an edge in the general election.

The third option was to ignore all announced or potential candidates and appoint a "caretaker," someone who would serve the remaining eight months of Williams' term and then give way to the newly elected senator. Even here I had many choices. I thought briefly of appointing the honorary chairman of my campaign, Cliff Case, who had served New Jersey in the Senate for twenty-four years. But Senator Case passed away only a week after Senator Williams resigned. Some people argued that I should use the appointment to reward a stalwart for service to the Republican party. By that line of thinking, several elder statesmen qualified, including former governor William Cahill; Bern Shanley, who had lost to my father in the 1958 senate primary; Webb Todd, former Republican party chairman who had ably shepherded the party through some of its darkest hours; and Peter Frelinghuysen, who had held the congressional seat that I had lost to Millicent Fenwick. Moreover, several of the younger Republican faithful were quite capable of making a mark in Washington. My old assembly mate Phil Kaltenbacher had agreed to take over as chairman of the state Republican party; former Paterson mayor Pat Kramer, whom I had defeated in the primary, was out of a political job; and, several women lobbied me to make national waves by appointing a talented young attorney named Marie Garibaldi.

The possibilities seemed endless. Not wanting to make a hasty decision, I decided instead to solicit advice from as many people as possible and to let both prospective candidates and their supporters lobby me directly on the merits of their appointment. I wanted to go slow in making my decision about my contribution to the most august legislative body in the world.

Mine was a risky strategy, and it didn't meet with approval from all quarters. Some people strongly suggested that the most prudent course would have been to interview and evaluate candidates before Senator Williams resigned, thus avoiding the deluge of suitors. Joe Sullivan, the venerable State House reporter for the *New York Times*, wrote in a front-page story the day of Williams' resignation that my lack of predetermination was "an invitation to the large field of those who would be Senator to increase their lobbying efforts. In this situation, Mr. Kean cannot help but make one person happy and bruise a number of egos."

I felt differently—that I needed to move slowly to allow good people to come forward. Making a decision as early as January, of course, would have been unseemly, because no one was sure that Williams was going to resign. Right up to the last minute there was a possibility that he was going to stay in the Senate and fight expulsion. Had he waited until he was expelled, the affair could have dragged on for months, perhaps even until November. Pete Williams was our senator until he said he wanted to step down or his colleagues expelled him, and I felt he should not have to worry about my appointing his successor while he still held office.

Within a week after Williams' resignation, however, I had a list of at least fifty people who warranted consideration, and began the process of narrowing the field. In the end, it was the state's and not the Republican party's interest I wanted to keep uppermost.

I decided that it made no sense for me to try to determine the outcome of the Republican primary. Jeff and Millicent were both people I had enormous respect for, and I couldn't choose between them. In any case, I believed that the situation called for the voters to choose, without the subtle or not-so-subtle influence of another elected official.

By the same token, I decided to rule out the appointment of any sitting representatives. In other circumstances my decision might have been different. But it made no sense to take a sitting Republican member of the House and appoint that person a U. S. Senator when there were two other Republican candidates actively opposing each other in a Republican primary.

But I also concluded that I could not afford to keep the seat open until after the Republican primary. The federal budget was then being put together, and major decisions were being made about spending priorities. We needed someone with clout to fight for programs that were important to New Jersey. The Senate Banking and Urban Affairs Committee had an open seat, for example, and a close vote was expected about whether to continue the Urban Development Action Grant (UDAG) program that provides help to cities. The new senator's vote could make the difference in the life of the program and could bring millions to New Jersey cities. Waiting until June would have put political advantage over the best interests of the state. I really couldn't do that.

I concluded that I had a chance to test a theory that went to the heart of my belief about democratic government. I've long been a believer in the Jeffersonian ideal of the part-time legislator, a person, accomplished in a world outside politics, who chooses to devote some time and talent to serving his fellow man by holding public office. After rendering service, the person returns to his chosen livelihood. I ran for the assembly with that sense of things, and my career has constantly moved back and forth between government service and private enterprise.

In our time, I worry that we have lost an appreciation for the Jeffersonian ideal. More and more, the only people in public service are ones who have made politics the only thing they do. Service in the U. S. Senate or House of Representatives is now a full-time job. Only on the state and municipal level is the citizen legislator that Jefferson envisioned still at work.

I have always felt that it is very hard to keep the public interest uppermost when your professional survival depends upon your reelection. At times you must do what is immediately unpopular in order to protect the long-term interests of the people you serve. Edmund Burke said it best: "Your representative owes you, not his industry only, but his judgment; and he betrays you instead of serving you if he sacrifices it to your opinion." Many public servants today fully exercise their best judgment, even if it flies in the face of constituency opinion; many others, unfortunately, cannot.

In particular I worry about the new breed of politicians, mostly lawyers who have never held a job outside the public realm. For them, the private sector presents no alternative. The new professional legislator, it seems to me, is blind to the experience of people outside of government, and is not only more susceptible to the pleas of special interests, but also more likely to use his or her office for private gain.

Many learned people consider the idea of a part-time Congress to be quaintly anachronistic. Issues, they say, are much too complex to master if a member can work on them only four or five months out of the year. Moreover, constituents' demands are much too great to satisfy on a part-time basis. I understand the objections. But as a state official, watching in frustration year after year as the federal government ducks major issues or conducts the same debate on the same issues, I cannot help but wonder if Congress' obsession with its own work has gone well beyond the point of diminishing returns. Moreover, most members sit in office too long. I feel the democracy would be well served by a limit of twelve years of service in the House and eighteen years in the Senate. Life is different away from the banks of the Potomac, and the professional legislator should experience it.

In the spring of 1982, I decided to look for someone who personified Jefferson's theory of the citizen legislator in the modern age. I wanted someone who was a national leader in a field of endeavor, the kind of whom others said, "It would be great if that person could hold public office." I wanted someone who had participated in politics, and yet had never run for office because of the time it took or the excess of publicity it generated.

I found precisely that person in my old friend Nick Brady, chairman of the board of the investment house Dillon, Read. I had known Nick since he was a teenager. He had attended St. Mark's six years before me, and was a friend of my brother. Moreover, Nick had impeccable credentials for the job. He had a brilliant intellect, having graduated near the top of his class at Yale and at the Harvard Business School. He was also respected on Wall Street, and knew every major player in the nation's financial community. On top of that, he was politically astute. One of George Bush's best friends, Nick had played a major role in the vice-president's unsuccessful presidential campaign in 1980. Nick had been gracious enough to serve as co-chairman of the transition team I had appointed to help me move smoothly into the governor's chair. Finally, he was respected in Washington, having as many contacts in power circles there as anyone in New Jersey.

About a month after Senator Williams stepped down, I met with Nick and asked if he would take the interim appointment. I told no one else of my decision. Nick said he was flattered, but he couldn't accept. He was worried about the myriad financial-disclosure statements he would have to prepare, and about the effect of leaving his business.

I was extremely disappointed, but determined to get Nick to reconsider. I had learned in government that when you find the right person you often have to persuade him or her to take the job. I asked Nick to call people he knew for advice. And from all over the country came the words, "Take it." So said the then White House chief of staff Jim Baker, who was traveling with the president in the Caribbean. Vice-President Bush weighed in. George Schultz called from California. Everyone who talked to Nick made the same argument: you just don't turn down an appointment to the U. S. Senate. Still, Nick was reluctant.

At the same time, of course, public speculation about who the next U. S. senator was going to be grew. Hardly a day passed without a newspaper making a guess. Most reporters had their own lists down to five to ten people who were under final consideration. No one, even my closest adviser, knew that I had picked Nick Brady. Only Nick and I knew that I had made my choice and that he had said no.

Even so, our secret did not stay one for long. Joe Sullivan of the *New York Times* broke the story, and to this day I still don't know how he did it. Maybe one of the people Nick called mentioned it to a reporter in Washington. More likely, though, it was good old-fashioned reporting. Joe probably called everyone on his short list and asked them if they were talking to Tom Kean about being senator. Perhaps everyone said no except Nick Brady, who refused to return his calls. Or maybe Joe simply guessed that Nick was the choice. So, while I was frantically calling every friend of Nick's I knew to persuade him to accept, Joe Sullivan was probably trying to convince his skeptical editors to run a story that Governor Kean was in fact going to appoint the Far Hills investment banker as U. S. senator.

The appointment story appeared on the *Times* front page on Friday, April 9, twenty-seven days after Williams resigned and one day after Nick had told me he wasn't interested. Joe Sullivan noted in the story that neither Nick nor I had confirmed the report, but he said that two other candidates had confirmed that Nick was the choice. I was nonplused. I felt sorry for Joe Sullivan. He was a diligent, thorough reporter who was out on a shaky limb. I suspected that on Monday I would simply have to face the press and say the *Times* was wrong and the appointment was going to someone else.

Maybe it was the pressure of the *Times* story, but I suspect Nick had been convinced to change his mind by my arguments and by those of his friends. In any case, he called and told me he would take the post and serve for eight months. But he made it very, very clear to me that he had no further interest in elective office, and that when his term ended he would return to his business. Nick Brady's appointment was applauded by Republicans, members of the press, and citizens alike. In the end, by refusing to rush things and to get involved in the Republican primary, and by choosing a caretaker with impeccable credentials, I had defused any potential ill will that might have been created by a Senate appointment. A few egos may have been hurt, but none was badly bruised. The state's interest and its collective ego were served.

I still find that I could not have made a better choice. Nick Brady carved out a unique place for himself in the Senate. He was recognized accurately as someone who was there to do nothing but the public good and who was utterly without personal political ambition. And his access always amazed me. New Jersey got things from the Reagan administration that had been impossible to obtain through Democratic senators Bradley and Williams. Moreover, Nick developed a reputation as one of the most thoughtful and candid observers of the Senate as an institution. He spoke out frequently about the problems plaguing the body and slowing its work. And when he talked, other senators listened intently. They recognized his objectivity and admired the way he could get to the roots of the body's ills so quickly.

I remember the day Nick asked me to Washington to have lunch with Republican senators. The agenda was the budget deficit. How serious was it and what should the Republican position be? I was surprised that again and again they turned to the freshman senator from New Jersey for his thoughts. In an incredibly short time he had become a well-liked and respected member of the club. His contacts and friendship made in those few months are still helpful to me and to the state of New Jersey.

I cannot leave the story of this decision without noting that the Republicans lost the Senate seat in the fall election. Millicent Fenwick, who defeated Jeff Bell in the Republican primary, began the campaign with a huge lead over a relatively obscure computer magnate named Frank Lautenberg. As summer turned to fall, her lead began to narrow. The rapidly slowing economy, her own refusal to accept PAC money, and Frank Lautenberg's relentless and well-financed campaign combined to produce perhaps the biggest upset of the 1982 campaign season. A few pundits looked back and speculated that things might have been different if I had appointed Mrs. Fenwick to the Senate seat in June. Yes, the speculation was warranted, but no, I would not have done things differently. It was the right thing to do.

☆

The Brady appointment was, overall, a political home run. The decision made party regulars, pundits, and good-government types very happy. Four years later I made another high-profile appointment. This one was far more controversial.

The issue was whether to reappoint the chief justice of the New Jersey Supreme Court, Robert Wilentz, who had first been appointed by Governor Byrne in 1979. Under the New Jersey constitution, a supreme court justice is appointed for seven years. If he serves competently during that time, he can gain tenure until he retires at seventy. Chief Justice Wilentz was fifty-nine. Therefore, my decision on his reappointment would in large part shape the conduct of the New Jersey Supreme Court for the next eleven years.

Since the new state constitution was adopted in 1947, governors have attempted in every instance to fill the court with respected jurists and to maintain, if not an ideological, at least a political balance. The state constitution requires that six spots on the seven-member court be divided equally between Republicans and Democrats. The chief justice runs the entire New Jersey court system and is immensely powerful.

Under ordinary circumstances, Bob Wilentz's renomination would not have posed a difficult decision. The chief justice was widely regarded as one of the most intelligent and able jurists ever in New Jersey. Wilentz was the scion of one of the most prominent Democratic families in the state. His father, David T. Wilentz, was a friend of my father. David Wilentz had served as attorney general and successfully prosecuted Bruno Hauptmann in the highly publicized Lindbergh kidnapping case in the 1930s. Robert had attended Harvard and then graduated from Columbia Law School, where he was a Harlan Fiske Stone scholar.

Robert Wilentz was serving in the assembly when I was first elected in 1967. He was a senior member of the other party, but extremely independent. I was impressed by his intellect and his self-assurance. We quickly became friends and I looked to him for guidance on a number of complex issues, particularly state education policy. Wilentz left the legislature in 1969 because the body had passed a conflict-of-interest bill that would bar lawyer-legislators or their partners from appearing before state agencies for several years after they left office. At the time, Bob had just assumed added responsibilities in his father's law firm, and thought the new law would hurt the firm's business. A measure of the strength of the man's character and his integrity was that Bob

Wilentz did not fight the new law when it was presented before the assembly. Instead, he voted for it and then, when it passed, left government. Here was belief in principle clearly triumphing over political ambition.

As chief justice, Wilentz had served admirably. His only weakness was that he was at times perceived as arrogant. True he did not suffer fools gladly and had little patience with some members of the legal profession. But the quality of his writing and opinions and research were superb, and his demeanor was appropriate to the office. Meanwhile, the court had adequately shouldered its administrative burden under his leadership. Judicial scholars were in virtually complete agreement that Robert Wilentz deserved reappointment. The state bar association publicly endorsed him.

Many members of the Republican party did not see things that way. To them, the issue was not Wilentz's competence as a member of the judiciary, but his ideology and his political affiliation. These Republicans argued that it was time for a Republican governor to remake the court in favor of his party. What's more, they saw in Wilentz the same kind of activist jurist and "liberal demonology" that national conservatives had seen in former chief justice Earl Warren and, more recently, in California chief justice Rose Bird.

Two cases in particular epitomized the kind of judicial activism and social engineering that Republicans, quite rightly, abhorred. The first was the social host liability case. In it, the court, under Wilentz's leadership, ruled that anyone in New Jersey who holds a party and serves alcoholic beverages is responsible for the behavior of any intoxicated guests. The more infamous and incendiary decision involved state housing policy. Designated *Mount Laurel II*, its impact could be felt by virtually every New Jerseyan and its significance reached far beyond our state's borders.

New Jersey is a state of contrasts, and nowhere is the contrast greater than between the noisy, crowded cities and the quiet, comfortable, and sometimes posh suburbs. Walk along some city streets and you will still see empty tenements, dilapidated housing, street corners populated by nothing but winos and young drug pushers—undeniable evidence of some of the worst urban decay in America. Yet less than a thirty-minute drive away, you can see the beginnings of long, winding driveways leading to the homes of some of America's most powerful corporate leaders.

By the end of the 1960s, many people, myself included, were troubled by the disparity between the wealthy suburbs and certain very poor cities. Some people felt that the historically strong instruments of home rule, particularly local zoning laws, were being used to keep minority and poor people out of the suburbs and locked in the cities. In 1972, the local chapter of the NAACP sued the then sleepy South Jersey suburb of Mount Laurel, which at that time had neither a post office nor a main street, arguing that its exclusionary zoning policies violated the state's constitution.

In 1975, the state supreme court, under Chief Justice and former governor Richard Hughes, handed down the original Mount Laurel ruling. Basically agreeing with the NAACP's contention, Hughes said that if communities retain the power to zone to protect the general welfare, any use of that power to subvert the general welfare is prohibited. Therefore, the use of zoning laws to restrict home ownership in a particular community to people with high incomes is unconstitutional.

Mount Laurel was praised by advocates for the poor as a courageous step that helped to move the state toward real equality. It was vociferously condemned by conservatives as social engineering on a scale never imagined by Marx or Engels. The practical effect was negligible because the interpretation of the law was as muddy as swamp water. While decrying exclusionary zoning, the court had offered no remedies. The decision remained a topic of debate among legal scholars across the country, but was of relatively minor significance to builders, town officials, or poor people.

Chief Justice Wilentz pulled *Mount Laurel* from the rarified air of theory into the rougher arena of practical politics in 1982, with the *Mount Laurel II* decision. In it, Wilentz, supported by a unanimous court, upheld the rationale of the Hughes decision and went several steps further. He ordered communities to revise their zoning ordinances to allow construction of a specific number of low- and moderate-income housing units. He then appointed three full-time judges and gave each the power to oversee implementation of the program in geographical thirds of the state. If a town refused to alter its zoning practices in a way the court thought proper, the court would allow what it called builder's remedies, under which a developer would be permitted to build more houses on the property than the zoning ordinance allowed, as long as the developer agreed to include in the project a certain number of low- and moderate-income dwellings. The builder's remedy was seen by the court as a carrot to get the powerful building industry behind the push for more housing in the suburbs. But the remedy ran roughshod over any local control.

Mount Laurel II exploded in the state like a giant hand grenade. Officials from every small town and suburb came to Trenton complaining that three judges were trying to make housing policy for every community in the state, and that generations of local planning were being overturned. This for me was clearly an instance of judicial activism at its worst. An unrestrained court had stomped on the toes of the executive and legislative branches of government.

I disagree with the decisions reached in both the host-liability and the *Mount Laurel II* cases. The former was just a good idea carried too far. The latter was a more serious dereliction of judicial responsibility. Certainly the court has a strong role to play in individual instances of housing discrimination. If people respond to an ad for a house or apartment and find they cannot buy or rent it because of their racial or ethnic background, they should have speedy legal recourse and the penalties should be harsh. But the idea that a court is going to lay down a law telling people where they are going to live is ludicrous, and smacks of judicial dictatorship. *Mount Laurel II* illustrated precisely what was wrong with judicial activism in general. How can a court possibly enforce this kind of social engineering? Such lofty decisions come to virtually nothing in practice. Invariably they clog the courts with expensive and needless litigation, while the lawyers benefit and the poor people get little or nothing in return.

If you want to change something like housing policy on a broad scale, you have to work through local governments or the state legislature. The court is impotent to act, because judges are in no way prepared to take over the functions of planners and local zoning boards. Among other things, they do not have hands-on knowledge of what areas in a community are environmentally sensitive. In any case, after the ruling, almost everyone was immediately suing everyone else. Builders eager to develop sued towns all over the state. Taxpayer sued taxpayer. The public advocate, funded by the public, sued various towns, whose defense was also paid for by the public. Builders thundered that unless they could build on this wetland or on the edge of that park they would sue under *Mount Laurel*. Builders often received concessions to forestall litigation, and so they built high-income condominiums but little if any low-income housing. Meanwhile, planning at the local level became impossible.

I deplored the chaos the court had created. I even publicly supported a constitutional amendment to remove the court's power in the area. But I always knew that, when the time came, no matter how much I disagreed with his individual decisions, I would reappoint the chief justice. The issue in my eyes was not *Mount Laurel*, but judicial independence.

The principle I was siding with is as old as our country itself. The Founding Fathers crafted a separation of powers precisely to prevent one branch of government from dominating the others. Judicial independence is a principle that is especially important in New Jersey. We don't elect judges. We never have, because we have tried to insulate them as much as possible from the caprices of public opinion and political pressure. Whenever I go into other states and talk to people worried about the courts, they always say that New Jersey may have the best judiciary in the country. I don't think you can have the best judiciary in the country without guaranteeing its independence.

Judges have to be totally free to make up their minds on a particular case. They should not have to think how their opinion will affect next year's election or even their reappointment. They should simply view the facts of the case and interpret the law. Accordingly, there has not been a judge since the constitution was adopted in New Jersey who has been denied reappointment based on court opinions or political beliefs. The day that happens, the New Jersey judiciary will be undermined. And I was not going to be party to any such event.

The principle of judicial independence always deserves defense, but mine was certainly not politically popular, especially with rank-and-file Republicans. I tried to explain to them that I was trying to prevent the destruction of an independent judiciary. Say I put a strong conservative on the bench, I asked them to assume. The next governor is a liberal and cannot wait to get rid of him. Or worse, the judge feels that if he rules a particular way, his reappointment will be reassured. To me, that is the easiest way to ensure a weak and obsequious judiciary and upset the delicate balance of power that makes democracy work.

My explanations fell on deaf ears. Three months before Chief Justice Wilentz's term was scheduled to expire, leading Republicans in the state senate mobilized a campaign to convince me to deny him reappointment, and they mailed letters to some ten thousand party activists. Because I didn't want a partisan campaign centered on the court, I let the press know early that I planned to reappoint the chief justice.

The reaction was predictable, if a little different than I had grown used to. Usually friendly Republican senators became critical. One,

Pete Garibaldi, announced that he might block the nomination by invoking an archaic practice called senatorial courtesy, under which a senator is allowed to "sign off" on any nomination from his home county. Meanwhile, my traditional antagonists, the Democrats, joined in rare approval of my decision. One said the reappointment belonged in *Profiles in Courage*.

I figured I could handle the angry Republicans. Many of the senators were also members of the bar, and they understood the importance of judicial independence. Most were privately very supportive. So once Senator Garibaldi's procedural roadblock was overridden, I expected smooth sailing for the reappointment. After all, the senate was controlled by Democrats who would be deeply embarrassed if the renomination was denied. Some spirited and vocal opposition would be heard, but eventually I thought the chief justice would be reconfirmed with thirty or thirty-five votes in the forty-member body.

Again I was wrong. The issue became not the chief justice's judicial philosophy, but where he slept at night. During his confirmation hearings, Justice Wilentz admitted that he had bought an apartment in New York in the early 1970s. Recently he had been spending an average of six nights a week in his apartment in Manhattan, and only one night a week in his home across the river in Perth Amboy, New Jersey. The reason? His wife had been diagnosed as having cancer and he needed to live in New York to be close to her treatment center. Understandably, the chief justice had decided to stay as close as possible to his wife during a difficult time.

Wilentz's honest admission of a very personal problem showed his candor and self-confidence. But it touched a nerve always raw throughout New Jersey's history. In other states, the question of a chief justice's residency under the circumstances might not have been a major issue. In New Jersey, it was political dynamite. Wilentz's saying he spent a lot of time in New York proved that beneath the patina of new pride lay a two hundred-year-old case of insecurity. To have the chief justice live outside the state was bad enough. But in Manhattan! To listen to some senators, one got the impression that it was grounds for impeachment.

Sadly, few senators seemed moved by Wilentz's reasons for living in Manhattan. Personal compassion finished a poor second to a parochial need to stand up and defend New Jersey. Almost overnight the mood in the senate shifted. Republicans who opposed Wilentz on ideological grounds now picked up allies in both parties who thought it was utterly embarrassing to have the state's chief judge living in another state.

The full senate took up the renomination question on the evening of July 31, 1986. I had just returned from a governors' conference and had stopped for the night to see my family on Fishers Island. But I stayed in constant contact with the State House as the debate proceeded. After six hours, it became clear that the vote was going to be much closer than I imagined. Nevertheless, I was still supremely confident that the nomination would pass. I knew the Democrats could not afford to let it fail. I also figured the leadership had a few votes in reserve, ready to switch if it became necessary. Bob Wilentz did not share my confidence. That evening I received an urgent call from the chief justice. The senate had recessed with the vote at twenty to eighteen with two senators undecided. Wilentz told me he thought his renomination was in deep trouble and needed my immediate intervention. I told him I was not worried about the eventual outcome, but that I would do what I could. I called the respective party leaders. The message was the same from the Democratic senate president and the Republican minority leader. Any hope of gaining the needed vote rested with some resolution of the residency issue. The wavering senators had doubts about whether New Jersey's chief justice would ever return to the state. A bill had been introduced in the legislature to force judges to live in the state, but there was no assurance that I would sign it or that the chief justice would abide by it.

I called Wilentz back. I asked him to agree to two things. First, if his wife's condition changed, he would move back to New Jersey. "Yes," he said, "that is my plan." Second, I asked him what he would do if I signed legislation requiring all judges to live in the state. "As long as it is constitutional," he said, "I would abide by the law." Armed with that, I called the senate leadership. The twenty-first vote was obtained and Wilentz was confirmed.

Some senators cried foul, and said that I had violated the separation of powers by interceding when a debate was raging on the senate floor. That was nonsense. Any governor or president has the right to fight for his nominees. I had never had a major appointment rebuffed by the senate and I was not going to start with the chief justice. In the end, I knew some would never forgive me for the reappointment. But I upheld the principle of the independence of the judiciary, something that will matter long after my term in office has expired.

After the Wilentz renomination, I did some thinking about the principle of the independent judiciary and how it ought to apply in the 1980s. I understand the movement toward a more conservative judiciary, because I believe that courts in the late 1960s and 1970s made some unfortunate decisions. Nevertheless, it makes me very nervous when candidates for the bench are required to respond to questionnaires or when they are given the third degree by the Justice Department or Congress.

Luckily, the practice doesn't have the effect intended. People are human, and once they get on the court they may change their minds on any number of issues. The history of the U. S. Supreme Court shows that presidents who thought they were appointing conservatives ended up getting liberals and vice versa. Once I had dinner with a reporter who had interviewed Dwight Eisenhower shortly before he left office. "Mr. President," he remembers saying, "in spite of all your other accomplishments, some of us believe you will go down in history as the man who appointed Earl Warren as Chief Justice." The famous grin vanished. "My God," said Ike, "I certainly hope not."

☆

The last decision I want to talk about was undoubtedly the most visible and sensitive of my first term: the decision to divest the state pension funds from firms that do business in South Africa. The choice involved a complex web of morality, economics, and politics. In the end, its significance reverberated from California to Cape Town.

Timing is everything in politics, and the bill reached my desk at the most sensitive time possible, in late June of 1985. In five months I was to face the voters for reelection. In the year preceding the bill's passage, events in South Africa had deteriorated and news about the country had moved from the foreign affairs page to page one. Americans grew familiar with pass laws and places like Johannesburg and Pretoria. Meanwhile, the Reagan policy of "constructive engagement" was being questioned publicly every day. In South Africa, violence and bloodshed were escalating and the Botha regime became increasingly defensive. I had two months, until the legislature reconvened in August, to decide whether to sign the bill, conditionally veto it, or veto it completely. While I pondered, the pressure mounted.

The bill, sponsored by Assemblyman Willie Brown of Newark, would be the most far-reaching state divestment law in the nation. It would require the complete divestment of all state pension fund money within three years in any company that had a loosely defined business presence in South Africa. At the time, eight states had already taken action against the South African government, but only three had opted for total divestiture. The rest had decided to divest only in those companies which did not abide by the "Sullivan principles," a series of guidelines to increase the employment and preferential treatment of black workers. But the three states were small potatoes compared to New Jersey. Our pension portfolio, worth at the time approximately $10 billion, was the forty-second largest in the country. Our pension division estimated that as much as $2 billion of the money was invested in either stocks or bonds of companies doing business in South Africa. In other words, our portfolio was ten times larger than that of Massachusetts, which had chosen to divest in 1983. Clearly, our decision would be watched by other states as well as by major companies, the financial markets, and even the Botha government.

My strategy was the familiar one. I took my time and sought counsel from people on both sides of the issue. The business community's position was obvious; they were opposed to the bill. I had been a pro-business governor and had spent a great amount of time trying to send a signal that New Jersey was the kind of state that went the extra mile to make businesses feel at home. Many times during my administration I had turned to some of our largest companies for help with my programs. Merck & Co. had played an integral role in education reform. Johnson & Johnson had donated an enormous amount of time and money to the management-improvement program during my first year in office. Both companies were trying to make a difference in South Africa. They were sincere, as were other New Jersey companies that did business in South Africa. All had signed the Sullivan principles, and they were actively recruiting black workers and helping with economic development and housing in black communities. I spent time talking with their representatives. But I noticed that the companies sent the usual community or legislative relations people. No chief executive officer came to discuss the issue.

I also sought the opinion of the public employee unions. After all, it was their pension money that was at stake, and I took my fiduciary responsibilities seriously. Because most government workers do not earn a great deal in their careers, the pension they receive from the state is often their only means of support in retirement. Under my tenure the pension fund had been earning a high return on investment. At times in New Jersey's past, politics had tainted pension decisions, and I didn't want that to happen again. Moreover, I disagreed with some of the bill's supporters who confidently predicted that we wouldn't lose a penny if we divested. To me, it only made mathematical sense that if our investment advisers had fewer stocks to chose from, they would not make as much money. Our best preliminary estimate was that total divestment could cause the pension system to lose up to $100 million over the next three years.

I told the union leadership not to ask me to sign the bill unless they were ready to absorb a loss of this magnitude. The unions took a selfless stance. With the notable exception of the New Jersey Education Association (NJEA), they chose to put the moral imperative of making a statement against apartheid above the interests of their pocketbooks. Al Wurf, of the American Federation of State, County, and Municipal Employees (AFSCME), leader and veteran of a thousand union battles, was the most articulate. He assured me that the union members would accept any potential damage to their pensions in return for sending a clear and unequivocal signal to a repugnant government that enshrined racism and attempted to subjugate an entire people on the basis of skin color.

Word also came from people in the White House, who did not like the approach I was taking. Politically, they were worried about the effect of the Republican governor of a large industrial state opposing them on a high-profile issue. This was months before the Republican Senate, led by Senator Richard Lugar, would rebuff the White House and replace the policy of constructive engagement with harsher sanctions. In the summer of 1985, the White House was still arguing that constructive engagement needed more time to work. Some White House officials also suggested that it was not the state's role to "meddle" in foreign policy.

Finally, I turned to a number of New Jersey community leaders who saw in apartheid the most profound moral issue of our time. I met with leaders of the religious community, particularly the black ministers. As I listened to those who had visited South Africa describe apartheid, how it robbed individuals of human decency and freedom, I thought back to my own childhood experience and the sense of outrage that I had felt as a young man on the fringes of the civil rights movement.

I also recalled growing up in Washington during the late 1940s, when our nation's capital had its own form of apartheid. I remembered my father's anger when a friend had come from New Jersey to see him on congressional business. They went out to lunch, only to be turned away from two restaurants because my father's friend was "colored." I remembered the nation's shame when the Daughters of the American Revolution denied Marian Anderson permission to sing in their Constitution Hall. I remembered as if it were yesterday my own feelings when my friends were turned away from a movie in downtown Washington because one of the seven boys with us was black. The manager of the theater, a large man with a bulbous nose, told us, "The coloreds have their own theater." I remembered as a graduate student at Columbia working at the first Northern chapter of the SCLC in an old Harlem storefront on 125th Street. Black friends and co-workers talked about the subtle vestiges of slavery that still undercut their basic human dignity. I listened and I thought about the fundamental assumptions of our Judeo-Christian tradition and about the writings of Thomas Jefferson and the dream of Martin Luther King, Jr.

On all sides I heard arguments that were thoughtful and deserved careful consideration. The problem facing me was complicated. I could veto the bill completely and argue that it was not a state's business to get involved in foreign policy. Or I could send the bill back to the legislature with a conditional veto, asking that we divest only from those companies that had not signed the Sullivan principles. This, the course I was most likely to pursue, would still allow us to make one of the strongest statements yet against apartheid and protect the interests of many good New Jersey companies. Yet as I pondered one of the more difficult decisions of my term, I changed my mind because of the actions taken by a man I had never met, who lived halfway around the world in a country I had never visited.

On August 15, P. W. Botha decided to respond to his international critics who demanded a change in his government's policies toward blacks in South Africa. Earlier in the summer he had declared martial law. From June to August the world had implored him to drop the order. Western governments, including that of the United States, had also urged him to take significant steps toward the ultimate goal of franchise and economic justice for black South Africans. They wanted, too, an end to the infamous pass laws and the release of the imprisoned black leader Nelson Mandela. Hopeful Western leaders looked for Botha's speech to provide the first concessions to the black majority. But P. W. Botha defiantly told the world to stay out of South Africa's business, offering not a glimmer of hope that things would change. With arrogance and belligerence he clearly implied that the racism and subjugation were going to continue: "I am not prepared to lead white South Africans and other minority groups on a road to abdication and suicide. . . . We have never given in to outside demands and we are not going to do so. South Africa's problems will be solved by South Africans and not foreigners. We are not going to be deterred from doing what we think best nor will we be forced into a position of doing what we don't want to do."

As I watched and listened to Botha that night, I concluded that any action other than complete and total divestiture would be morally indefensible. New Jersey had to speak out. Our state had to end the Reagan administration's tacit endorsement of "business as usual" in South Africa.

At the press conference announcing the decision, I tried to answer each of the objections I had heard over the course of two months. I made it clear that the action was not aimed at the companies which do business in South Africa, but at the behavior of the South African government. To those who argued that a state had no business meddling in foreign affairs and that New Jersey should not politicize fiduciary decisions, I said: "This is a profoundly moral issue—one so compelling that the economic arguments against divestiture, no matter how persuasive they may be in some kind of fiscal sense, pale in comparison to the moral imperative of working at every level to end apartheid. . . . There are instances in human history when the gravity of an evil is so clear, and the cost of its continuance so great, that government—at every level—must use every tool at its disposal to combat it."

At the same time, I didn't want to wring my hands, wash them of the issue, and then walk away from it. So I asked the legislature for a companion bill that would permit the state to reinvest pension funds in companies that continued to do business in South Africa, if the country should take significant steps to end apartheid. I felt the bill gave us the flexibility we needed to react to possible developments over the long term.

When I signed the divestment bill the next week, the reaction was immediate. The business community was disappointed and angered. Some within it argued they would stay in South Africa to support their black employees. A few reacted as if my decision had been aimed specifically at them. But in general my action was well received. Many ordinary people, both white and black, felt that we had taken a clear stand on a moral problem that required personal sacrifice. The *Trenton Times* summed up the response by saying, "New Jersey has every reason to be proud of its Governor. . . ."

In retrospect, I believe a couple of things were noteworthy about the decision. First, I know New Jersey's leadership influenced others. Since our divestment, General Motors, IBM, and Coca-Cola have pulled out of South Africa and other states have come around to total divestiture. The federal government has also changed its position. Bishop Desmond Tutu himself has told me that everywhere he goes, both here in the United States and abroad, people are aware of what New Jersey did and support it.

Second, I believe the state has lost money because of the divestment decision. How much is almost impossible to calculate. We sold many blue chip stocks that powered much of Wall Street's rally in the first eight months of 1987. Yet the public employee unions have remained staunch supporters of divestment, standing behind the moral statement all the way.

As for events in South Africa, there has been no progress since New Jersey divested. In many ways, things have gotten worse. As I write, the Botha government seems to have become more secretive while recent elections show increased minority white support for even more oppression.

Some look at these developments and conclude that divestment has backfired, arguing that by divesting we have lost all leverage to move the South African government toward desired change. But this only echoes the arguments that used to be made by apologists in the Old South. Then as now, we must ask the question: Just how long do we have to tiptoe around a problem before justice is served? For twenty years we accepted business as usual in South Africa and apartheid stood triumphant. What we desperately need, and what we don't have, is a coherent policy of the United States toward apartheid. The federal government needs to work with the states and every major corporation in a coordinated, long-term approach to the problem. But that is not happening. We are missing an opportunity; the stakes are high and the time is short.

President Reagan says proudly, "America is great because America is good." He is right. He's right about the source of American power, and it's been that way since the beginning. During the nineteenth century,

Americans supported "freedom fighters" in countries like France, Poland, and Italy; they found friends in America because their cause was ours: democracy is incompatible with racism or dictatorship. In the 1860s, Lincoln's antislavery crusade was applauded around the world; later, Woodrow Wilson was believed when he asserted that the United States helped to fight the war to make the world "safe for democracy." Our decision to resist Nazi Germany and imperial Japan had its roots in very special beliefs about our place in the world. And after both world wars, these same beliefs led the American people to support Herbert Hoover's feeding of Europe's thousands of hungry and Harry Truman's Marshall Plan.

In the 1960s, the vision of John F. Kennedy and Martin Luther King received moral endorsement around the world. Why? Because at our best we do hold up a torch of liberty for everyone. As Herman Melville wrote, "We Americans are the peculiar chosen people—the Israel of our time—we bear the ark of liberties of the world."

My father taught me that. In 1943, a time when too many Americans wanted to turn away, he rose on the floor of Congress and condemned the Nazi atrocities against the Jewish people. Forty years later, I was invited by the Israeli government to watch a sacred candle be rekindled in my father's honor at Yad Vashem, the Israeli memorial to the Jews murdered during the Holocaust, located outside Jerusalem.

After the ceremony honoring my father, I was taken through the Yad Vashem museum, a cold, foreboding place, by Gideon Hausner, the man who prosecuted Adolf Eichmann. Gideon showed me the record of the years leading up to the Holocaust: the early anti-Semitic statements; the horrible cartoons filled with awkward humor laced with hate; the written restrictions on where Jews could live, where they could work, and how they could practice their faith.

Returning to my hotel room, I got a surprise visit from a Jewish refusenik who had just left the Soviet Union and was a close friend of a refusenik I had recently "adopted," Boris Klotz. When a prominent American official takes responsibility for a refusenik, the chances increase that he will be treated well and even let out. Boris Klotz's friend told me what life was like for Boris Klotz in Russia—how Boris's children could only attend certain schools, how his family could not practice their religion, and how Boris could only apply for certain jobs. As I listened, the terrible parallels became obvious. After that conversation, I worked for four years until Boris Klotz and his family were finally allowed to leave the Soviet Union. We met in Washington and, at Boris' request, I adopted two more refuseniks. The entire adventure reminded me of what my father had said in Congress in the 1940s: we in this nation have a special responsibility. Whether it is the Soviet Union, South Africa, Afghanistan or Nicaragua, we must always be there when other human beings are robbed of their freedoms and their dignity. If we in the United States are not vigilant in defense of freedom and liberty, no one else will be.

☆

I have talked about just four decisions out of the thousands I have made during my tenure as governor. They may be remembered longer than others, but they show my mode of operation. First, I actively encourage a diversity of opinion among my staff and advisers. In other words, I like disagreements to emerge and I want them clarified as various recommendations are brought before me. If people feel strongly about something, I want to hear the arguments pro and con myself. If someone disagrees with a position I am likely to take, I want to know why. The only time I get really upset is when I learn that I was not given all the information before I made a decision. In other words, I don't want yes-people working for me.

If there is a weakness here it is like Hamlet's. Like him, I tend to be "sicklied o'er with the pale cast of thought." Once in a while I will ponder a decision to death. On those occassions, I have to close the door to my office, sit down, and decide. That's when a governor's job become lonely. You can't hide behind the vote of a fellow legislator or your own rhetoric. If you choose to sign the divestment legislation, then you take the credit—and the blame.

Second, I believe there are times when you have to put aside politics and everything else, and simply do what is right for the state. It may involve the reappointment of a chief justice; more likely it will mean vetoing a popular but unconstitutional school-prayer bill or pinning down the site for a toxic waste incinerator. I don't like to settle for short-term advantage and convenience, because I believe that voters deserve a long-range perspective. An independent judiciary, for example, is good for New Jersey. On occasions like these, you simply tell your political friends that you can't be with them on the issue.

Third, I believe that governors cannot afford the comfort provided by an absolute devotion to any ideology. One has to have basic principles, to be sure. I, for one, feel that the private sector should be allowed as much freedom to do what it wants as possible. But government must provide the level playing field, to help people starting out or people unable to make it through no fault of their own. I believe in these basic principles and apply them to various situations as I encounter them.

In politics, I feel that Emerson was right when he wrote that "a foolish consistency is the hobgoblin of little minds." Because facts and circumstances change, an open mind is essential. The death penalty is one example. Another is highway safety. I don't believe government ought to tell people how to behave in their private lives. So I always opposed mandatory seat belt laws. In 1982, parents' organizations and the State Police confronted me with some statistics. They showed me a study, by the federal Department of Transportation, stating that 10,000 lives a year could be saved if 70 percent of Americans were to wear seat belts. In this case the opportunity to save a human life overrode my reservations about government intrusion into private behavior. I signed the second mandatory seat belt law in the nation.

Three months after I signed the legislation, I got a letter from a woman in Irvington. She told me that when I first signed the seat belt law she felt "angry and violated" that her rights had been taken away. Her attitude changed when she got into an accident on the Garden State Parkway. Her jeep tipped over. Because she was wearing a seat belt, she only sustained cuts and bruises and a slight concussion. "If you had not signed that law, my seat belt would not have been used," she wrote. "Thanks for saving my life."

I went through the same process with teenage drinking. I believe that most eighteen- or nineteen-year-olds are responsible. We count on them to defend us in war and most can handle the responsibilities of an adult. But the statistics about young people who are drinking and driving can't be ignored. I changed my mind on the issue and raised the drinking age. As a result of this and other measures, teenage deaths on the highways have been cut by almost 50 percent. I have deep respect for public officials who are willing constantly to ponder and probe their beliefs and conclusions, and I respect those who have the strength to change their minds.

I am not saying that politicians should be totally open all the time to all manner of viewpoints or to every shift in public opinion. But I do believe that the general public will respect you if you change your mind forthrightly and explain why you changed it. In the end, the public is the final judge and the public is much more aware and enlightened than most sophisticated political observers realize.

8

The Education Governor

I once had a conversation with a black businessman who owned and ran a chain of successful grocery stores. He had grown up in a rough inner-city neighborhood and was one of the few lucky enough to make his way out. Now he wanted to give other black teenagers a chance to do the same. So he went back into his old neighborhood to offer good jobs in his stores. He was swamped with applications from kids who didn't want to live off public assistance or have to sell drugs for a living. They wanted to work. The businessman interviewed the kids, and asked two questions. First, if oranges are four for a dollar, how much does one orange cost? And second, if a woman buys $8.40 worth of groceries and gives you a $20 bill, how much change do you give her? Two out of three kids he asked couldn't answer either question, and the businessman had to send them away. It tore him apart, he told me. He knew what happened to kids in the ghetto who couldn't find work. He asked me, "How long are we going to tolerate this? How long are we going to let our children pay the price for our failure?"

Those two questions go to the core of my worry about our country's future. The same two questions prey on the minds of millions of Americans as the next century approaches. Our urban schools furnish the most egregious examples of failure, but a pervasive feeling exists that things are far from right in schools all over, from the cities to the suburbs to the rural towns. Critics include business leaders, who will soon spend $25 billion a year to teach basic reading and arithmetic skills to new workers. They include the armed services, which report that one quarter of new recruits cannot read basic safety instructions. Most important, they include mothers and fathers, who are afraid that their children may be the first generation in our history to get a poorer education than their parents.

Out of this worry has grown an education reform movement. From Maine to Hawaii, business leaders, college presidents, teachers, school board members, and political leaders have gone to work to improve the American school. The stakes are high. Success or failure may well determine our country's future and the way our children will live.

I have been part of the reform movement, viewing the problem as a member of the most distinguished policy commissions, and getting another perspective in countless hours spent with teachers and students. Because of my background as a teacher, I had thought about education for twenty years before I became governor. So when I assumed office, the issue naturally became my top priority. Only a few months after the release of the federal government's heavily publicized *A Nation at Risk* report in 1983, I called the New Jersey legislature together in a rare joint session to lay out a comprehensive blueprint to improve the state's schools. Virtually every part of that blueprint has been put in place. As New Jersey's reputation as an education leader grew, I shared my ideas with other states and in turn brought good ideas back to New Jersey.

I spent a year talking to teachers across the country as chairman of the Education Commission of the States. I also headed a panel on teaching for the National Governors' Association, and I was the only sitting Governor invited to serve on the distinguished Carnegie Task Force on Teaching as a Profession. Accordingly, I had the chance to work with an eclectic group of thinkers; the erudite John Gardner, secretary of health, education and welfare under President Eisenhower and the founder of Common Cause; Bill Honig, the witty iconoclast who has single-handedly made education the priority issue in California; Al Shanker, the head of the American Federation of Teachers, who has emerged as a sort of elder statesman of the reform movement; and Secretary of Education Bill Bennett, the controversial gadfly who has done much to shake the education establishment out of its complacency. Working with them, and listening to thousands of teachers and students, I have developed some ideas about schools and how they work.

Here I want to share my views on three important questions: Why must education become the most important domestic priority for the next twenty years? What have we learned so far to improve the schools? And what more must we do? Of course, I don't pretend to have all the answers, but I hope I can add some reasonably clear thinking to an issue that sometimes lacks clarity for political leaders.

Before I share my thoughts, let me tell you about my own education. A governor's thoughts about education, or anything else, reflect his own experiences. With me, the observation here applies doubly because I have spent my life in and out of classrooms as both teacher and student.

My own education was very much in the tradition of the English public school. My father did not like the schools found in Washington. So, at the age of twelve, I found myself shipped off, against my will, to a boarding school in Southborough, Massachusetts. My father had attended the same St. Mark's some forty years earlier. I guess he believed what had been good for him would be good for me. As I saw my parents disappear down the long school drive, I realized I was going to spend the next six years where I was left standing. I didn't know a soul, student or teacher.

The school consisted of two buildings. One housed the dormitory for two hundred students, the classrooms, and the headmaster's living quarters. The other was the gymnasium. Unless you played hockey, you could spend January and February indoors, which was often advisable in the woods of New England.

St. Mark's put a lot of emphasis on building character. The Christian athlete was the ideal: somebody who prayed on his knees in the morning and excelled on the football field in the afternoon. We prayed together every morning and then had chapel every afternoon. On Sundays we dressed in blue suits for mandatory church services at ten in the morning and again for another service at five in the afternoon. Students who were especially devout awoke early on the Sabbath for the Holy Eucharist, at 7:00 A.M. Popularity, at least in the younger classes, depended on some sort of success in football, baseball, or hockey. I wasn't very good at any of them.

Meanwhile, all of us lived in a spartan manner. Boys lived in alcoves, which consisted of basically two walls, one bureau, and a bed. A long corridor down the middle of the building separated the alcoves from each other. This was our world. Three years passed before I was allowed to leave school for a weekend.

Discipline was strict. If a student misbehaved, he was sentenced to spend Wednesday and Saturday afternoons shoveling coal into the school's

furnace. My usual sins were an inveterate tardiness and a messiness that tended to make my room look a little like a Jackson Pollock painting. So I spent my first eight weekends at school shoveling coal. It was awful. Only in the most extreme winter blizzard were we spared the coal pile, when we were punished by having to copy page after page of the *Congressional Record*. Here is where I first began to question the value of congressional debate.

Seniority was a large part of the St. Mark's tradition. The first-termers lived in constant fear of the older students. Seniors had the power to inflict any form of discipline, including paddling in extreme cases. About an hour after bedtime you would hear the slapping of paddles along the dormitory wall and a voice would yell out your name in the darkness. You would emerge in your pajamas from your alcove and be taken off to be whacked by the seniors. The experience was to be avoided at all costs.

So old boys terrorized new boys. The worst tradition was something called Bloody Sunday, which was held the first Sunday of the school year, when most of us were still confused and homesick. New boys were given twenty minutes to hide in the woods, after which the old boys would try to find us. Dire consequences were promised to anyone who was caught, because the old boys spent a great deal of time developing ingenious forms of torture for the captives. On Bloody Sunday, I hadn't yet made any friends, so I went off alone, while most of the boys hid in pairs. I lay shivering in the damp woods for hours but was never found. I thought I had passed a great test of manhood, until a few days later I realized that my secluded lair had been lined with poison ivy.

The curriculum was grounded in the classics. Three or four years of Latin and French were required, and courses in religion were part of each year's study. We became steeped in the King James Bible and the Cranmer Book of Common Prayer. Study halls were mandatory during any free period and from 5:00 to 6:00 and 7:00 to 9:15 at night. During study hall, you sat at your desk under the watchful eye of a member of the faculty and did your homework. Daydreaming was a disciplinary offense. I can still remember being yelled at in front of the whole school because I had committed the great sin of looking up for too long from the book I was studying.

It was a rough environment for a twelve-year-old who had never been away from home for very long. I was miserable for the first two years. I had few friends. I was not a good student or a good athlete. I was confused and lonely. Small kindnesses took on great importance.

Latin was my worst subject. Dean Towner, the young Latin teacher, took the time to give me extra help. Sensing that Latin was not my only problem, he would invite me to his room to have a cup of tea and talk. His guidance, along with that of William Gaccon, another splendid teacher and human being, helped get me through those early years.

St. Mark's had attracted an extraordinary faculty, people who cared greatly about their students. One was Fred Ulen. I had been in school about four years and was doing unusually well in his English course. Up to that time, I had been content with C's in the subject; with Mr. Ulen making English literature come alive, I was suddenly getting A's and B's. Then one day, about two-thirds of the way through the year, he announced that the rest of the term would be spent on poetry, which I had never liked or understood. I worried that the rest of the term would be boring and that I would get low grades. I guess something in the way I carried myself must have betrayed my thoughts, because Mr. Ulen asked me to stay after class. After some prodding on his part, I told him about my fears. For the next few weeks, he made a point of working with me. During free periods we met and talked about Shakespeare's sonnets or Pope's and Dryden's couplets. We explored the beauty of Shelley and Keats, and Mr. Ulen imparted to me a love of poetry that has lasted to this day. Never again did I settle for anything less than a B in any English course.

Not all the lessons were easy ones. I remember a tough math teacher named Roland Sawyer. One day we had a test. We were asked to write the answers only on one sheet of paper, and I knew I had gotten all of them right. I looked forward confidently to the next class. When Mr. Sawyer handed the tests back, I was crushed. Instead of 100, I had gotten a 50. His explanation: I had copied down both the questions and the answers. "Next time," Mr. Sawyer said, "follow directions." I left class mad as hell, but I never again forgot to read and listen to directions carefully. St. Mark's was not pleasant, but I learned. Teachers made the difference.

As the years went on, I gained confidence. I grew to love the chapel, where I gained a faith that sustains me even now. The school was small so that I knew every student at least by face and name. I made close friends. I became a class officer and even an athlete of sorts, graduating with four varsity letters.

When I returned to St. Mark's as a teacher, I found a better school than the one I had left. The student body was more diverse. Paddling and Bloody Sunday had been done away with. But the school kept many of the great teachers. I worked long hours in my first teaching year, sometimes keeping barely a period ahead of my students. I loved the work. Nothing can compare with the excitement you feel when you see that first glimmer of understanding in a student's eyes or when you find out that after the bell rings the kids want to stay and finish the discussion. Once the headmaster had confidence in a teacher, that teacher had almost unlimited freedom in the classroom. One year in my early European history course I was allowed to set aside over two months for reading the *Iliad* in translation. I wanted the students not just to read this great work of literature, but to understand the relationship between literature and history. I did the same thing in another class with Dickens.

Every Monday night all the school's teachers would meet with the headmaster. We would hash over school problems and how we might do a better job. Then we would talk about individual boys who were not doing well. We tried to share what we knew about students' emotional problems. Maybe there was a problem at home or perhaps other students were picking on a boy. Maybe a boy who was having trouble reading was also having trouble hitting a baseball; glasses would solve both problems. My point is, teaching was a complete team effort. If there was a way to help a student, we would find it.

I have never worked harder in my life. Besides teaching, I coached two sports, was faculty adviser to the school newspaper, started a photography magazine, and, with a brilliant young English teacher named Jay Engel, started an evening club to discuss the great philosophers. As if this weren't enough, I advised both the student council and the senior class. The job took seven days a week.

To leave teaching was the hardest decision I have ever made. Yet I knew I had to get some credentials if I was to pursue the profession the rest of my life. So I forced myself to make the break and applied to Columbia University to enter in the fall semester of 1963. The class of 1962 at St. Mark's dedicated their yearbook to me and gave me a standing ovation at graduation. Anyone who has ever been a teacher will understand the lump in my throat that day. Twenty-five years later, as governor of New Jersey, I joined the class of 1962 for their twenty-fifth reunion. They told me their twenty-five-year gift would be to start a fund, in my name, to bring noted public servants to the school.

I still miss the classroom. Teaching is the only job I have ever had that can compare to being governor of a great state. You feel good knowing that your infant nutrition program is keeping babies healthy or your transportation program is putting people back to work. But it still doesn't beat getting a letter from a former student telling you that something you did made a difference in his life.

Obviously, St. Mark's was unlike most public schools in a number of ways. But in all good schools there are certain common elements. In order to teach well, a teacher needs discipline. Without it, even the best teacher is bound to fail. And teachers' creativity must be encouraged, not stifled. They must also have some say in the running of the school. A collegial relationship between administrator and teacher is essential to good education. Finally, the curriculum must be built on the fundamentals—English and math are the basics, but also important are science, history, language, and arts. Until these are mastered, further education is impossible. All of this we had at St. Mark's, and all of it contributed to my own education. John Kennedy said that every American should want for all children what they want for their own children. I see no reason why what is good in a St. Mark's education shouldn't be integral to every public school.

☆

The fall of 1962 found me enrolled at Columbia University, preparing for a lifetime of teaching. During the next two years, I earned my master's and completed almost all the course work for my Ph.D. Along the way I took courses that I didn't like but that were necessary for my teaching certification. Many seemed to have little or no relationship to the teacher's job in the classroom. Far too much time was wasted in required courses like The Psychology of Education, sometimes taught by a man or woman who hadn't been inside a school classroom for fifteen or twenty years.

Perhaps it was my Brantwood experience that made me aware of another problem. The Teachers College faculty talked endlessly about the good schools on Long Island with which they had formed relationships, and where most of the student teaching was done. Meanwhile, only a few blocks from Columbia was one of the most troubled schools in Harlem. You could not walk those few blocks without being solicited by drug dealers or prostitutes. So far as I could find out, there was little or no relationship between Columbia Teachers College and that Harlem school.

It was easy to see what was wrong. My classmates were among the best teachers in the country, idealistic young women and men dedicated to education. Often in the evenings we talked about why we wanted a master's or a doctorate. One young woman said she had been teaching in the city for five years, and was threatened a number of times by students and physically attacked once. The school administration treated the violence as routine. Her degree, she told me, would be a ticket out of the city, to a good school in a safe suburb on Long Island. She wouldn't have to worry about being mugged, and the pay was higher. How sad, I thought. We desperately need good teachers in our cities to deal with our most troubled young people. And yet here was a great teacher who was leaving the city for the suburbs. Our society works by incentives, yet in education they pointed in the wrong direction.

After I left Columbia and was elected to the state legislature, education, along with conservation, became my chief legislative interest. I lobbied for and won a seat on the assembly's education committee. Within a year, I was chairman. It was a time of intellectual ferment in education, because a huge influx of children was pouring into the schools, and teachers were in short supply. Meanwhile, educators were calling for a move away from the basic curriculum and for new programs to allow students to realize what was regarded as more of their innate creativity. "Access" and "equality" were the big themes, as colleges and universities lowered standards to allow in more students. High school students were given almost unlimited choice in curriculum, which naturally included frill courses. Homework assignments became less frequent. And in some schools, walls between classrooms were torn down, to create what was thought to be a more open and relaxed learning environment.

It was a time of grand and good intentions and big mistakes. In Newark after the riots, for example, a great hue and cry went up that the children were somehow being cheated because schools had few minority administrators. The response was to immediately hire a number of minority administrators, many of whom had no qualifications; these people have stayed in the school system for two decades. Change is now their enemy and a threat to their jobs. In other words, Newark's children suffer because the school system contains too many people who care more about protecting their jobs than educating kids.

The schools were being buffeted by the same winds roaring through the rest of society. On one level, schools are the most conservative institution, utterly resistant to change. On another, they reflect nearly everything going on in the world around them. So the social turbulence of the Sixties naturally became part of the classroom. Codes of discipline disintegrated as student activists demanded full freedom of expression, while teachers and principals, in extreme cases, were forced to carry weapons. In general, the settled convictions about education seemed to have vanished overnight. Often the new ideas sweeping through the schools meant that everything new was not only permissible but good. Educational therapists of various sorts and students felt a new freedom to experiment, as hundreds of years of experience were set aside.

In New Jersey, what was going on in the classroom was often obscured by what was perceived to be a more important question: who was going to pay for it? By the mid-1970s, most New Jerseyans concluded that property taxes alone could not support good schools, especially in the cities. But many legislators thought that if the state was going to pay for education, they ought to have some control over it. So along with the income tax, New Jersey passed a sweeping new education law. This time the state established a complex, centrally controlled, and almost quantitative definition of "educational quality." Things got even worse. As more attention was paid to the bureaucratic definition of quality, less and less attention was being paid to what was actually going on in the classrooms.

By 1981, when I ran for governor, disillusionment with the schools was widespread. On the campaign trail, of course, you hear a lot of complaints, because people don't hesitate to tell you what they feel is wrong. Teachers complained that the state cared more about paperwork than about children, and many parents, as I said, felt strongly that their children were not getting as good an education as they themselves had received. That startled me. Our country had made great progress politically, economically, and technologically. The suggestion that education, the underpinning of all of the improvement, had gone backward really made me wonder how long the advance in other areas could continue.

I was not alone. Governors in other states were hearing the same complaints. Lamar Alexander in Tennessee, Chuck Robb in Virginia, Jim Hunt in North Carolina, Dick Riley in South Carolina—all realized that the access and equality of the Sixties and Seventies had been purchased at the expense of quality. Governors had to fight to put the emphasis back on quality.

Education has always been a political enterprise. That fact is the source of some of its problems, but fewer than you might suppose. There is no subject more important, more worthy of the attention of political leaders at any level. The idea that good schools will cure society's ills is quintessentially American. In his farewell address, George Washington gave primary importance to the promotion of "institutions for the general diffusion of knowledge." Thomas Jefferson argued that "no other sure foundation can be devised for the preservation of freedom and happiness" than good schools. John Adams said that educating the poor was more important to society than the wealth of all the richest citizens.

And as long as Americans have had schools, there have been people who have wanted to reform them. Beginning with Horace Mann's crusade for public high schools in Massachusetts in the middle of the nineteenth century, American education has constantly responded to pressures for change. The most memorable outburst of reform in my lifetime followed the launch of the first artificial satellite, Sputnik I, by the Soviets in 1957. In the United States, government, industry, and education then joined forces to promote programs in science and technology.

Today's reform movement stems from the same basic motives that spurred Jefferson and Mann and later John Dewey—with one difference. The circumstances of our modern world have put even greater pressure on the schools. Today, American education can't be just good; it has to be great. Never has the link between education and the economy been clearer or more compelling.

As everybody knows, we have lost a great many blue collar jobs. No longer do we make cars, textiles, and television sets better and cheaper than the rest of the world. In New Jersey, for example, as recently as the early 1970s, more than 40 percent of our workers were employed in manufacturing industries; today that percentage has shrunk to 20 percent.

Where did those jobs go? To find out, I was part of a trade mission to the Far East in the fall of 1986. In Seoul, Korea, I stood on a shop floor and watched young women build television sets. The women work twelve hours a day, six days a week. Like the immigrants who came to America at the beginning of this century, the South Koreans today are willing to work for extremely low wages, because grinding labor is the only chance they have to lift their children out of poverty.

So we are not going to compete with a country like South Korea by lowering wages. Our workers don't want to toil sixty hours a week to bring home a $150 paycheck, nor should they want to. The only thing we can do is move our economy away from brawn-based manufacturing and toward high-wage, brain-based manufacturing and service industries. We can compete in steel and autos, for example, but only if our factories are run by highly skilled workers backed by robots and other forms of advanced technology. We also need well-educated, adaptable people who can run the new growth industries like biotechnology, supercomputers, and materials science. And we need professionals to handle the flow of services like medicine, finance, and information. All of this has to happen in a world economy, because economic isolationism today makes no more sense than political isolationism did in the 1940s. We cannot turn back any clock. If we cannot compete successfully, we will fall by the wayside. As H. G. Wells said, "Human history has become more and more a race between education and catastrophe."

What this means for our schools is that students need to acquire high-level skills if they are going to hold jobs tomorrow. In New Jersey, for example, we expect 600,000 new jobs to be created by 1993. Yet, according to one study, four out of five of them will require better than a high school education. The skills required to get work, never mind prosper, are getting more complex. As the National Academy of Education concluded in 1985, what was probably a satisfactory level of literacy in 1950 will be only marginal by the turn of the century. The same applies to mathematics. We need workers who don't just know how to punch the keyboard of a computer, but who can program it and understand the mathematical principles behind its operation. We need workers who are flexible; who can learn easily on the job; who can evaluate or make complicated arguments; who are not just literate, but can write well; who cannot only multiply and divide, but can figure out how a computer works. We need, to quote the report of the Carnegie Task Force on Teaching as a Profession, "a massive upgrading of the work force."

Compare such requirements to some of the things that recent studies tell us about American schools, students, and workers. In an international comparison of student achievement in industrialized nations, completed in the 1970s, our students never finished first or second on nineteen standard tests. They did finish last seven times.

By specific subject area the situation doesn't look much better. According to one survey, for example, only one out of ten American students takes calculus, whereas in Japan you cannot graduate from high school without it. Moreover, fewer than 10 percent of all American high school students take even one year of physics or chemistry. According to a study released in 1985, the average math scores for American eighth-graders ranked nearly 20 percentage points behind the Japanese and behind almost every other industrialized nation. A *Reading Report Card*, released in 1985, concluded that while 98 percent of seventeen-year-old students could perform simple reading tasks, only 40 percent could understand, summarize, and explain complicated information.

In general, student performance involving higher skills has been declining at precisely the moment when our economy requires the opposite. This is the crux of the Carnegie report, called, appropriately, *A Nation Prepared*. It leads to the conclusion that American schools do not just need repair, they need to be rebuilt.

To put it another way, we can expend enormous effort and money to erect trade barriers, open foreign markets, invest in research and development, or modify our antitrust laws. But if our schools fail, then all else will mean nothing. A highly educated work force offers our only real hope of competing with low-wage countries or with high-wage countries like Japan that enjoy higher productivity.

But it is not enough simply to compete economically. I get uncomfortable whenever schools are viewed as nothing more than an extension of industrial America—a vast oven from which emerge thousands of gingerbread men and women ready to work. The narrow, technocratic view ignores the equally important role that education plays in glueing a democracy together. As Will Durant put it, "Education is the transmission of civilization." A democratic government depends on a citizenry that not only can read and write, but has some common body of knowledge and experience, some sense of its own history. Eighty-five percent of the governments in the world will survive without an educated citizenry. Dictators, whether from the left or right, rule by force: no reading skills are required to understand what a tank means. Democracy is different. It requires knowledge, understanding, and common belief. When they don't exist, democracy is in danger.

Our Founding Fathers fought to make us free so that the deliberative might prevail over the arbitrary. Liberty, as Louis Brandeis was fond of pointing out, is both an end and a means: "They believed liberty to be the secret of happiness, and courage to be the secret of liberty." Freedom to think and speak are indispensable to the discovery and spread of political truth. This in turn is the greatest protection against the loss of freedom. But what if people don't understand the terms of the debate?

What if they are not educated enough to take part in the democratic process? To Brandeis, the greatest menace to freedom was an "inert" people. To me, without good public education, an inert people is a distinct possibility, and then neither freedom nor justice can survive.

That's why I worry so much when I see a recent survey of high school juniors that shows two-thirds of them did not know when the Civil War was fought. One half could not point to Great Britain, West Germany, or France on a map of the world. One half thought Karl Marx's phrase "From each according to his abilities, to each according to his needs" came from the U. S. Constitution. And a vast majority were totally ignorant of Dante, Dostoevski, Austen, Whitman, Hawthorne, Melville, and Chaucer.

Our democracy faces some tough choices and maybe some tough times in the years ahead. How can we be expected to deal with them if our citizens lack a common set of beliefs and a core of common educational experience. Historians love to quote de Tocqueville's epic work on America but they seldom bring up the last sentence in the book. He wrote, "It depends upon themselves, whether equality is to lead them to servitude or freedom, knowledge or barbarism, prosperity or wretchedness." I will add, everything depends on the schools.

Finally, I am troubled by the absence of the teaching of ethics and values. A recent study pointed out that none of our five leading world history textbooks provides students with more than a brief mention of Plato or Aristotle. Almost every debate over right and wrong or the individual's place in society is centered in the basic ideas of Judaism, the ancient Greeks, and Christianity. Yet you seldom find the timeless ideas of our common heritage expressed in textbooks or in the classroom. In the name of purging religion from our schools we have also purged the values on which our society is based. By ignoring our basic values we send a message to our children that they are not important—that morals are, after all, relative. Accordingly, our children become morally anemic. "We are talking," says Albert Shanker, "about thinking, about understanding our ideals, about knowledge of the past. The unfortunate and the evil as well as the good. That is not indoctrination: that is education in the best sense of the word." If we are to remain the world's moral leader, we have to instill in our young people an appreciation for the values that have served us well for two hundred years. That, along with our economic and political needs, is why education should remain at the top of the nation's political agenda for the rest of the century.

☆

When I was first elected, education was far from the top of any policy agenda. People were complaining, yes, but only a few political leaders were responding. I sat down with my education commissioner, Saul Cooperman, and tried to make some sense of what was happening, what was right with American education and what was wrong.

In the end, we put together some fifteen school reforms, several of which were controversial. I had hoped to unveil my ideas during my annual state-of-the-state address to the legislature, but my plans changed when the federal government released *A Nation at Risk*. In the report's most memorable line, the authors wrote: "If an unfriendly foreign power had attempted to impose on America the mediocre educational performance that exists today, we might have viewed it as an act of war."

The report cried out for a response. The question was, would anyone seize the initiative? I decided to call a special joint session of the legislature when school opened in September. Normally, joint sessions convene twice a year, during my budget message and the state-of-the-state; only during a budget crisis is a special session ever called. I decided to break precedent. I wanted to provoke a crisis atmosphere to get the legislators to think about education and nothing else. The gamble paid off. Virtually every one of my fifteen proposals would become policy within two years. More important, I was able to fix the state's attention for the first time on the quality of our schools.

Ideas are important in education reform, no question. But a governor's job is also to shape the political environment needed to support education. During the next few years I not only pushed my ideas, I visited classrooms once a month, met with teachers, spoke to principals and parents, and encouraged people to run for school boards. My message was that reform wasn't going to happen unless everyone bought into it.

I also deliberately set out to influence national policy. I hired one of the brightest young minds in the Department of Education, Dr. Rick Mills, and brought him on my personal staff. He became my liaison to other states. As word of New Jersey's reforms spread, other governors called me up and asked for advice. I also lobbied for and won the chairmanship of the Education Commission of the States. I used that position to become the only governor on the Carnegie Forum Task Force on Teaching. There I tried to give some intellectual consistency to the spate of reports that were coming out on education. For example, in New Jersey we had modified teacher certification to attract talented people from industry and higher education to the classroom. Other states were copying the idea, so I made sure it was in both the Carnegie report and the report I helped write for the National Governors' Association. The former endorsed the idea of a national board to certify teachers, while I helped to ensure that the national board would also be the centerpiece of the governors' recommendations.

I didn't go to conferences simply to talk, but to learn as well. Jim Hunt told me about North Carolina's governor's school program, where talented high school juniors get together for one month each summer to study the arts or sciences. I wanted a similar program in New Jersey. But we were still facing a $600 million deficit and there was no way I could get the legislature to fund a new program of this sort. So with the help of Assemblyman Doc Villane and the cooperation of Monmouth College we organized an inaugural ball, and donated the proceeds to starting a governor's school. Later others from the private sector pitched in. Today, we have three governor's schools, including the first ever in public policy. I visit the schools every summer and marvel as our most talented young people exchange ideas.

Six years later, the education reform movement remains strong. That in itself is noteworthy. Also important is the intensity of interest all across our society. Business leaders like Ross Perot and David Kearns, the chairman of Xerox, have joined union leaders in a common effort to improve our schools.

What have we learned? In many instances, it is too early to tell. Politicians like to see the results of their work in one or two years, but the reforms in education will take many years to evaluate. We do know that some of our efforts have been misguided; others have died for lack of broad-based political support. But overall, a fragile consensus has emerged on three things we have to do: restore teaching to its rightful status as a high calling; increase expectations on performance of our students, especially from poor backgrounds; and change the environment within the schools themselves.

Teachers are the key. A simple proposition, but true. You cannot have great schools without great teachers. For much of our history, we didn't have to worry about a shortage of qualified teachers. If you were

an able woman who wanted a career, you had a choice: become a
nurse or a teacher. So our children were taught by bright, enthusiastic
women who worked for little pay. These "dedicated missionaries," as
Al Shanker calls them, did an extraordinary job, but now they are retiring.
Now with other fields open to ambitious young women, too many of
the people replacing retiring teachers are not of the same quality. A
1983 study, for example, showed that college students entering the teaching profession scored lower on their average verbal SATs than students
going into social sciences, engineering, or business. In other words, far
too many of our recent teaching candidates come from the bottom 25
percent of their college class.

What's happened is that teaching has become in many minds a
second-class profession. During my chairmanship of the Education Commission of the States, I started a series of "talks with teachers." It seemed
to me that nearly everyone knew how teachers could do a better job,
but no one was asking the teachers themselves what they thought. So I
sat down with groups of fifteen of the very best teachers we could find,
and I'm proud to say that sessions of the same sort have since been
held in more than twenty other states.

A few teachers that I listened to complained about the money. One
black woman who taught in a city school said she had left teaching for
a job that paid $10,000 more in the private sector. She took a cut in
pay and returned to the classroom because she missed the kids. Now
she had another even better offer from the private sector. "If I leave
this time," she said, "I'm never coming back." While pay was a problem,
most teachers spoke emotionally about the working conditions, the lack
of recognition, and how administrators never listened to them. One
woman said, "In twenty-eight years of teaching, the superintendent put
his head in my classroom door only once to say hello. My principal
sits in his office all day with his newspapers. And we have some teachers
getting tenure who are no more qualified to teach than your pet dog."
Another said, "I've been teaching English for twenty years, but when
the Lions Club wants to recognize someone, they always pick the football
coach." These were talented, dedicated professionals, seeking recognition
for their work. As I listened, I thought of the words of Jacques Barzun:
"Teaching is not a lost art, but regard for teaching is a lost tradition."

Our lack of regard for teachers and for the profession of teaching
demonstrates the bizarre shape of priorities in our society. We are the
only society in the history of the world that has put entertainers at the

top, in both pay and prestige. I assume it is that we need to be distracted and diverted, and we reward those who do it well. So Michael Jackson earns more than $100 million on one album, while more than twenty ballplayers now get paid more than $1 million a year. Boxers get $10 million for one fight, and actors and actresses are routinely guaranteed $3 or $4 million for a single movie. Yet we entrust our children to people who make $14,000 a year.

It doesn't make sense. Even more troubling to me is that our ablest young people are being lured into fields intrinsically less productive. One of my former students graduated near the top of his class in college and made law review at one of our nation's top law schools. He was hired by a big New York law firm, where he spent a number of years developing ingenious ways to defend companies against a takeover. He works long hours, but is paid handsomely, nearly $180,000 a year. I saw him one day on a Manhattan street. I congratulated him for doing so well so few years out of law school, noting that he was earning more than twice my salary. "Are you happy?" I asked him. "Not especially," he replied, "but I will be making even more next year."

The fact is, many of our brightest young people are being chained by golden handcuffs to big law firms or investment banking firms. The money they make is astonishing, but in the end, they don't seem to me to produce very much. They are not developing or selling a new product, working on a car to compete with Hyundai, trying to find a vaccine for AIDS, or teaching an illiterate person to read. I have a fantasy: What if the incentives were reversed? What if all those brilliant young people were attracted into teaching, or government, or manufacturing? How different would our future be? Quite different, I suspect. But there is something dreadfully wrong in a society where the best and brightest people are encouraged to go into unproductive economic activity.

Don't get me wrong—I have nothing against investment bankers personally. I don't begrudge Michael Jackson his millions and I will pay fifteen dollars to watch Lawrence Taylor chase a quarterback around a football field. But my real heroes are teachers, and my favorite play is *A Man For All Seasons*. I love the scene where Sir Thomas More, the lord chancellor of England, is confronted by Richard Rich, an ambitious and not very virtuous courtier, who desperately wants to find his way to riches and fame. More is fresh from court and in no mood to dally when Rich asks him what he should do with his life. More replies, "Be a teacher." "A teacher," says Rich, "why? And if I were good, who would know?" More responds, "Your pupils, your friends, God—not a bad public, that."

Not only is teaching unattractive compared to other professions, but within the education profession itself teaching is often slighted. I remember a young man I knew at Columbia Teachers College. From our conversations, I could tell he was a wonderful teacher. He had a great relationship with his students, both past and present. But he had come to Columbia to study administration. Why? Because he had just gotten married and his wife was expecting a child. As much as he loved the classroom, he explained, he could earn twice as much as a principal or superintendent. He was reluctantly making the switch. I remember thinking that the system has to be upside down if the best teachers are quickly encouraged to leave the classroom.

The only way we are ever going to improve our schools is to set the incentives straight. Pay teachers more money. Give them a role in the operation of the school. Reward the best teachers. Let them work in a professional work environment. In return, teachers must commit themselves to higher standards of performance. Too many teachers complain about disruptive students, or students who are zombie-eyed from watching reruns of Johnny Carson, or who are hungry or on drugs. The truth is that every profession contends with factors that are beyond immediate control. But in return for power and prestige, teachers have got to stop making excuses and start getting kids to learn.

In my speech to the special session of the legislature, I proposed that we guarantee that every new teacher in the state be paid a minimum of $18,500 a year. The teachers union, of course, loved the proposal—the new governor was willing to put money behind the rhetoric about education. But I told union officials that the minimum-salary bill had to be accompanied by some kind of program to recognize and reward the very best teachers. I have always believed that great teaching should be recognized, just as standout performance is recognized in everything from baseball to novel writing. As Lamar Alexander likes to say, "Teaching is the only profession in which you are not paid one extra cent for being good at your job." If I had my way, the teachers with advanced education credentials, competence, and talent would earn $70,000 to $80,000 and incompetent teachers would be eased out of the classroom. The teachers union does not agree with me. They argue that it is impossible to determine who the best teachers are, and they oppose any recognition program. We negotiated for several months. I badly wanted the higher minimum salary, because I knew it would attract good young people to the classroom. But I wasn't willing to budge on teacher recognition. Great teaching must be supported and rewarded. At the eleventh hour, we compromised. Starting teachers would earn $18,500. Once each year the state would award $1,000 grants to the best teacher in every school in New Jersey, with teachers choosing how the money is to be spent. It can be used on a field trip or on new uniforms for the band, whatever the good teacher wants.

Every year I hold a convocation for the state's great teachers in Princeton. I remember the first one. More than a thousand teachers attended. The atmosphere was electric. These people had been working to help kids all their lives, and now someone was finally saying thank you. It took me thirty minutes just to work my way to the podium. Every time I moved, teachers wanted to tell me how excited they were, and how they would use the state money. The next day New Jersey newspapers were dotted with biographical sketches of the winners. It was probably the first time that people in many of the communities recognized the caliber of the people who were spending all that time with their children.

The teacher recognition program was the first of a number of programs to revitalize the profession. We followed by offering $5,000-a-year college scholarships to top high school students who promised to go into teaching as a profession. With my conversations at Columbia in mind, we offered to forgive loans of students who agreed to teach in urban schools. We also opened an academy where teachers could go to improve their skills, which was oversubscribed before it even opened its doors.

We also changed the way we recruited teachers. Again I thought back to my days at Columbia. So many of the education courses I had been forced to take were dull and meaningless. We changed the curriculum at our teachers colleges to stress courses in the subject a person would teach. At the same time, we made admission requirements tougher. The prevailing wisdom said this was risky. I was asked how I could possibly raise standards for the profession when we were facing a teacher shortage. I figured that one of the major reasons people were not going into the profession was that the standards were too lax. I gambled that higher standards would attract more teachers. I was proved right.

We made one other change to improve the quality of our teachers. For years, people of real ability have been excluded from the classroom. For example, someone who has taught science for twenty years at a private school like St. Mark's could not teach in a public school without spending time in teachers college taking education courses. Under the system, an Isaac Stern couldn't teach music and a John Updike couldn't teach English in a New Jersey public school.

Many men and women, after years in another profession, are drawn to the challenge of public school teaching. But no matter how experienced or qualified they are, we require them to quit their jobs, take education courses for a year, and then apply for a new position. Few put up with the rigamarole. Our schools lose talented people and our children suffer.

We decided to reach beyond the teachers colleges and tap the deep pool of teaching talent hidden in unlikely places: large corporations, retirement villages, and our most prestigious liberal arts universities. Now, through an alternate route, prospective teachers can teach without a traditional education degree. They do have to have hold a bachelor's degrees in the subject they want to teach, pass the National Teachers Examination, and undergo approximately two hundred hours of classroom instruction before the school year begins and while they are on the job. By the time they are finished with our program, they have undergone as much training as a graduate with a degree in teaching.

Again, the teachers unions initially responded negatively. They argued that we were using our children as guinea pigs. But within two years, more than two thousand people had applied for the program and over four hundred had been hired to teach. And the candidates are scoring higher on the National Teachers Examination than their counterparts from traditional teacher-training programs. Typical is a young woman named Nancy Pfeil, who holds an MBA and had worked as a chemical engineer with the Exxon Corporation. Another alternate-route teacher is Gaylord French. A graduate of the prestigious Eastman School of Music and a former director of the U. S. Navy band, he is now teaching music at a high school in Montclair. In the first year alone, New Jersey schools hired a Fulbright Scholar, five Harvard graduates, and a scientist with two patents. New Jersey is, in short, attracting bright, ambitious people with experience into teaching. Today, one out of six of our new teachers is being recruited through the alternate route. What's more, because of it, New Jersey has more than enough able people looking for teaching jobs, and the shortage the experts predicted never developed. In the spring of 1986, for example, the number of prospective teachers taking certification tests was up 31 percent over the previous year. The New Jersey experience proves that higher standards and the alternate route can attract more and better people.

New Jersey was one of the first states to raise teachers' salaries and reward good teachers, and the very first state to create an alternate route. Other states are now following us. One of them is Iowa. The farm economy there is depressed, but Governor Terry Branstad convinced the legislature to approve nearly $100 million in teacher salary increases. A large chunk of the money was used to raise the average starting salary from $14,000 to $18,000. But some $20 million is going to what Governor Branstad calls performance-based pay. Local school districts have set up committees of citizens, school board members, administrators, and teachers that establish objective criteria to determine which teachers work the hardest and which do a better job than their peers. The best teachers get raises.

Recruitment reforms will help attract better instructors into the class-room. Raising salaries and rewarding performance will help keep them there. Still, I doubt that these reforms alone will allow teachers to take their place beside business leaders, lawyers, and doctors as the most valued professionals in a community. For that to happen, we need a national board for professional teaching standards, which is the heart of the recommendation made by the Carnegie Forum.

The board would be made up of the nation's best teachers, chosen by their peers in each state. It would also include other education professionals and members of the public. The board's major responsibility would be to set standards for excellence in the profession. Applications for national board certification would be submitted voluntarily by teachers, and would be open only to those who have been certified by boards in their own states. As more teachers pass the rigorous certification requirements, a teacher's reputation will grow. And just as architectural firms compete for the certified elite of their profession, schools will compete for nationally certified teachers. That will drive salaries up. Schools will have to offer certified teachers contracts that give them more control over curriculum and the operation of their school and more responsibility in training and overseeing the work of new teachers. Having a national board will increase the prestige of every teacher. My goal is a day when every teacher in America makes it a priority to receive national certification, and school board members brag to parents about the number of certified teachers on a school's staff. But the program has to be voluntary, not forced on unwilling teachers. The board offers the one chance to revolutionize teaching in this country and to bring a substantial improvement in our children's education.

☆

As states work to improve teaching, educators and public officials agree that we must demand more from our students. And we must pay special attention to the needs of poor, minority students. This country is rapidly becoming blacker and browner. By the turn of the century, one out of three Americans will be nonwhite and the vast majority of the bulge will be younger. The minority children will be filling tomorrow's jobs and will be paying Social Security taxes to keep a huge number of senior citizens comfortable. The point is, there are no longer any "spare" people in America.

So far we haven't done very well with minority children. Drop out rates are much higher for blacks and Hispanics than white children. Four out of ten black children live in poverty; six out of ten are raised in a home with only one parent. Black Americans represent slightly above 1 percent of degree holders in the doctoral sciences; Hispanics, .6 percent. Here we sit, the most affluent generation on earth, ready to pass our future to a group of children with many characteristics of a third world country.

What do we do? The worst thing we could do is to lower our expectations for black and Hispanic children. The reforms of the Sixties and Seventies inadvertently left us with a system in which a great many students were automatically passed from one grade to another, regardless of whether they could perform even the most basic skills. School curriculums became loaded down with courses like "Bachelor Living," as students sat in classrooms learning how to cook TV dinners, when some of them couldn't read the directions on the package. Many of them eventually received high school diplomas and left school believing they were prepared for the world.

That was a hoax. We led youngsters to believe they were ready to become participating members of our society, when all they were prepared for was a lifetime of only the most menial employment at best, or at worst, total dependency. For years, our schools' response to the problem was the same. Pass students. Give them a diploma. Push the problem off onto someone else. Which is why American industry will spend $25 billion a year on basic-skills instruction. It is also why when I ask the New Jersey Turnpike commissioners to hire more city kids as toll takers, they tell me that they can't because the kids fail the simplest arithmetic test.

As the education reform movement gained steam, it became clear that states must demand results. Too many local schools were content to give diplomas to illiterates. But between 1980 and 1985, at least forty-three states strengthened their high school graduation requirements, and New Jersey was one of them. When our program was being debated back in the 1970s, I agreed to vote for the income tax to pay for education if, in turn, the state would administer a minimum basic-skills test for high school students. The test turned out to be ridiculously easy. In 1985, the last year it was administered, the failure rate among ninth-grade students was less than 1 percent. Anyone who had spent an hour in our urban schools knew the result was absurd. Virtually every student was passing, including students with no proficiency whatever in math or reading.

As part of my blueprint for reform, I proposed a much tougher test, this time to include writing skills that would be mandatory for high school graduation. The test measures basic ninth-grade-level skills. If a sophomore fails, he or she can take the test again as a junior or senior, but must pass the test in order to receive a high school diploma.

The initial reaction of educators to the new test was extremely negative. They predicted failure rates as high as 70 percent in our urban schools. Faced with those odds, the argument went, urban teenagers would drop out of school even faster. It would be a disaster for the schools and for the students. Educators lobbied me strenuously to delay the test, or better, to cancel it.

A close look at the argument shows an insidious tendency to put the image of schools above the welfare of the students. If you abandon a strict test, the only thing you can do is continue passing the youngsters from grade to grade and then to graduate them. In effect, the educators' lobbyists were telling me that city students—mostly black—cannot possibly learn the basic skills required of an average high school sophomore. I couldn't believe that. The argument borders on racism. If two-thirds of high school students fail a ninth-grade basic-skills test, that is the schools' fault. It is time to stop blaming the children.

Some argued that preparation for the test could dominate the high school curriculum, with its entire focus devoted to preparing students for testing. Again, the argument doesn't hold water. The test is not some esoteric measure of high-order skills, but is instead a measure of simple reading, writing, and math ability. So for me, until high schools can teach such skills they should not worry about the rest of the curriculum. Let's learn to read first. Then we will study Faulkner or take sociology.

We went ahead with the test despite the critics. And I added some

$50 million to my budget to help tutor children who failed so that they could eventually pass. Even here we tried a new twist. New Jersey, like other states, had always provided more money to schools that needed remedial help. So schools had no incentive to teach the needy children. If the need lessened, your school lost money. We tried adding more money to reward schools whose students succeeded. The idea was to teach the basic skills early, so the graduation tests would become easy.

So far, the results of the graduation test have been promising. The first year, 38 percent of the ninth-graders—31,000 students—failed, far below the 42,000 who had been expected to flunk. The second year, the failure rate had dropped to 20 percent. The lesson for me is that schools, when properly motivated, can teach, and children, with proper incentive, can learn.

Minimum-skills tests are sort of a necessary evil. The danger is that the entire back-to-basics movement can lead to doing away with classes in music, art, poetry, or even history. That is especially misguided. Of course students need to know how to read and write, but it is also important that they understand why the Civil War was fought, why Hamlet was sick at heart, what DNA is, and maybe even why we honor Michelangelo and Beethoven.

You can't read or write unless you know something about the world around you. You can recognize words without having the foggiest notion of what they represent. *Moby Dick* is just a story about a whale unless you know a little bit about history and psychology. And you cannot understand Milton or Eliot without some knowledge of the classics. Education, as Barzun put it, is what turns grammar into literature, a list of dates into history, a sheet of formulas into the natural sciences. These are not the idealistic ramblings of an elitist. We ought to expect a first-rate education for every child, from the cities to the suburbs. Bertrand Russell, who knew that habits praiseworthy in a poet are not necessarily useful to a postman, nevertheless argued that education ought to provide everyone with four virtues: vitality, courage, sensitivity, and intelligence. You don't acquire them by simply learning how to read and write and multiply.

We may be lulled into thinking that once 90 percent of our high school students pass a basic-skills test, we have done our job. So if you hear a politician talking about "back to basics," be skeptical. Remember, basic skills yield only basic jobs. If you passed the arithmetic section of New Jersey's high school test, you may be able to get a job as a turnpike toll collector. In no way are you qualified to work as a computer program-mer. As the Carnegie report concluded, the latter is precisely the kind of job we need to compete in the world economy. If American or New Jersey children are not qualified for it, the job will go elsewhere.

If we are serious about providing opportunity to minority children, we have to solve the problems of our urban schools. Indeed, calling some of them schools is a travesty. They are more like warehouses, storing children for ten or twelve years until they are sent out, unprepared and unable to compete.

Money is only one problem, and not the most fundamental. In New Jersey we've almost doubled spending for urban schools since I took office. The real problem is that some schools just do not work. Too many simply provide jobs and money for urban politicians. I've learned of schools in New Jersey where students read from textbooks that are thirty years old, while the school spends $50,000 on a custodian and pays salaries to administrators who seldom show up for work. One school claimed to have no money for classroom supplies, but spent $10,000 on a fancy reception for the school board.

This is nothing short of educational child abuse—schools producing third-world kids to compete in a first-world economy. It used to be we blamed the children: "Poor black kids just can't learn" was the not-so-subtle refrain. That's nonsense. I've seen poor kids learn more at Brant-wood Camp in two weeks than they learn in our inner-city schools in two years.

I've proposed a radical solution to the problem, namely, that if a school district repeatedly fails the state monitoring process—if by every measure it is not educating children—then the state should come in and run the school. I've asked for the power to remove the school board, the superintendent, and, if we have to, the principal.

Not everyone sees it my way, of course. Some argue that school intervention usurps the rights of local citizens to choose local representa-tives. My response is that those rights pale next to a child's right to a good education. Others have said that school takeover is a racist conspiracy to take political power away from the blacks and Hispanics who now run city schools. I don't care whether administrators are white, black, or polka-dot; if they are not educating children, they should be removed. My purpose is not to have the state run schools, but to make sure the schools are run right. That means providing expertise and forming alliances with parents who care about their children's education and are right now stifled by the wall of patronage. As I write, the New Jersey legislature has not yet passed the school-takeover legislation. But I will keep on fighting. I hope eventually they will grant me the full power I need, because I welcome the responsibility. If anything is said of Tom Kean as governor, I hope it is that I did not sit by and watch another generation of city children treated like pawns in a political game, the resulting ignorance enslaving them just like the chains that once bound their great-grandparents.

☆

The third area of reform is probably the most difficult. We have to change the actual work environment within our schools. Again, I think back to my teaching days at St. Mark's and I recall those once-a-week meetings. Teachers shared information with one another and the coaches. The headmaster was there and always ready to help. We talked together about ways to help individual children.

Compare that with the environment in many of our public schools today. Teachers have told me they never see the principal in a classroom; on the football field, yes, but in the classroom, never. The only time teachers, administrators, and school board members get together is over the collective bargaining table. Then the air is filled with animosity over salaries, pensions, and working conditions. Teachers have become, in the minds of school board members, nothing more than greedy philistines who don't care about kids. Teachers whisper about the stingy ogres the public elects to work on school boards. The situation is best captured by a joke they tell about a teacher who was hospitalized for surgery. He got a card that read, "After much discussion, and a five-to-four vote, the school board has decided to wish you best luck for a speedy recovery."

Funny maybe, but our children suffer from the poisoned environment. One answer is to strengthen the role of the principal dramatically. All good schools have one characteristic: strong leadership in the principal's office. Weak schools invariably have weak principals—maybe a retired football coach or a favorite teacher who has never managed people. A principal's job is in many respects like being governor or the CEO of a major corporation—you need to know how to motivate people. Now we are changing the principal certification requirements to require a master's in public administration. A strong, respected principal ought to be able to help manage the problems that develop between teachers and administration.

Too little attention has been paid to the problem of school management. In New Jersey and elsewhere, we spend a considerable amount of money creating tension and then resolving it. Let me give you an example. Every time a teacher is denied tenure, the dispute is heard by the Department of Education. We even have a Bureau of Controversies and Disputes handling the cases. Millions of dollars are spent every year to settle these and related matters, the majority of which are brought just because a teacher or administrator is angry and wants to bug somebody. Once a suit is settled, the ill will generated among the school administration, the teacher, and the department lingers for quite a while. It is disastrous. Now we are spending money on a program to have the state sit down with teachers, administrators, and boards outside the bargaining process and the courtroom. The idea is to get the three sides to focus on their common goal—educating the kids—and try to cool the animosity they feel for each other.

This is just a first step. The Carnegie report painted a picture of what the schools of the future ought to look like. Envisioned was a school in which principals go from classroom to classroom, motivating teachers, while lead teachers, certified by the national board and earning over $50,000, spend free time putting curriculums together and helping new teachers. Interns and associate teachers monitor the cafeteria, teachers work together on courses and problem students, and individual help is available for students falling behind academically. Collegiality is everywhere.

I remember the meeting at which the Carnegie staff described the dream school. It was the fall of 1985, and my political advisers were angry that I would take time from my campaign to go to a national education meeting. After the school was described, a few members of the Carnegie task force said it was impossible. I said, "Not only can we create it, we have to create it." From then on, that vision became the centerpiece of the report.

We have a long way to go before we have public schools like those we want in America. But some states are trying. In 1987, Booth Gardner, the governor of Washington, unveiled his proposal for model "collaborative schools" in a few districts. Governor Mike Dukakis is trying a similar pilot program in Massachusetts, and actually calling them Carnegie schools. My dream is that one day such schools will be the rule, not the exception. A student who went to school in the 1980s will step into a twenty-first-century classroom and feel like someone today trying to control a pair of oxen. He will wonder how we could have been so backward.

Governors are active in education all over the country. Some governors, like Rudy Perpich in Minnesota, are letting parents choose the public schools their children attend. Lamar Alexander was able to establish career ladders, so that able teachers can earn more pay and more responsibility in Tennessee. These reforms are close to radical. Others, like the use of basic skills tests, reflect a return of nothing more than common sense to the classroom.

The education reform movement has been with us now for most of the 1980s. We won't know its real impact for years. Nevertheless, we can pause at this point and see what lessons we have learned and what challenges lie ahead.

Perhaps the most promising lesson is that it is possible to move a nation, and you don't have to live within the District of Columbia, 202 area code to do it. Ten years ago, education reform mattered only to educators while the political community showed no interest whatever. Then a few prescient governors, like Jim Hunt, Dick Riley, and Lamar Alexander, began to experiment. Now these men have left office, but governors like Bill Clinton and John Ashcroft have taken their place. Meanwhile, governors Terry Branstad of Iowa and Rudy Perpich of Minnesota continue to lead. These governors have shared their success with others. In the process, they have given the movement a coherence and a purpose it might otherwise have lacked. I should add that governors have taxpayers' support on this one. Between 1980 and 1986, the states have increased spending for schools by $27 billion. We already spend more per capita on education than any other country and we are willing to spend more. The taxpayers' only demand is that they see results.

A fragile consensus now exists about the initial steps needed to improve the schools. According to a recent National Governor's Association survey, every state has taken some action to pay teachers more and to reward the best teachers. And virtually every state has minimum skills standards and is looking for a way to help minority students. The bolder states are turning to the sensitive problem of the school environment. We have come far. Although progress cannot yet be measured in the test scores, it has been made. Yet major challenges and questions remain.

The first is a philosophical one with pragmatic implications. We have yet to define the purpose of education in this country. We are afraid of Japan. We talk about teaching Billie and Susie how to read and write, but in the back of our minds lie Toro and Shuichi. Or, as one educator put it, the invisible Toyota orbiting the earth. So economic implications dominate too much of the reform debate. As a result, the liberal arts are undervalued and curriculums are being shifted toward business and vocational education. Education is more than modern-day anthracite—the fuel, as politicians like to say, that drives modern factories. A resilient democracy and a country with a fixed moral compass are just as important as a positive balance of trade. We need to think more about the broad implications of education. Once we do, the reforms will become more profound.

Then too, many recent reforms have come from the top. Governors have made efforts to include teachers unions and other players in the reform, but the best reforms come from the grass roots—from schools that on their own give teachers more authority or require tougher skills tests for students. The teachers and administrators within each school will determine if the reform movement succeeds or fails. They must become the driving energy behind the movement.

Let me give you an example. I met a teacher named Bernadette Anand at one of the Talks with Teachers in Washington, D. C. Early in her career, Bernadette had taken it upon herself to get teachers more power in her school. She had given up, mostly out of frustration. The Talks with Teachers renewed her spirit. She asked her fellow teachers to hold a Talks with Teachers in her district in Montclair. The union resisted. So on her own, she hosted a meeting for parents, teachers, and members of the school board. She talked about ways teachers could get more involved in the operation of the school. Now she is preparing to lobby the school superintendent to create a demonstration school to be run only by teachers. Education reform will succeed, and more, if we can only recruit many more Bernadette Anands to the cause.

We also know too little about what makes a good education. We know that an emphasis on reading and writing in the early grades lays a foundation. But we don't know enough about the relationship between good teaching and learning.

Finally, there is the question about the role of the federal government. Until now, the federal government has been a noisy but relatively inactive partner. Secretary of Education Bill Bennett has contributed greatly by asking tough questions and forcing the education community to engage in some healthy introspection.

But what of federal education programs? Can they be expected to make any contribution, with Washington paralyzed by the budget deficit? I think they can and I believe they must. The key is to build on the work already going on at the state level. Every candidate for president, Republican or Democrat, ought to endorse the National Board for Professional Teaching Standards. It is probably the single most important long-term step to improving teaching in the country. The board deserves a strong advocate in the White House.

Washington also has a vital role to play helping the vast underclass of minority children. The problem is simply too large and important for states to handle on their own. Once we saved the paralyzed and hungry of Europe with the Marshall Plan. Now we must summon similar resources and energy to save the education of our own poor. We need a federal Marshall Plan, a concentrated effort to educate our most vulnerable students. Right now, Chapter I education aid is spread like buckshot around the country, going to rich and poor school districts alike. I think it is time we begin to target that federal aid to the neediest districts, perhaps those where a majority of students repeatedly fail basic-skills tests. These districts should voluntarily apply for special assistance, to prove that they recognize problems and are willing to change. Together the states and federal government should provide educational leadership for these districts, perhaps lending them teachers and principals who have run good schools in other cities. Then we must strip away all the state and federal regulations and come up with a schoolwide plan of action. Just as a patient who is gravely ill won't be helped by a nasal spray, a school in which 50 percent of the students drop out won't be saved by just a new compensatory education program. The entire school needs therapy. We should provide small grants to get the plans under way, then step back and watch. If, after two years, improvements are made, such districts deserve big increases in federal aid. If miserable performance continues, let the local mayor and other elected officials answer to the taxpayers. Let the voters punish the adults who year after year fail the children.

One final area is ripe for federal involvement. Our young people need to know that school leads to something. If they study hard and stay at it, they can go to college and get a better job than their parents. The entire education community has been following a wonderful real-life story that demonstrates what I mean. A few years ago, a successful New York businessman named Eugene Lang returned to an East Harlem sixth-grade class to speak. He had prepared the usual rhetoric about how if students studied hard, they could do anything. When the business-man looked out across the classroom at the sixth-graders, he knew the speech was meaningless. These kids were black and Hispanic; they were all poor. Most came from broken homes. They were bored; they saw no reason to study. The girls might already be thinking about a baby; the boys, about how to earn some spending money on the street. They would no sooner believe they could go to college than they would fly to Mars. Eugene Lang tossed his prepared speech away. Instead, he simply said, "Anyone in the class who will study hard enough to be accepted at a college can go. I'll pay for it." The class stared in silence, then broke into cheers. Six years later, forty-eight of the sixty-one students are expected to graduate from high school and twenty-five have been accepted at colleges, several on full scholarships. The story has become legend in education circles. Just knowing that college was possible had turned those kids into good students.

Unfortunately, today more and more young families, especially mi-nority families, feel that college is out of reach. Private colleges are now asking $20,000 a year in tuition alone. How many families can afford two children in college at that price? Meanwhile, federal assistance has shifted from grants to loans, as graduates of private schools in 1987 find themselves burdened with an average debt approaching $10,000.

Paying off the debts is going to require a substantial income, and career choices will be narrowed. On their own, states are scrambling to find a solution to the problem. The most popular answer appears to be some type of prepayment plan, under which children as young as four sign up to attend a specific college and their parents put aside a specific amount for tuition every year until the child actually enters the school. This approach has problems, primarily because it precludes choice, which has been the hallmark of American higher education. Many plans protect the financial needs of the colleges while doing little to guarantee the students' right to a quality education tailored to their needs. A better alternative would be a national IRA for education, which would allow students to save and choose the college they favor, or the bonding approach favored by Vice-President Bush.

The federal government has to get involved here. Every major educa-tion advance in this country, from Lincoln's land-grant colleges to the

G.I. bill, was made with federal leadership. Without an education reformer in the White House, the education movement may be to the 1980s what disco was to the 1970s—a temporary phenomenon, a fad.

It is my profound desire that that not happen. Too much is riding on the outcome. American education made some big mistakes, no question about it. But to paraphrase John F. Kennedy, our job now is not to fix the blame for the past, but to fix a course for the future.

What are we trying to do? The pay raises for teachers, the basic-skills tests, and the collaborative schools point to a larger purpose. We are trying, in various ways, to reform modern American culture. Affluence breeds many diseases, the most insidious of which may be an indifference to the next generation that borders on contempt. It's often rough being a child in America today. If you are under the age of fourteen, you are six times more likely to be poor than if you were over sixty-five. Chances are you have only one parent. The possibility of college or a good job may seem about as real as *Fantasy Island* on television. We're pushing the problems of illiteracy and poverty off on little kids who don't even know how to fight back. Our indifference is plain at a very personal level. City teachers are not the only ones who complain that parents don't give a damn about their children. Suburban teachers say it too. We seem to have forgotten that one of the responsibilities of adulthood is to care for the generation to follow us.

At heart, that is what the education reform movement is all about. Will it work? Nobody knows. But every time a bright young college student says no to investment banking and yes to teaching, I smile and feel a little bit better about our future.

9
The Politics of Inclusion

Politics in America is best when it brings people together. Our greatest leaders, such as Washington, Lincoln, Theodore Roosevelt, and Martin Luther King, had a vision that unified us. Each touched values imbedded in the American character. Washington fought for freedom and independence; Lincoln and King stood for liberty and equality; and Teddy Roosevelt stood for individualism and the little guy against the forces of monopoly and privilege. All of them became leaders during a time of uncertainty, yet thanks to the strength and clarity of their vision, our nation moved forward.

The leader who dominated much of our century, of course, was Franklin Delano Roosevelt, someone my grandfather did not support. He felt that Roosevelt's policies were the wrong medicine for a sick economy. So, while Len Coleman's grandfather hid his money in a mattress, my grandfather put money for his grandchildren in the Bank of Nova Scotia. But what my grandfather and other wealthy Republicans could not understand during the Depression was that Roosevelt's reforms and his optimism helped to save capitalism. FDR did that by envisioning a future in which government could be used to extend the advantages of a free-market economy to what he called the average man. As a result, the Democratic party, once the party of sectionalism and reaction, captured the allegiance of millions and became the majority party for the next forty years.

As the New Deal turned into the Great Society, the excesses and weaknesses of the liberal welfare state gradually became obvious. The federal government, used by Roosevelt to serve the "average man," grew so large that it became the average man's oppressor. Government was no longer a means to individual advancement, it became an end in itself. Working men and women saw more and more of their paychecks going to feed the federal government's ever-bigger appetite. Moreover, using taxpayer money, the Great Society moved the federal government toward not just guaranteeing opportunity, but trying to ensure that every American led a comfortable life. In other words, government began to try to guarantee not just equality of opportunity, but equality of result. Not only is this impossible, it goes against the American experience. That people lose initiative and independence when they depend on government for support is for me only common sense.

Finally, politicians stopped talking of the needs of people and began to devote themselves to calculations about what the organized interests wanted. The Democratic party split the electorate into segments—labor unions, teachers, minorities—and tried to appeal to them on narrow issues. FDR's common vision was lost as the Democrats tried to stitch together a majority coalition of special interests. Meanwhile, we Republicans looked to our own groups for support. We tried to win white males through the Southern strategy, and wrote off the black community. We went after business by criticizing organized labor. We pitted the suburbs against the cities. If the economy was strong, we could win by relying on the support of swing voters: primarily white, ethnic, lower- to middle-class suburbanites. If the economy was weak, we didn't have much of a chance.

While both strategies may have won a few elections, neither provides a way to create the kind of broad coalition that dominated American politics in the past, and neither is designed to appeal to the whole electorate today. Moreover, neither approach seems to produce a workable way of governing America in the 1980s. Torn from within by a society that seems increasingly fractured, and challenged from without by fierce economic competition, the old style of politics won't work. America wants and needs a new vision, one that will unite us and move us forward.

President Reagan understood that yearning. Underestimated for so many years, he united our country by embodying two enduring American virtues: pride and optimism. After years of more and more reliance on the federal government, he reminded us that America's real strength lies in the people whom government serves. He thereby shed the Republicans' reputation as the party of doubt. The Democrats, led by President

Jimmy Carter, talked about an era of limits. Ronald Reagan talked about growth and optimism, about an American era that was just beginning. Reagan's new style of leadership struck a chord, particularly among young voters, 60 percent of whom cast their votes in 1984 for this country's oldest president.

President Reagan changed the terms of our nation's ongoing debate. Now even the most liberal Democrat hesitates before endorsing major new federal programs, because the voters now ask how much government programs cost, not just what they do. Nearly all agree that the unfettered expansion of government is unacceptable. But while Reagan has altered the agenda, he has not supplied FDR's unifying vision. The voters are not willing to reject government completely, because they know that government can be used constructively to solve some of our most pressing problems. So, despite Reagan's appeal, the American people are still looking for a new consensus. And the political party that provides the basis for it could become the dominant party for a long, long time.

Where should we look for the new philosophy? Well, for me, the past is often our best guide to the future. The presidents I admire shared at least two things: they were optimists about America and they worked to create economic opportunity for the average man and woman. Abraham Lincoln inspires me the most. His whole political philosophy could be summed up in one word: opportunity. During the tremendous bloodletting of the Civil War, Lincoln was asked how he could possibly justify a conflict in which brother killed brother. "It is a struggle," Lincoln said, "for maintaining in the world that form and substance of government whose leading object is to elevate the condition of men . . . to afford all an unfettered start, and a fair chance, in the race of life." Lincoln believed every person ought to be given the opportunity to succeed, not a guarantee of success.

The first bill passed by a Republican-controlled Congress and signed by Lincoln was the Homestead Act of 1862. This act offered settlers a tract of land, provided they cleared, plowed, cultivated, and improved it for five years. To become an owner a person had to become a pilgrim, a seeker, a pioneer, and thousands did.

The Homestead Act was rooted in the ideas and principles that should guide us today. It was open to any head of a family—man or woman, white or black. No new federal bureaucracy was created, and no huge outlay of money from Washington was required. In other words, sound basic values lay behind a program that widened the opportunities for people without increasing the size of the federal government. We did the same thing eighty years later with the G.I. bill. What is government doing today to make people's dreams real? What are we doing to create opportunity?

Any program centered around the principle of opportunity is inclusive. It appeals to the dreamers, those who see a chance for a better life for themselves and their families and who are willing to work for it. The appeal is the same for the black father or single mother in Newark working to send their kids to college as it is for the young suburban woman living at home, saving money for law school. It is the same for the entrepreneur who has invested his savings in a small store or the farmer who has borrowed money to plant more peach trees. All are willing to work hard and make sacrifices today for a better tomorrow.

We should encourage dreamers and workers. And it is against their deepest yearnings that the success or failure of the two great political parties should be measured.

I know all of this sounds simple, and few of our political leaders would disagree with what I have said. Yet the reality is that much of our political energy is devoted to narrow issues that divide the electorate: abortion, school prayer, the ERA, gay rights, the death penalty. These are important issues and every serious candidate owes us his or her views on them. But they should not be the issues that decide elections, because they divide us when we need to be united. We all do agree on certain things: a chance at a decent job, a good school for our children, a comfortable home, a neighborhood free of drugs and crime. We want our air, soil, and water clean. After a lifetime of work, our senior citizens want to live out their lives in dignity. Government must create a climate in which these things are possible.

That is what we have tried to do in New Jersey. After cutting taxes and watching the economy boom on the strength of the private sector, we invested our bounty in everything from roads and research to welfare reform and infant nutrition. We did it all in the name of opportunity.

The idea of a government that promotes and creates opportunity, while remaining compassionate and responsible, is as old as our country. It is a vision particularly suited to the philosophy and history of the Republican party—a philosophy that allows Republicans to go beyond the country clubs and the suburbs. We can talk about our ideas and programs in barrios, in labor union halls, and in black churches. My campaign staff worked hard in 1985—everyone, that is, except my speechwriter. That's because I used the same basic message everywhere. I used the same themes for labor and business, the same vision of the future to rabbis and black clergymen.

In short, interest-group politics must not determine our future. Neither can we afford a system where government abdicates and leaves all of our collective problems to the private sector. The alternative is a responsible government that invests wisely in the things that matter to people. We must improve schools, clean up our water and air, and care for the ill and infirm, all without strangling entrepreneurs in a welter of red tape or stifling initiative with layer after layer of taxes.

The political party that successfully balances the needs and responsibilities of the private and public sectors will claim the allegiance of American voters of every and all sorts. Let me give you an example.

For years I have had one great political frustration. The black community has been treated by both parties as somehow different from the rest of the electorate. Democrats have looked upon the black community as their own special fiefdom, and deal with a few leaders at the top. For a small price, usually a minor appointment or elected position, Democrats get the support of black leaders. Then the party works through them to gain community support. But in the really important political positions, only token black representation is allowed. It's as if an invisible barrier existed, one disenchanted black Democrat told me: blacks are allowed to rise, but only so high.

New Jersey is typical. We have twice as many registered Democrats as Republicans. Before my election, Democrats had controlled the State House for twenty-four out of the last twenty-eight years. We have a large black population, 13 percent of the state's residents. In the twenty-eight years, on average, blacks supported Democratic candidates with 75 to 90 percent of their votes. And yet the makeup of New Jersey government during the time shows no black congressmen and few black legislators, and those only from districts where blacks were overwhelmingly in the majority. Meanwhile, Democratic governors in Trenton appointed blacks to a few visible positions of leadership, but they were kept out of the important subcabinet positions where real policy is made. Only once since Reconstruction have the Democrats allowed a black to become either assembly speaker or majority leader, and there has never been a black majority leader or president of the state senate. There were also few black judges, no black prosecutors, one black county chairman. I could go on. My point is that Democrats have come to take the black vote for granted. The result? Blacks continue to get short shrift, because Democratic leaders don't really have to pay attention to the issues important to the state's black community.

For the Republicans the story is different. The common wisdom for some time now has been that no matter what we do, there is no way Republicans can win more than 10 to 15 percent of the black vote. Party officials in Washington told me, "Ignore the black vote. You'll never get them anyway." Which, of course, is a self-fulfilling prophecy. And when Republicans get into office, we usually ignore the black community except for a token few. Why? Party leaders in Washington believed that to reach out to blacks could threaten our tenuous blue-collar base in the North and undermine our new gains in the South.

For too long, my party has hewed to this line. Quite simply, it is wrong. No political party that ignores more than 10 percent of the electorate can be or should be the majority party. I've been told that if Republicans were able to attract only 25 percent of the black vote, we would not only control the Senate but be very close to control in the House. Look at 1986, when we lost control of the U. S. Senate. In six close races, from Georgia to California, Democratic candidates won at least 85 percent of the black vote.

When the Republican party practices the politics of exclusion, we deserve to lose. The results for the black community are even more severe. Where do you turn when one party ignores you and the other party takes you for granted? Many groups in the past have made their way in America because the two great political parties had to compete for their votes. I knew this and I wanted to prove my party's conventional wisdom wrong. So in 1985 I deliberately went after the black vote. I felt that if I could win 25 percent of it, I could destroy the myth that black voters would never respond to a Republican.

Two people especially shared my belief that black voters would respond to Republicans who listened. One was Len Coleman. The other was a white, cigar-smoking ex-army pilot named Frank Holman, the chairman of the state Republican party. Gruff on the outside, Frank Holman looks and talks like the classic old-style politician. To me, on the inside he represents the new style of the Republican party; he is absolutely committed to reaching out to the people Republicans have always ignored. With help from Len and Frank, I came up with a strategy to tear down some of the barriers that blacks had always faced.

First, I made sure that there were a record number of minorities in policy-making positions. Second, I appointed far more able blacks to judgeships in four years than any Democratic governor had done in eight. This was especially important. The law represents authority. For decades blacks had been told that justice was color-blind, but white was the only color behind the bench. Third, I tried to be sensitive to specific problems in the black community.

For example, I once noticed that the Port Authority of New Jersey and New York showed in its minutes that it was disallowing the low bid of a New Jersey small businessman for a cleaning contract in the Authority's bus terminals. I held up signing that part of the minutes and later learned that the small businessman happened to be black. Malcom Dunn's cleaning company had been the low bidder on the contract. The Port Authority rejected his bid because it did not conform to prevailing wage rates in Manhattan. I invited Malcolm Dunn to my office to hear his story. We hit it off right away. He told me he thought he was on sound legal footing in challenging the Port Authority's decision. He also told me that New Jersey contractors routinely lost work to New York contractors, even though the Authority was supposed to be a bistate agency. Although he was prepared for a costly legal battle, he worried that his one lawyer would be no match for the Port Authority's massive legal staff. He asked for my help. I told him I would provide it. I refused to sign the minutes authorizing that the work be performed by the higher bidder. The Port Authority commissioners were annoyed, because New Jersey governors had almost never meddled in their business. It took nine months of tussling, but eventually Malcolm Dunn's company got the contract.

I didn't help Malcolm Dunn because he was black, but because he was right and because it was my job to stand up for New Jersey. After our success he told me, "I've been a Democrat all my life. I don't think any Democrat would have gone out on a limb for me." Since then, he has become one of my most reliable supporters. Although the press hardly noticed, the story spread quickly through the black business and political community: a white Republican had gone to bat for a black businessman. The truth is that too many blacks and Hispanics, even successful businessmen like Malcolm Dunn, still feel, sometimes for very good reasons, that the corridors of government have a "No trespassing" sign on them. Republicans should take down such signs and listen to blacks.

During my campaign, I resolved to spend more and more time in the black communities. At one point Ken Gibson, the former black mayor from Newark, said, "This Republican goes places we have never seen Republicans before." And I took a simple message to the churches and to the streets. It was basically the same message I delivered everywhere, but for blacks it had special meaning. I talked about ways to bring jobs into the neighborhoods through enterprise zones and to expand job training. Most poor people want to work but they need help up the first rung of the ladder. I talked about better city schools. Black parents, even if they have dead-end jobs themselves, want more than that for their children. Like many Americans before them, blacks see school as a way out for their children. Nothing destroys their dream faster than failing urban schools. I promised to try to do more for their children.

Finally, I talked about public safety. I remember one large black gathering I addressed in Newark. At the end I asked what was the most important thing I could do for them as governor. A older woman raised her hand. "Governor Kean," she said, "I try to work hard. I don't make a lot of money but I make enough to make do for myself and my two children. I walk one block to get to my bus to go to work. Three times I've been mugged on that block on Fridays before I can get home with my paycheck. Governor, the most important thing you could do is get a policeman at that corner so that we can get these thugs off my block and put them away where they belong." The audience applauded for nearly three minutes. Politicians have to remember that people in the black community are the most frequent victims of crime. I promised mandatory sentences and additional jail cells and they responded by voting for me. Later I signed a bill that provided two thousand extra police for our state's cities.

So I was talking basics. I promised a program of more jobs, greater public safety, and better schools. After I finished speaking in a black church I would take the same speech to union halls and the Chambers of Commerce. My programs presented a common vision for the state. They included everybody, because everybody accepts opportunity as one great meaning of America.

To me, that is what the politics of inclusion is about: a realization that we are all here together. From the time when my ancestors arrived on these shores more than two hundred years ago to the 1980s when the Vietnamese boat people became Americans, we have always been a country of extraordinary diversity, and yet we are one in purpose.

One July evening in the summer of 1986, a group of Americans stood in the unexpectedly cold, biting wind of New York Harbor, waiting for the president to relight the torch on the Statue of Liberty. On one side of me was an old friend, Coretta Scott King; on the other, a new friend, President Reagan's budget director James Miller. But as we waited, political differences meant nothing as we talked about our hopes for this good and great country. I was reminded then, as I have been just about every day, that there is a powerful sense of unity in America, which the surface feel of things sometimes obscures. When our common values are tapped and their energy released, we can do anything.

Government remains one of the few institutions that can tap that energy. And so it is not at all inconsistent to believe that the strength of this country is its people and the free market economy in which we labor, and yet understand and accept government's awesome ability to inspire our people and to enhance the performance of our free market. I have tried to show during my political career, and especially my years as governor, that responsible government can meet people's needs and bring them together, that government can make a difference in the way we live.

The Republican vision of responsible government has worked in New Jersey. And if it has worked here, it can work anywhere.

Index